D1163661

THE TEACHING AND LEARNING OF PSYCHOANALYSIS

The Guilford Psychoanalysis Series

Robert S. Wallerstein, Editor

Associate Editors
Leonard Shengold
Neil J. Smelser
Albert J. Solnit
Edward Weinshel

The Teaching and Learning of Psychoanalysis: Selected Papers of Joan Fleming, M.D.
Stanley S. Weiss, Editor

Forty-Two Lives in Treatment: A Study of Psychoanalysis and Psychotherapy
Robert S. Wallerstein

In Preparation
From Safety to Superego: Selected Papers of Joseph Sandler
Joseph Sandler

The Teaching and Learning of Psychoanalysis

Selected Papers of Joan Fleming, M.D.

Edited by
STANLEY S. WEISS, M.D.

Foreword by Robert S. Wallerstein, M.D.

THE GUILFORD PRESS
New York   London

© 1987 The Guilford Press
A Division of Guilford Publications, Inc.
200 Park Avenue South, New York, N.Y. 10003

All rights reserved.

No part of this book may be reproduced, stored in a retrieval system,
or transmitted, in any form or by any means, electronic, mechanical,
photocopying, microfilming, recording, or otherwise,
without written permission from the Publisher.

Printed in the United States of America

LIBRARY OF CONGRESS CATALOGING IN PUBLICATION DATA

Fleming, Joan, 1904–1980
   The teaching and learning of psychoanalysis.
   (The Guilford psychoanalysis series)
   Bibliography: p.
   Includes index.
   1. Psychoanalysis—Study and teaching.
2. Psychoanalysis—Study and teaching—Supervision.
I. Weiss, Stanley S.   II. Title.   III. Series.
[DNLM: 1. Psychoanalysis—education—collected works.
WM 18 F597t]
RC502.F556 1987   616.89'17'071   86-14910
ISBN 0-89862-326-X

ACKNOWLEDGMENTS

Dr. Fleming and I had planned to write a monograph on psychoanalytic education together. However, before we could do this, Dr. Fleming became ill and died. I was especially pleased, therefore, to learn from Drs. Edward M. Weinshel and Robert S. Wallerstein that they felt a volume of Dr. Fleming's writings on the pedagogy of psychoanalytic education would be a timely and valuable contribution, and I did not hesitate when they asked me to edit such a volume for The Guilford Series in Psychoanalysis. I wish to thank them for suggesting that this be done and for their help, support, and encouragement throughout its preparation. Dr. Wallerstein has also contributed the Foreword, a somewhat personal document that chronicles so well the significant influence Dr. Fleming had on many distinguished professional careers, such as his own.

I also wish to express my sincerest thanks to Helen (Mrs. Frank M.) Summers for her cooperation and interest in this volume about her sister's work. I am very grateful to Miss Toini E. Kari, Dr. Fleming's secretary and close friend, for her thoughtful and competent secretarial help. To my wife, Marilyn, who also enjoyed Dr. Fleming's friendship, I express my deep appreciation for reviewing the manuscript and for her many helpful suggestions.

I am grateful to the following journals and publisher for permission to reproduce Dr. Fleming's papers: *Journal of the American Psychoanalytic Association, Psychoanalytic Quarterly, The Annual of Psychoanalysis, International Review of Psycho-Analysis*, and International Universities Press.

Stanley S. Weiss

FOREWORD

If anyone at all has merited the title "Pedagogue of Psychoanalytic Education," it is Joan Fleming. Her abiding influence upon all of us within organized psychoanalysis who were privileged to know her and to work with her lay in the fierce respect with which she imbued us all for the pedagogical aspects of the entire psychoanalytical training endeavor, pervading all of its interlocking components, including even the properly therapeutically focused training analysis. It was as a teacher that Joan began her professional career, teaching biology, physical education, anatomy, and physiology in a succession of Midwestern colleges; it was as a psychiatric psychoanalytic teacher that she inspired generations of students in Chicago and in Denver with a devotion for the clinical therapeutic activity. Beyond all that, it was as a philosopher of the psychoanalytic educational enterprise (she would not have used so pretentious a phrase) that she gave so many friends and colleagues fresh and deep understandings of the experiential nature of the teaching and learning of psychoanalysis, where the learning is of the optimal use of oneself in an interpersonal helping context, and the teaching is intricately imbricated with treating, both when it is called teaching (in supervision) and when it is called treating (in personal analysis).

In this book Stanley S. Weiss, Joan Fleming's closest collaborator and frequent coauthor through her Denver years, devotedly lays out and annotates the corpus of Joan's most significant papers on the educational process in psychoanalysis. My foreword can perhaps best serve to illustrate how these multiple contributions to the educational philosophy and techniques of psychoanalysis were actually given life and impact through a personalized account of the various ways in which one career (my own) was constantly influenced by, and in signal respects significantly shaped by, Joan's presence and her voice.

I first met Joan Fleming in the mid-1950s, when Rudolf Ekstein and I were struggling to form the manuscript of our own book on the supervisory process, *The Teaching and Learning of Psychotherapy*, which was published in 1958. It was Joan Fleming, senior to us both, whom Ekstein knew and whom we involved in consultation (from Chicago to Topeka, where we were at The Menninger Foundation) to discuss our planned book and to review our ideas on the supervisory process with us. Her help and encouragement were generous and unstinting. Our ideas resonated with hers, and her admonition (which we needed) was to go full steam ahead. She indicated that it was exactly such a book that she had been planning with her own psychoanalytic mentor in Chicago, N. Lionel Blitzsten, just as Ekstein was then one of my mentors; with Blitzsten now dead, she felt that she would never write her own book, and wanted very much to see it (or at least its essence) written through ours. As is so well known, of course, her prediction about herself proved faulty: She shortly thereafter was involved in her own intensely productive collaboration with Therese F. Benedek, out of which emerged in 1966 their jointly authored landmark book, *Psychoanalytic Supervision: A Method of Clinical Teaching.* Here she gave full voice to her own very particular philosophy of psychoanalytic education and her methodology for its intensive study.

In that same time period, Joan was also centrally involved in two parallel educational studies—one in psychoanalytic psychiatry, the other in psychoanalysis itself. Within psychiatry there were, during that time, a series of five annual so-called Onchiota Conferences organized by José Barchilon, an academic psychoanalyst, then with the Albert Einstein College of Medicine in New York. These conferences were designed to assess the place of psychoanalysis within psychiatric teaching in the departments of psychiatry of the medical schools and teaching hospitals across the United States. I was privileged to be invited to one of them in 1963, and there I found Joan Fleming (with the strong support of Roy Astley of Pittsburgh, who served with her as Secretary of the Board on Professional Standards of the American Psychoanalytic Association during Joan's term as Chairman of that Board) to be the ideological spokesperson who centrally articulated the psychoanalytic educational vision for psychiatry that infused the conference.

It was during that same period that the American Psychoanalytic Association created a Survey Steering Committee, chaired by Joan Fleming, to survey, via six Preliminary Commissions, the overall state of our formal psychoanalytic educational structure in the six topical areas of Organization and Administration; Curriculum; Faculty; Students; Evaluation; and Related Fields. It was the December 1955 report of this Survey Steering Committee, dubbed the "Rainbow Report" from the multicolored paper by which the reports from the six individual commissions were coded, that created the famous field study of psychoanalytic education carried out over a span of several years by Bertram Lewin of New York and Helen Ross of Chicago (on grant funds secured by the Survey Steering Committee from the National Institute of Mental Health). The field study eventuated in the publication in 1960 of their book, *Psychoanalytic Education in the United States.* It is no hyperbole to state that the impact of Lewin and Ross's book on the structure and conduct of formal psychoanalytic education under the aegis of the American Psychoanalytic Association was fully comparable to the impact of the famed Flexner Report on the structure and conduct of formal medical education in the United States early in the century.

Though one of the central recommendations of the Lewin and Ross book—the establishment of a permanent Office of Education within the American Psychoanalytic Association (to be initially staffed by Lewin and Ross)—proved abortive, another enduring result did emerge in 1961. The body within the Association charged with the oversight of all organized psychoanalytic training in all affiliated Psychoanalytic Institutes, the Board on Professional Standards (of which Joan was Secretary in 1953–1955, and which she chaired in 1961–1964), established a new committee, the Committee on Psychoanalytic Education (COPE). Unlike all the other Board Committees, which had major action and decision-making charges in relation to the various facets of the psychoanalytic educational structure, COPE was to be purely a study committee, dedicated via various Study Groups that it would organize to a process of scholarly study of all the components of the psychoanalytic education process and to the promulgation of recommendations via the mechanism of reports and published articles and books. In 1971, I participated in a plenary panel at the annual meeting of the American Psychoanalytic Association in Washington, D.C., celebrating the activities and accomplishments of COPE over its first decade. It was natural that Joan Fleming should be invited to be a member of that panel, and she entitled her talk "The Birth of COPE as Viewed in 1971." She began her presentation with this sentence: "Talking to you about the birth of the Committee on Psychoanalytic Education is a pleasure—not because it takes me back over a span of 20 years, but because so much has happened in that time." Her full talk, along with all the others, was published in Volume 20 of the *Journal of the American Psychoanalytic Association* in 1972.

When one of COPE's first Study Groups, a Study Group on Psychoanalytic Supervision, was established in 1964 with Emanuel Windholz of San Francisco as Chairman and myself as Secretary, it was again natural that Joan would become one of the Study Group's members. The group was small (initially, eight people; later enlarged by three more). It met intensively, a day or two at a time, and three times yearly, over a goodly span of years. It is fair to say that Joan Fleming was at all times the central principled voice, around whom—and at times, against whom—everyone else's ideas were always bounced off, considered, and usually refined. When the book produced by the Study Group, *Becoming a Psychoanalyst: A Study of Psychoanalytic Supervision*, was finally published in 1981, it was unhappily after Joan's death. It was dedicated by us to her, in memoriam.

With her intense feeling for the need for a constant dialectical process and interchange among psychoanalytic educators in regard to the psychoanalytic educational process, Joan Fleming was the prime mover in the organization of the Three Institute Conferences (Chicago, Pittsburgh, Topeka) on the problems of training analysis. I attended the first of these, in Pittsburgh in 1965, as a then newly appointed Training Analyst in the Topeka Institute for Psychoanalysis. It was characteristic of Joan that she would be instrumental in insuring the presence alongside all the psychoanalyst educators of a professional educator, Ralph Tyler (then Director of the Center for Advanced Study in the Behavioral Sciences at Stanford, California), in order to ensure that broad educational perspectives from cognate realms outside the inner parochial investments of psychoanalysis per se would be brought to bear on the educational deliberations. There was a second Three Institute Conference (with the same participating Institutes) held at The Menninger Foundation in Topeka, Kansas, in 1969, but in that year Joan also left Chicago for Denver and these conferences lapsed. It was a disappointment to Joan that these small regional educational conferences were not picked up and emulated by comparable Institute groups around the country.

In the early 1970s, the American Psychoanalytic Association undertook to organize another nationwide conference, to be called the Conference on Psychoanalytic Education and Research (COPER), as a follow-up to the earlier Survey Steering Committee (chaired by Joan), which had been convened more that 15 years earlier and had produced the "Rainbow Report." This undertaking was to be more ambitious. A conference would be held, involving approximately 200 individuals, in the fall of 1974 at The Homestead in Hot Springs, Virginia. It would be organized around the planning work and the position papers of Preparatory Commissions in nine designated areas: The Tripartite System of Psychoanalytic Education; Child Analysis; Psychoanalytic Research; The Ideal Institute; Age and the Psychoanalytic Career; Relationship of Psychoanalysis to Current Changes in Medical and Psychiatric Education; Relationship of Psychoanalysis to Universities; Psychoanalytic Education and the Allied Disciplines; and Relationship of Psychoanalysis to Social and Community Issues. As Co-Chairman of the COPER Planning Committee (along with Herbert Gaskill of Denver), I felt that there could be no one more suitable to chair Preparatory Commission I on The Tripartite System of Psychoanalytic Education than Joan Fleming, and the rest of the Planning Committee was of like mind. The position paper prepared by this group of 19 (which at Joan's request included Ralph Tyler) has been one of the most enduringly influential, as well as provocative, of all the COPER documents; though all 19 Commission members participated variously, the final product bore the unmistakable stamp of Joan Fleming and her chosen secretary for the Commission, Stanley Weiss (who is also coauthor of four of the nine papers in the present book, as well as the book's editor). The volume of COPER's proceedings was published in 1977, with Stanley Goodman of San Francisco as editor, under the title *Psychoanalytic Education and Research: The Current Situation and Future Possibilities.*

I trust I have traced sufficiently the guiding role of Joan Fleming in the evolution of psychoanalytic training in America, its structures and its processes, as experienced by one person (myself) who was privileged to be with her and to learn from her in a sequence of professional and educational endeavors over a professional lifetime: in writing about supervision; at an Onchiota Conference; as an observer to the "Rainbow Report" and the Survey of Psychoanalytic Education; in the creation, evolution, and assessment of COPE; in the long labors of the COPE Study Group on Supervision; in the Three Institute Conferences; and in the extraordinarily stimulating COPER. And Joan's influence bids fair to extend beyond its North American borders. Under the presidency of Serge Lebovici of Paris (1973–1977), the International Psycho-Analytical Association first articulated a concern for the establishment of agreed-upon procedures and practices for psychoanalytic training around the world, which could lead to agreed-upon and adhered-to training standards for professional and scientific excellence in our discipline. This has been carried further under the presidency of Adam Limentani of London (1981–1985), who established two successive Working Parties on training requirements and standards, each chaired by Janice de Saussure of Switzerland. The first of these Working Parties produced the document *IPA Standards and Criteria for Qualification and Admission to Membership*, and the second one produced the document *Minimum Requirements for Acquiring and Maintaining the Function of Training Analyst*. As one of the American members of those Working Parties, I can attest to the central role played in their thinking by ideas and convictions that originated with Joan Fleming. All of this is reason enough, I think, to happily re-present to the psychoanalytic world the distillation of Joan Fleming's pedagogical thinking as represented in the nine papers in this book. Her thought is admirably embedded between an illuminating prologue and epilogue by her coauthor and book editor, Stanley Weiss, who has also created brief connecting texts that relate these papers one to another and to the evolution of psychoanalytic thinking about the educational process. Joan's voice should now speak for itself.

Robert S. Wallerstein
San Francisco
June 1985

PROLOGUE

Joan Fleming, M.D., a distinguished psychoanalytic clinician and educator, was born in Bloomington, Illinois on March 24, 1904, and died peacefully in her sleep on August 11, 1980, in Denver, Colorado. Her creative and professional life was devoted to the science and practice of psychoanalysis, and especially to the educational process by which it is taught and learned.

Psychoanalytic education is unique: "In no other field is the educational process so complex, so involved with the imbrication of inner and outer worlds, so firmly rooted in knowing oneself in order to use oneself in therapy, in scientific discovery, and in teaching the what and how of psychoanalysis" (Fleming, 1972, p. 547). Dr. Fleming played a most significant role in the history and evolutionary character of American psychoanalytic education, and her influence was also felt in other parts of the world. Through her foresight and leadership in the American Psychoanalytic Association; as chairman of many important committees, panels, and commissions; as Dean of Education at the Chicago Institute for Psychoanalysis; as a member of the Editorial Board of the *Journal of the American Psychoanalytic Association*; as Editor of the Section on Education of *The Annual of Psychoanalysis*; and as an inspired teacher and esteemed faculty member at the Denver Institute for Psychoanalysis—in all these capacities, Dr. Fleming worked tirelessly and creatively to seek solutions to the complex and unique problems in teaching and learning psychoanalysis, the scientific discipline created by Sigmund Freud.

In 1905, a small group of interested persons began meeting on Wednesday evenings at Freud's home, Berggasse 19, Vienna, to learn about psychoanalysis. Psychoanalytic education, though not called by that name at the time, had begun. The students were usually practicing psychiatrists who wanted to apply Freud's new ideas in their work with patients. The technique of free association and the interpretation of resistance and transference phenomena became the primary principles of the treatment process. Freud's teaching methods involved small-group discussions and consulta- tions about cases. The first group of students rapidly became the teachers of the next group, and for a time the method of education was that of an apprentice system in which the teaching analyst performed the functions of analyst, theoretician, and case consul- tant. As the science developed and its significance and value be- came more widely appreciated, interest grew, and there was soon a need for more formal training. Training by individuals was replaced by group responsibility for educating students. The Ber- lin Institute was formed in 1920, and the Vienna Institute in 1922. The educational process gradually evolved into three phases: the training analysis, didactic courses, and supervised analyses. This training was codified by the International Training Commission of the International Psycho-Analytical Association in 1925.

Education at the European Institutes led to the founding of the American schools. (For views of the early history of American psychoanalytic education, see Bandler, 1960; Benedek, 1969; Gitel- son, 1964; Henrick, 1955; Knight, 1953; Lewin, 1962; Quen & Carlson, 1978.) The New York Psychoanalytic Institute was or- ganized in 1931, and the Chicago Institute and the Boston Insti- tute during the next two years. Due to the Nazi persecution, there was a marked emigration of analysts from Europe to England and America during this time, strengthening psychoanalysis in the United States and weakening it in Europe. Psychoanalytic educa- tion was no longer predominantly European. The American Psy- choanalytic Association began in 1911. By 1932, it was a federa- tion of constituent local societies. These societies had extensive local autonomy and controlled training for their own students. In 1938, the American Psychoanalytic Association gained its auto- nomy from the International Psycho-Analytical Association and began to take more interest in educational standards. With the reorganization of the American Psychoanalytic Association in 1946, the Board on Professional Standards came into being. Dr. Fleming joined the Association in 1947 and soon began to devote her energy and skill to organizational and educational matters.

Following the end of World War II, the few Institutes were confronted with many applicants desiring psychoanalytic train- ing. Most were young psychiatrists who had been stimulated by the usefulness of psychoanalytic understanding while in the military (Greenacre, 1961, p. 672). The Board was pushed by this new and unusual situation to consider what constituted a well-organized and well-equipped Institute, so that high-quality training and high-quality faculty could be maintained. As Secretary (1953–1955) and Chairman (1961–1964) of the Board on Professional Standards, Dr. Fleming played an active and significant role in this endeavor.

Dr. Fleming was the Chairman of the Survey Steering Committee (with Drs. Norman Reider, M. Ralph Kaufman, and Richard L. Frank), which recommended to the Board on Professional Standards in 1955 that after about 30 years of organized training in the United States, there was now a need for awareness of the philosophy underlying training standards and knowledge about specific policies and procedures in all approved training facilities. Psychoanalysts knew very little about the organization and educational philosophy of Institutes other than their own. Dr. Fleming's committee suggested a field study consisting of visits to each educational facility. This stock-taking effort was based on Dr. Fleming's conviction that the education of candidates is an investment in the future of psychoanalysis. Good analytic education would help candidates acquire the skills to use the analytic method for both therapeutic and investigative purposes, and would stimulate a spirit of inquiry. Dr. Bertram Lewin and Miss Helen Ross were chosen to devote their full-time efforts to this fact-finding study. Their task was admirably accomplished and resulted in an important publication, *Psychoanalytic Education in the United States* (1960). The field study focused on facts and not on a critique of the observations made or on suggestions for change. Such generalizations were beyond its scope, but Dr. Fleming's belief that psychoanalytic education is worthy of systematic study had caught the attention of psychoanalytic educators. Arlow (1973) has noted, "During the years 1956 to 1959, Dr. Lewin and Miss Ross created an intellectual and educational ferment in the Institutes . . . they helped break down the prevalent parochialism and suspicion" (p. ii). Their visits around the country became unique and exciting consultations (Keiser, 1969, p. 253). The Report of the Survey Steering Committee to the Board on Professional Standards (Survey Steering Committee, 1955; usually referred to as the "Rainbow Report," since the six commissions' reports were printed on different-colored paper), the fact-finding survey, and the published volume all played an important role in shaping the future of psychoanalytic education.

Dr. Fleming was also Chairman of the Planning Committee (with Drs. Sarah S. Tower, Otto Fleischmann, Maxwell Gitelson, and Norman Reider), which recommended to the Board on Professional Standards and Council in 1959 the establishment of a Committee on Psychoanalytic Education (COPE). The aim of COPE was to define and study the wide range of educational problems and make its findings available to all psychoanalysts. Since its birth, COPE has been successfully working to educate the educators. The Planning Committee also recommended that an Office of Education be set up within the structure of the American Psychoanalytic Association and administered by the former survey directors, who would serve as consultants to Institutes and to the Association, and would develop and carry out long-range programs to advance psychoanalytic education. This part of the recommendation did not materalize. Dr. Fleming was disappointed and felt that this was a setback for psychoanalytic education, but she was pleased with what had been accomplished thus far in getting analysts to communicate with one another about educational matters. Dr. Fleming believed that analysts possessed a resistance to sharing clinical experiences openly and were often reluctant to conceptualize the analytic experience as well as the educational experience: "Perhaps we are rooted so deeply in the intimate emotionally charged one-to-one relationships that we cannot shift to the multiple person situation and to a conceptual level of generalizations which would make it possible to discuss objectively the phenomena and processes of teaching and learning" (Fleming, 1972, p. 554). In an attempt to overcome this, Dr. Fleming was a prime sponsor (with Drs. Royden Astley, Charlotte Babcock, George Pollock, and Ishak Ramzy) for organizing a conference to study the training analysis, an especially sensitive area of the educational system; it was described by Lewin and Ross (1960, pp. 46–52) as a syncretistic dilemma for psychoanalytic educators, since both treatment and education are so intimately involved. Two Three Institute Conferences on Training Analysis were held, in 1965 and 1969, and two important publications emerged (see Babcock, 1965, and Ramzy, 1973). These conferences represented the first time that a group of training analysts had come together to share knowledge and experiences in an atmosphere of mutual learning. The two conferences were highly successful, and, once again, provided evidence for Dr. Fleming's belief in the value of discussions on national and local levels to explore in depth all aspects of training problems. Dr. Fleming felt that an essential part of good conference planning should involve ongoing, built-in continuity that allows for follow-through on various questions, especially those that are controversial. Dr. Fleming hoped that the two historical Three Institute Conferences would stimulate discussion in all Institutes on the training analysis, the keystone of psychoanalytic education. She believed that all too often there is of very little diffusion of the results of conferences to the local level and the individual training analyst, supervisor, and teacher.

The study of supervision, one of the main methods for teaching clinical psychoanalysis, was especially close to Dr. Fleming's heart. Dr. Fleming (with Dr. Therese F. Benedek) wrote in 1966 a monograph, *Psychoanalytic Supervision: A Method of Clinical Teaching*, which was reissued in 1983 as a classic. The didactic problems of supervision had never before been subjected to such systematic investigation. Dr. Fleming believed that what really happens in the supervision of a particular student with a particular patient is what needs to be scrutinized and conceptualized as an interactive process of communication, with teaching and learning as its goal. Already, in 1953, Dr. Fleming (with Dr. N. Lionel Blitzten) had focused attention on supervision in "What is a Supervisory Analysis?" Dr. Fleming believed at that time that the supervisor should take an active part in the interpretation of countertransference to the student, whether or not the candidate is in training analysis. Dr. Fleming knew that this was controversial and that many of her colleagues did not agree with this view. The 1953 paper stimulated two panels on the Technique of Supervised Analysis at a subsequent meeting of the American Psychoanalytic Association, and the handling of countertransference in the student analyst by the supervisor dominated the discussion. The predominant view today, with which Dr. Fleming came to agree, holds that the supervisor should rely on confronting the student with the presence of a blind spot or defensive reaction to his patient, rather than making transference or genetic interpretations in noting the student's countertransference problems; the management of such problems should be left to further training analysis or to self-analysis. Dr. Fleming had the ability to effect changes in how psychoanalytic educators view all Institute educational policies and procedures by illuminating and clarifying the underlying psychoanalytic principles. Dr. Fleming could also alter her own views following discussion and study of the data from the vicissitudes, successes, and failures of the psychoanalytic educational program.

Just after Dr. Fleming's death, The Study Group on Supervision of the Committee on Psychoanalytic Education published *Becoming a Psychoanalyst: A Study of Psychoanalytic Education*, edited by Robert S. Wallerstein, M.D. The volume was dedicated to Dr. Fleming, "who was one of the principal architects and far more than just the author of one of its chapters" (Wallerstein, 1981, p. x). The dedication—"To Joan Fleming, friend, colleague, mentor, who shared this labor and whose spirit inspired us all"— was to be a surprise, but, sadly, Dr. Fleming died without being aware of this tribute from her colleagues.

While at the Chicago Institute for Psychoanalysis, Dr. Fleming helped devise a new curriculum. The curriculum followed the historical development of psychoanalytic thought, but also considered degrees of difficulty, new knowledge, and the importance (not fully appreciated at the time) of combining both theory and clinical data in all aspects of analytic teaching and learning. Also, at Chicago, Dr. Fleming began to do research on selection criteria and the selection process. It was a pioneering effort in focusing attention on the applicant's ego functioning and on the ego functions required to become a competent psychoanalyst. Dr. Fleming's original work on the selection of candidates for psychoanalytic education stimulated much debate in this important and controversial area. In 1969, Dr. Fleming relocated to the University of Colorado School of Medicine, where, as Professor of Psychiatry and as Training and Supervising Analyst at the Denver Institute for Psychoanalysis, she influenced greatly the functioning of a beginning Institute. Dr. Fleming was instrumental in the education of a new generation of students as well as the teaching of psychoanalytic principles to other mental health professionals, especially social workers.

Dr. Fleming was the guiding force of Commission I on the Tripartite System of Psychoanalytic Education for the 1974 Conference on Psychoanalytic Education and Research (COPER), sponsored by the American Psychoanalytic Association. Once again, Dr. Fleming was creatively involved with a group of psychoanalytic educators in exploring the goals and methods of the tripartite system of psychoanalytic education, identifying strong and weak points, and making recommendations for changes. The Commission re-evaluated each phase of the educational program and re-emphasized its basic validity. The Commission noted that with all its complexities, the Institute still offers the best structure and setting available for psychoanalytic education. However, the Commission believed that the educational program would be strengthened by increasing the integration of each of the three phases of the educational experience into an overall educational process. Dr. Fleming believed that further study of the policies and procedures for doing this would be undertaken. She also felt that the continuing and careful assessment of the quality of teaching and learning could be improved, and that more attention should be given to organizational structure and group process. Psychoanalytic educators should work together toward developing a cohesive educational group interested in the common goal of improving the educational program. This group task is not easy to accomplish. It requires thought, effort, and constant review. Dr. Fleming felt that some of the most serious weaknesses in the educational system and potential for splitting a group exist in this area.

COPER was another successful conference of self-evaluation, and of intense review and re-evaluation of educational policies and practices. The condensed reports of Commission I and the eight other preparatory commissions have been published in a volume edited by Stanley Goodman, M.D., *Psychoanalytic Education and Research: The Current Situation and Future Possibilities* (1977).

Only two years after COPER, in 1976, Dr. Fleming was urgently called upon to chair an ad hoc committee (with Drs. Maurice R. Friend, Frances H. Gitelson, James T. McLaughlin, and Nathan P. Segel, and myself) to help an Institute in serious trouble. Site visits had pointed to educational difficulties that had persisted, and a substandard training program was now in great difficulty. Dr. Fleming observed that the Institute in question had not made use of the advanced educational and organizational concepts to which all evolving Institutes should give serious attention. Dr. Fleming referred especially to the application of evaluation as an educational tool in the formulation of criteria for assessing outcome of analyses; the qualifications of training analysts, supervisors, and teachers; and the ongoing review of the effectiveness of policy making and implementation.

Through the processes of consultation and demonstration to facilitate the joint appraisal of their educational and organizational procedures, Dr. Fleming and the committee were able to convert the difficulties that this Institute was having into a learning experience profitable for all psychoanalytic educators. Also, Dr. Fleming actively encouraged the participation of the candidates in evaluating the educational process that so deeply affected them. Dr. Fleming believed in the principle of involving all students in the learning process.

On the basis of this experience, the ad hoc committee proposed that the Board on Professional Standards consider a new mode of relating to each of its Institutes. This new mode should provide a continuum of communication, ranging from liaison consultation at one end for an optimally functioning Institute, to an advisory consultative relationship requiring shared responsibility in crucial decision making when an Institute is in trouble. This ongoing collaboration between Board and Institute would provide an opportunity for more rapid confrontation of educational difficulties, and would, it was hoped, prevent the problems that almost destroyed an important learning center.

The present book is about Dr. Fleming's contributions to psychoanalytic education. Dr. Fleming devoted her professional life to helping students gain competence in using the psychoanalytic method for therapeutic purposes, for extending the area of understanding of behavior, and for applying psychoanalytic theory to other fields of knowledge. A picture of Dr. Fleming emerges through her writings. She was a gifted educator, innovator, administrator, clinician, and writer. In accordance with Dr. Fleming's philosophy of the importance of discussion and interaction with colleagues, many of her papers were written together with other psychoanalytic educators. I was one of those colleagues who worked closely with Dr. Fleming, and we collaborated on four of the papers included herein. It was a rare privilege to have had the opportunity to observe Dr. Fleming's love for psychoanalysis and to participate with her in creative and scholarly endeavors. This volume is offered to her memory with deep affection and respect.

Dr. Fleming would be pleased to know that some of her contributions to psychoanalytic education are gathered together for the first time in one volume. Her hope would be that these papers will contribute to the ongoing dialogue about the problems of psychoanalytic education, encourage new solutions, and thereby safeguard and advance the science and profession of psychoanalysis.

CONTENTS

xxiii

·1·

THE EXPERIENTIAL NATURE OF PSYCHOANALYTIC LEARNING

(with Therese F. Benedek)

In this chapter taken from the monograph she wrote with Dr. Therese F. Benedek, *Psychoanalytic Supervision: A Method of Clinical Teaching*, Dr. Fleming clearly presents her philosophy of psychoanalytic education. It was first published in 1966 but remains, I believe, as fresh, important, and timely as when it was written.

Dr. Fleming had a deep appreciation for the magnificent psychoanalytic situation and method discovered by Sigmund Freud for studying and treating the human psyche, and knew that it can only be taught and mastered by learning experiences of a special nature. Traditional instruction, as this chapter notes, is inadequate. Learning primarily by experience is necessary for becoming a psychoanalyst. Dr. Fleming believed that the Institute has the responsibility to provide a proper learning environment and learning experiences for candidates that will help them attain a scholarly and research approach to all phases of their analytic work.

This chapter emphasizes that each part of the educational program—the training analysis, course work, and supervision—makes a specific contribution to the total learning experience of the candidate, and that each phase provides different kinds of learning experiences that contribute to professional development. The training analysis lays the foundation for the development of sensitive, emphatic understanding, which is then linked with cognitive, explanatory understanding, taught during the second phase of the learning program. Both of these kinds of learning experiences are further developed and

Reprinted by permission from *Psychoanalytic Supervision: A Method of Clinical Teaching* by J. Fleming and T. F. Benedek. New York: International Universities Press, 1983, pp. 20–34. (Originally published, New York: Grune & Stratton, 1966.)

1

integrated into clinical skills that lead to therapeutic effectiveness and psychoanalytic scholarship. The basic goal of these educative experiences is the development of an analytic instrument (Freud, 1912) or "work ego" (R. Fliess, 1942; Fleming, 1961 [see Chapter Three, this volume]), in which the skills of introspection, empathy, and interpretation are highly developed.

The nature of psychoanalytic work requires knowledge and skills which probe the world of psychological experience—a world not knowable through the usual sensory pathways, a world of processes which influence behavior and well-being without the subject's awareness of what is motivating him. Freud discovered that when a person became aware of previously unconscious motivations, he could change his behavior so as to be no longer at the mercy of the forces which created his symptoms. This discovery is the assumption basic to psychoanalytic therapy. To learn how to enter this intimate inner world, to discover what was unknown and to make it knowable is the goal of psychoanalytic treatment. To learn how to help another person achieve this kind of self-knowledge and mastery is the objective of a student-analyst, an objective that can be accomplished only by learning experiences of a special nature. For such learning traditional instruction is inadequate, since the means of exploring and influencing the inner world of psychological experience cannot be achieved by reading a book, hearing a lecture, or observing someone else do it. Cognitive processes are essential but play a role secondary to learning by experience during the greater part of the development of a psychoanalyst [Ferenczi and Rank, 1927].

Intuitively we understand what is meant by experiential learning: to know by testing it.[1] For purposes of clarifying the educational process, however, we shall attempt to identify the significant experience a student-analyst goes through to attain his

---

1. *Oxford English Dictionary*—from the Latin: *experiri*, meaning to try, to put to the test. Several illustrative quotations have bearing on our thesis regarding experience as a source of knowledge and a means of learning. 1736, Joseph Butler—Analogy of Religion I. ii. 35: It is not so much a Deduction of Reason as a matter of Experience. 1826, Benjamin Disraeli—*Vivian Grey*, v.i., Experience is the child of thought. 1874, William Carpenter—*Principles of Mental Physiology* I. ii. 58, The experiential acquirement of knowledge.

goal. We shall also attempt to distinguish the elements of learning-by-experiencing from learning-by-cognizing, and to identify the part played by each in the education of an analyst.

Although it goes without saying that a student of psychoanalysis should possess the aptitudes necessary for the job, it is not a simple matter to define these aptitudes. Several authors have emphasized psychological sensitivity, a capacity for empathic understanding and tactful responsiveness (R. Fliess, 1942; Fleming, 1961 [see Chapter Three]), as being related to the special tasks of psychoanalysis. Discussion of these and other selection criteria, however, is beyond the scope of this study, since our main concern is with the best way to develop a student-analyst's aptitudes into freely accessible, useful tools for his professional work.

The psychoanalytic training program at present is divided into three phases, each of which makes a special contribution to the total learning experience of the student and each of which emphasizes a different aspect of his professional development. In sequence the training analysis comes first, imbricated with a period of theoretical instruction and clinical demonstrations, which overlap with the culminating phase of analyzing patients under supervision. Although the structure of the system could evolve only through trial and error without a formulated rationale for the total program until Eitingon's proposals in 1925 [Eitingon, 1926], history reveals that the educational philosophy behind this training system has been "experiential" from the beginning.

Development of the training system has paralleled in many ways the development of psychoanalysis as a clinical science. The empirical observations made by Freud in collaboration with Breuer [Breuer and Freud, 1895] led to discovery of a method which could reach below the surface and was found useful not only for observing behavior not previously observable, but also for discovering its motivations. Freud's earliest observations became foundation stones in the theoretical structure which gradually evolved; yet this structure might never have been built if Freud had not had the fortitude to "experiment" by testing out his new method of observation on himself. His letters of those early days [Freud, 1887–1902] reveal more authentically than his studies in hysteria the "origins of psychoanalysis" in the depths of his own experiences.

In Letter 130, written on November 3, 1900 [Freud, 1887–

1902, p. 312], he describes a period of incubation and preconscious working through of resistances he could feel but whose origins he did not know. His tactics correspond to the "regression in the service of the ego" which Kris [1952] holds equally significant for analytic and creative work in general—an activity of mind in which synthesis and integration proceed subliminally before illumination of the problem by conscious recognition. Freud says, "I adopted the expedient of renouncing working by conscious thought, so as to grope my way further into the riddles only by blind touch. Since I started this I have been doing my work, perhaps more skillfully then before, but I do not really know what I am doing." This shift in working occurred in a period of frustration following a realization that "all the hypotheses that until then had seemed plausible" had to be thought through further. In this example of Freud's observation of his own reaction and behavior, we see again his record of experiencing a process which calls forth discovery of hidden meanings in manifest behavior. His urge to find the master keys of concepts and theories by experiencing this hitherto unexplored world met the resistances with which he became so well acquainted and later conceptualized with such benefit to psychology and analytic therapy.

Freud's genius expressed itself in his ability to observe and to objectify his own emotional responses. His driving curiosity and his reactions to self-observations became the material for his "self-analysis." By means of introspection and interpretation of his own dreams he arrived at insights on which far-reaching conceptualizations could be based. With this introspective beginning, he was able to empathize with similar phenomena in others, and from these observations he gradually developed a psychological theory and a method for investigation of human behavior that has revolutionized the study of man.

Since his own learning was so firmly rooted in the examination of his own experience, it is not surprising that from the earliest days of the student meetings at Freud's house, the experiential nature of the learning necessary for becoming an analyst was recognized. It was accepted that the student should try the method on himself, "analyzing" his dreams, slips of the tongue, and emotional reactions to the new ideas and the discussions about them. Such personal experiences convinced his students that behavior was unconsciously determined, that some process of censorship existed, and that emotions could interfere with objective thinking. They kept at it, spurred by the pleasure of discovery and by their attempts to anchor the fleeting phenomena of experience in the cognitive framework of concepts and theory.

The complexities of analyzing patients soon confronted the early analysts, as they had Freud, with the phenomena of "blind spots" [Stekel, 1923] or "countertransferences" [Freud, 1910]. They realized that experiencing the method through "self-analysis" was not enough. They went through all of the vicissitudes Freud described in his letters to Fliess before 1900 and began to understand how often something of which they were not aware crept into their communication with patients. Thus, these first analysts learned that to associate freely was not easy in the face of ever-present resistances and, consequently, that a deeper examination of their own inner life was necessary. In 1910 Freud emphasized the therapeutic aims of self-analysis. He said: "We have become aware of the 'countertransference' which arises in him [the analyst] as a result of the patient's influence on his unconscious feelings, and we are *almost* [italics ours] inclined to insist that he shall recognize this countertranference in himself and overcome it. Since analysts have begun to exchange observations with each other we have noticed no psychoanalyst goes further than his own complexes and internal resistances permit; and we consequently require that he shall begin his activity with a self-analysis and continually carry it deeper while he is making his observations on his patients. Anyone who fails to produce results in a self-analysis of this kind may at once give up any idea of being able to treat patients by analysis" (p. 145). This statement is still a long way from the concept of a training analysis as we think of it today. Freud's tentative insistence on a therapeutic aim seems related to his experience of internal resistances in himself and to his experience with public opposition to psychoanalytic theories, which many persons, including some early analysts, found intolerable because of what tended to be stimulated within themselves [Freud, 1914a].

Freud had learned by experience what the struggle with resistances involves and that outside assistance can help [Freud, 1887–1902, p. 229], but there was no one to help him as he helped others. The use of a therapeutic relationship as an aid in the self-analytic process was advocated in 1912 when he said, "I count it one of the many merits of the Zurich School of Analysis that they have laid increasing emphasis on this requirement and have embodied it in a demand that everyone who wishes to carry out analysis of other people shall first himself undergo an analysis by someone with expert knowledge" [Freud, 1912, p. 116]. Thus the principle fundamental for psychoanalytic education gradually took shape, the principle that a personal analysis is a prerequisite, a *sine qua non* for professional learning.[2] The therapeutic aim, strongly enunciated by Nunberg in 1918, became established as a standard practice by the International Training Commission in 1925 [Eitingon, 1926] about 30 years after Freud's first entrance into this unexplored territory.

How knowledge is derived from the noncognitive experience of analysis was described by Freud in his attempts to communicate to Fliess his excitement in discovery and the ideas so generated. He said in Letter 72, dated October 27, 1897 [Freud, 1887–1902, p. 226], "I am now experiencing myself all the things which as a third party I have witnessed going on in my patients."[3] In Letter 74, dated November 5, 1897 (p. 228), there is recognition of the absence of conscious cognitive work: "At the moment I can neither read nor think. I am sufficiently absorbed in observation. My self-analysis is stagnating again, or rather it trickles on without my understanding its progress." In this statement he alludes to a shadowy awareness of which he was only partially conscious. In *Remembering, Repeating, and Working Through*, Freud (1914b) comments on the remark many patients make when something forgotten is being recalled: "As a matter of fact I've always *known* it; only I've never *thought* of it" (italics ours) [Freud, 1914b, p. 148].

Letter 75, dated November 14, 1897 [Freud, 1887–1902, p. 230], describes the birth of a new piece of knowledge: "Truth to tell, it was not entirely new, it had repeatedly shown and then withdrawn itself again; but this time it remained and saw the light of day. In a strange way I am aware of these events sometime

---

2. The terms applied to this experience with analysis, such as "didactic," "preparatory," "preliminary," "training," etc., are matters we cannot discuss here. The choice of term is often influenced by extraneous issues. We will use the term "training analysis" most frequently, since this is the commonly accepted one.

3. Why did Freud call himself a "third party"? Perhaps because he saw in the patient two persons as protagonists.

in advance." His language suggests something that moves in and out of conscious awareness, something only partially visible before it becomes clearly so—something that is experienced as actively working inside of himself but whose cognitive connections are only slowly established and cannot be *known* before the preconscious process of creating a new gestalt has taken place. Thus the process of experiential learning by introspection and interpretation in self-analytic work was put into communicable form by Freud, "the chief patient I am busy with" [Letter 67, 1887–1902, p. 218].

This primary stage in the education of an analyst could be described as an *in*-the-job learning experience compared to the *on*-the-job learning provided in supervision. Immersed in the analytic process, the student learns something of the analytic method of investigation by applying it to himself. From his experience as a patient he learns what it means to make an effort to associate freely, to speak out loud against the various resistances aroused by inner conflicts and anxieties. As he works in his training analysis to understand his own developmental experiences, he re-experiences them in relation to his analyst. Through the many levels of that recapitulation he learns to understand his own life history and himself as an active and passive agent in it. What he experiences as a patient introduces him to the tools of analytic work: introspection, empathy, and interpretation.

Introspection takes precedence in the training analysis, but the task of a patient in the psychoanalytic process involves more than looking into oneself by oneself alone. It includes communicating to someone else what has been "seen" by introspection. The patient's success in putting his introspected experience into words, saying it out loud in the presence of another person, expands the field available for awareness and cognition. As a patient the student-analyst realizes that psychoanalysis includes interpersonal communication based on an alliance with another person who also does introspective work.

The second tool, empathic understanding, which develops out of vicarious introspection by the analyst [Kohut, 1959] as a supplementary instrument for the patient's self-observation, becomes a part of the student-analyst's experience. In this beginning phase of training it is usually not integrated cognitively, but through first-hand experience the student learns that an analyst can hear meanings not recognizable to a patient and can empathically translate his understanding into an interpretation which enlarges a patient's area of awareness.

The experience of being understood empathically by his training analyst is fundamental for the development of the student's own capacity for empathy. He learns to listen not only to his analyst's interpretations but to himself as well, to interpret his manifest behavior in terms of its latent aims and its genetic roots, and to observe his own experience with empathic understanding for the childhood selves he once was. Empathy with those parts of himself that belong to the past, that he has outgrown, dislikes, or even rejects is an essential ingredient for self-understanding; it opens the way for the understanding of others. By way of experiencing himself against something else that is also himself, new awareness, new knowledge, and new professional skills emerge for the student-analyst. He discovers from direct intimate experience what it means "to make the unconscious conscious" [Freud, 1916, p. 282] and to build ego where id used to be [Freud, 1932].

The concept of the analyst's personality as an instrument of the analysis is not a new one. It was clearly recognized by Freud when in 1912 he described how "blind spots" in the analyst interfere with his use of himself as an instrument of therapy. But the earliest aims of the training analysis, to demonstrate the analytic method (didactic) and to relieve neurotic conflicts (therapeutic), have been expanded by the professional aim to develop the specific functions of the analyst's mental apparatus that are "instrumental" in the analytic process. This addition to the goals of the training analysis is possible because of advances of psychoanalytic psychology which afford increasing insight into the structure of the personality, with concomitant insight into the interpersonal dynamics of the therapeutic process. Thus, with new knowledge gained from clinical work, the educational objective of the training analysis can be formulated in terms of providing an experience which develops the ego functions of introspection, empathy, and interpretation that are essential for work as an analyst.

Regardless of how thorough-going a training analysis may be, it is just a beginning of an interminable process of self-analysis. This aspect of the training analysis, which has its personally protective as well as its professional value, has not been given its due emphasis in discussions of the first phase to training. An analyst may be confronted by any of his patients in any period of his professional life with one or another vulnerable area in his own personality. Healthy defensive systems and character traits are never completely immune to pressures which may be generated by work with patients, and changes caused by aging, fatigue, illness, or other external events may increase the analyst's vulnerability to the challenge of a patient's demands. In self-defense, his resistance to these demands may bring about technical mistakes which are generally called countertransferences. Or these challenges may stir up symptomatic responses which could disturb the analyst's balance between health and illness. Protection against these hazards of the profession is provided primarily by the training analysis and continued in the development of his self-analytic function during supervision.

One might say that although past and present experience plays a part in all learning, the student in the first phase of psychoanalytic training makes his own experiencing a primary object of study. In the analytic "experiment" he is the subject as well as the observer of the nature, language, and mechanisms of the unconscious, and his discoveries in this situation constitute basic learning about the psychoanalytic method and its tools— introspection, understanding, and interpreting.

After the experience of analysis from the position of patient has laid the groundwork,[4] the second phase of the training program refines the instrument still further. The chief objective of the second phase is concerned with learning to articulate the behavioral data of an analysis with explanatory concepts and theories. This task has been described by Bruner [1957] as "going beyond the information given." He defines this as a cognitive operation which seeks the coding system that establishes the relationships between the information given and the concepts which permit generalizing from one case or a prediction of probabilities. Such a cognitive operation enables the student to make sense out of an otherwise overwhelming mass of particulate phenomena, which often seem to be unrelated to each other or to any "known" frame of reference. The patient's individual personal experiences

4. To discuss the criteria for progression from training analysis to theoretical and clinical learning experiences is beyond the scope of our present study. Their formulation, however, is essential to the total educational process. In practice, the personal analysis may continue all through or beyond the other phases.

are brought into the analyst's field of cognitive scrutiny, where he can find equivalences in more general terms. In this way he correlates an analytic event with his learned concepts of dynamics, economics, and the genetics of behavior, and he so deepens his understanding of the dimensions of a specific phenomenon. Concepts and theories provide the student with a store of new information which gives explanatory power to the knowledge acquired by experience.

Two lines of experience, developing two kinds of knowing—empathic and cognitive—are continuously active in the process of analytic interaction. These two lines are essential for the analyst's work toward a diagnostic understanding of his patient. In the second phase of his education, the ability to experience introspectively and empathically that began in the training analysis is continued and organized into cognitive structures. One might describe these two tasks, whether in the analytic situation or in the learning situation, as making first an "experiential fit" and second a "cognitive fit." They have many operations in common. Both use synthetic, integrative, and introspective functions of the ego; both are inferential and interpretive in their aims; both deal with meanings "beyond the information given"; both start from a specific behavioral event, whether in the past or present, and attempt to enlarge the scope of understanding and knowing. Empathic understanding, however, leads to a different kind of knowing than the explanatory coding which the cognitive process involves. The message from the patient, whose latent as well as manifest meanings are "heard" with the analytic ear, is often responded to without any cognitive mediating step. The patient and the analyst can and do interact intuitively and "unknowingly," often with very beneficial results. The "experiential fit" facilitated by empathy enables the analyst to identify the communication behind the patient's words and translate it into words not yet available to the patient. This cognitive step in the process of interpretation provides explanatory answers to the questions *why* and *how*, sometimes to be communicated to the patient and sometimes not. Making a "cognitive fit" builds a bridge between otherwise incongruous and contradictory behaviors and renders them understandable. An analyst moves back and forth across this bridge as he reconstructs the life story of the interactions of innate and environmental forces on his patient.

In the stage of active learning, traveling back and forth between these two kinds of knowing is more conscious and explicit than it becomes later. To know what one knows and how one knows it becomes part of the process of learning [Bateson, 1942], and to be able to express this level of insight in words becomes a significant (albeit often ideal) part of the interaction between teacher and student. The pedagogic task is to provide the situations and experiences which facilitate this learning.

One source of material for building this bridge between direct experiencing of unconscious forces and organizing the experience into more general frames of reference is the student's personal analysis. Subjected to secondary processes of thinking and to correlation with a theoretical system, the student's experience in being an analytic patient can be objectified and given more meaning when cognitive understanding of that experience becomes a goal of learning. On the other hand, concepts and theories take on added significance when compared and contrasted with a student's personal experience. This level of insight is not an explicit aim during the personal analysis, although it may happen with a rare analysand and in rare moments as described by Kris [1956a] when he speaks of the ego observing its own functioning. For a student of psychoanalysis, however, this kind of understanding should become a learning goal. When it is accomplished, a dimension is added to his professional work ego.

This new level of self-knowledge may take shape preconsciously either late in the training analysis or after it is terminated; it may become conscious and explicit without active incentive supplied by classroom teachers or in clinical situations. A sudden recall of an event in his own analysis may occur to a student while he is listening to a lecture and illuminate with new meaning both the analytic event and the ideas being presented by the lecturer. A step in the cognitive organization of experience has taken place; the synthesizing function of the ego has "gone beyond the information" to a new level of integration; and knowledge has been created from experience.

Such a moment of learning gives intimations of the active preconscious metabolizing of stored experience with the inflow of new information which is the core of a creative process. Learning at this level can be compared with the therapeutic experience of working through [Jones, 1962], in which defenses against change are gradually eroded, permitting shifts of energies, modifications of structure, and development of more mature modes of experiencing. How to utilize the creativity of the preconscious [Beres, 1957; Kramer, 1959; Sachs, 1942] and build the cognitive structures that will make it more effective for the practice of analysis is the pedagogic problem at this stage of a student-analyst's development. The bridge between what happened in his analysis and a cognitive understanding of it can be facilitated by teaching which directs the student's attention to a scrutiny of that experience as a source of valuable information about technique and the analytic process. Many training analysts will disagree with this point of view, raising the objection that the emphasis on cognitive learning in the classroom encourages intellectualizing resistances which interfere with the affective experience essential for a good analysis. Such an outcome may occur, especially if the student is still in analysis. On the other hand, that outcome becomes material for interpretation and can be treated as such.

The crucial question is the teacher's method of approach to this kind of learning experience. In terms of timing, it seems to belong to courses on the theory of technique and can be introduced by the teacher's raising the question, "What did you learn about technique from your training analysis and how did you learn it?" The answers will be varied and the class discussion can be used as an exercise in on-the-spot self-observation. Such an exercise touches upon part of an analyst's job: a constant need to tolerate self-examination and to learn from it—vividly experienced in the training analysis and reinforced in classroom and supervision.

Strangely enough, many students are startled at being confronted with this question, which seems never to have occurred to them consciously. Moreover, they respond as if the objective examination of their own experience were a forbidden activity, a transgression of the role of "patient" in analysis. This is understandable in view of the fact that many students overcome resistance to "being a patient" only after great effort, but the resistance to observing that experience is also something that needs to be overcome. What the student experiences as a patient must be related to the process of experiencing and to the process of change. The factors that modify both the experiences of childhood and the childhood mode of experiencing must be identified and organized into schemata of concepts and cognitive structures that construct a framework of theory relevant to the work of psychoanalyzing.

This kind of classroom activity does not involve "analyzing" the student by expecting free associations or by making interpretations. It consists more appropriately of a confrontation with an attitude of self-inquiry and the value of generalizing from one's own experience. Such an exercise in a classroom situation goes only a short distance on the road toward the skill in self-analysis that belongs to a competent analyst, but it takes the first steps in a direction that continues in clinical conferences and supervision. Moreover, Freud provides an excellent model for identification in this phase of cognitive learning. His own experiences in self-analysis as well as with his patients were his chief source of data for theroy building. Motivated by scientific curiosity and a search for truth, he freed himself from his transference identifications with Fliess [Buxbaum, 1951] and subjected his generalizations to continuous revisions in the light of new knowledge.

It is well recognized that identification is a vital factor at all levels of learning, but its mechanisms and processes are not clearly understood. Since identification takes place unconsciously, we see only the effects rather than the process itself. We can, however, recognize the source and often the motivational determinants of behavior as it reflects the shadows of persons and events belonging to childhood development. The psychoanalytic method of reconstruction facilitates discovery and recall of the developmental experiences influential in the formation of psychic structure. Moreover, through recapitulation in the transference, a patient's childhood identifications can become conscious and the phenomena of identifying with the analyst can be observed. As these identifications are examined with all of their positive and negative carry-overs, the building of regulatory systems and modifications of ego functions can be traced.

Identification, however, is not confined to childhood, but plays a part in learning experiences throughout life. It is a powerful force in every teacher–student relationship at all levels of education and in other life situations as well. It is important for the student of psychoanalysis to learn not only about his childhood identifications, but also how he uses his analyst and his other teachers as a source of supply for incentives, knowledge, and objects for imitative learning. When he achieves this degree of self-insight, he will be able to differentiate his primitive transference identifications from present-day models, and his motives for learning by identification can be more consciously integrated with his professional aims.

However, since the process of identification is such a powerful and pervasive force, and since it operates unconsciously, it becomes a problem in psychoanalytic education for teachers as well as students. Many authors have recognized it as a factor in countertransference problems seen in training analysts and supervisors. Balint [1948], Glover [1952], Benedek [1954], and Szasz [1958], to mention only a few, have called attention to the tendency of analytic teachers to permit and even subtly to encourage their training candidates to establish idenfications with their own points of view and techniques. Whether or not this results in perpetuation of infantile patterns of behavior depends upon the immaturity of the candidate, which may be manifested in uncritical imitation of the behavior of the individual identified with or in intense resistance to a differing point of view. Anxieties and defensiveness at the root of such patterns are difficult to deal with except in the analytic situation; yet the dangers of their persistence, described by Balint [1948] as stultifying to the individual student and to psychoanalysis as a science, present clear-cut problems for psychoanalytic educators.

Educators are confronted with a particularly difficult but interesting challenge, since the problem stems from forces basic to psychoanalysis and related to its value systems as a developmental and clinical science. The aim of psychoanalysis—to increase the field of conscious knowledge and consequently to provide freedom for more reality-oriented choices—is at stake, but is threatened by the very forces which have positive as well as negative value for growth and learning [Grotjahn, 1949]. There is no simple solution to this problem, since it is so closely related to the question of insight into resistances in both analytic teacher and student—a question which has plagued analysts from the days when Freud struggled with his own conflicts and when he recognized that an analyst can learn only as far as his complexes permit [Freud, 1910].

There are many variables which influence the factor of identification in the learning of psychoanalysis. Only two will be mentioned here. One factor is the stage of resolution of the transference neurosis at the time the student begins his theoretical and clinical work. The other factor is the relative skill of the classroom teacher and supervisor in helping the student overcome resistances stemming from transference reactions.

In the classroom, displacement of transference identifications and various forms of defense offer resistances to learning rooted in dependency conflicts and ambivalences. If these inevitable conflicts and their corresponding anxieties have not been worked through in the training analysis, progression to the next phase of training will not result in optimal learning. In a recent article, Langer *et al.* [Langer, Puget, and Teper, 1964] describe this problem as they saw it in a seminar on the theory of technique. This paper is of interest because it is the only one of which we are aware that discusses classroom learning experiences. Lewin and Ross [1960] discuss "school problems" but describe them in general terms applied mainly to supervision. Langer [*et al.*'s] paper is interesting because it describes an effort to encourage an attitude of unprejudiced objectivity toward differing points of view, a basic attitude for an analyst and for a learner in any field.

The principal problem for the classroom teacher lies in his ability to differentiate the various phenomena of identification in terms of their facilitation of learning or their obstruction of it. This diagnostic task is especially difficult in a classroom situation because of the individualized aspects of the problem and the number of persons likely to be involved simultaneously. The techniques relevant for an analytic situation do not apply, yet the mechanisms of identification which operate ubiquitously demand that the classroom teacher of psychoanalysis understand both the positive and negative aspects of the role of identification in learning and that he develop techniques for using the process constructively. The same consideration holds true for the supervisory situation and the supervisor, as will be discussed later.

In the theoretical phase of training, the clinical conference provides a variation on the classroom situation which is comparable to the laboratory in other sciences. Here the correlation of theory and practice is closer to the work of analyzing, and the student has an opportunity to practice, in the sense of rehearsing—to exercise his diagnostic understanding and his interpretive technique. In the classroom he learns the cognitive language of psychoanalysis, while in the clinical conference he identifies the behavioral cues which he can then categorize as anxiety, resistance, defenses, transference, etc. He follows vicariously the technical maneuvers of the analyst, assesses their therapeutic effectiveness, and makes trial interpretations of his own. This "laboratory" experience has a stimulating effect on the student's self-observation and correlation of his own experiences, past and immediate, with that of the patient being presented or with that of the student-analyst whose work is under scrutiny. How far each individual goes in investigating his personal reactions in a clinical conference situation cannot be made explicit. Each student must follow his own path in this direction. It is to be hoped, however, that he possesses the attitude and the ability to let his preconscious processing come into consciousness. Many of his responses to the immediate situation will remain on a preconscious level, to become available for insightful closures as he achieves an integration of learning from all of these different kinds of experiences.

In the third phase of the training program, the phase of on-the-job practice of analysis under supervision, learning by doing continues the experiential testing out, which has been emphasized as the basic component of learning to become an analyst. In the supervisory situation the student tries out his "analytic instrument" *in vivo*. With his psychic processes clarified and refined in his training analysis, exercised and strengthened by theoretical learning tasks, the student enters the final step in the sequence of training experiences. He is called upon to carry forward what he has learned in other situations to performance as an analyst with a patient, a level of learning that presents its own hierarchy of objectives and teaching techniques.

A third line of experience comes into prominence as the student enters the clinical phase of his education. This line involves learning how to translate intuitive and cognitive understanding back into "experiential" language for communication to the patient. Such a task requires an integration of empathic (affective), cognitive, and executive (decision-making) functions into the act of "making an interpretation." The various principles to be followed in arriving at technical decisions about what, when, and how to communicate with a patient will be discussed later.

The two kinds of learning, experiential and cognitive, continue to confront both student and supervisor. Learning in supervision combines experiential testing of the tools of introspection, empathy, and tactful interpretation with recognition and coding of "what works" and "what does not work." Making a "cognitive fit" in clinical learning includes increasing awareness of why "this works" and "that does not." In other words, a good learning experience in supervision goes beyond following rules of thumb or imitation of what someone else did or might have done in similar circumstances. It increases the student-analyst's awareness of himself in the interaction with his patient. In the supervisory situation, the student travels back and forth across the bridge between his knowledge of how it should be done and what he actually did. There is a constant oscillation between experiencing and observing that experience, between empathy, introspection, and insightful choices for technical action, and between analyzing his patient and himself in an effort to correct his mistakes and develop creative skill in his professional work.

Both student and supervisor become involved in "instrumental" learning—how to use what has been learned and how to make the instrument work. "The concept of the 'analyzing instrument' recommends itself," according to Isakower [1963b, p. 1], "primarily on the grounds of its heuristic value, as a point of reference for clarification of the psychic processes which constitute the foundation of the specific analytic activity." These processes that make the instrument work operate unconsciously but can be observed through their effects and can be studied retrospectively. This retrospective view of the analytic instrument in operation is a major focus of attention in supervision. The training analysis begins to assemble the tools for functioning as an analyst; the clinical phase of training puts these tools to work and develops their instrumental use; and the process of self-analysis initiated in the training analysis is continued in supervision.

In *Analysis Terminable and Interminable*, Freud [1937, p. 249] referred to the importance of an analyst's capacity to analyze himself: "We hope and believe that the stimuli received in the learner's own analysis will not cease to act upon him when that analysis ends, *that the processes of ego transformation will go on of their own accord and that all further experiences will be made use of in a newly acquired way.*[5] This does indeed happen and in so far as it happens, it qualifies the learner who has been analyzed to

5. Translated from the German by Maria Kramer and quoted in her paper.

become an analyst." Kramer [1959], in her beautifully elaborated, significant paper describing observations on the continuation of the analytic process in herself, explains what she means by the analytic process going on of its own accord. Because of the automaticity of the process and the spontaneity of resulting insights, she has coined the term "auto-analysis," and defined it as an independent ego function existing only in those persons who have been analyzed.

To define this process of intrapsychic activity and structural change as an ego function is an interesting question which would take us beyond the scope of this book. The total process is, of course, a complex operation employing various ego functions, each contributing to the total result. Since we are interested in how these ego resources can be developed for professional work, we find it more useful for our purposes to concentrate on the separate learning experiences that will help a student-analyst acquire the ability to use these "processes of ego transformation . . . in a newly acquired way."

The chief obstacles to overcome are the inevitable resistances. Kramer paints a vivid picture of these resistances. Freud does also in Letter 71 [Freud, 1887–1902, p. 221]: "My self-analysis is the most important thing I have in hand, and promises to be of the greatest value to me, when it is finished. When I was in the very midst of it, it suddenly broke down for three days, and I had the feeling of inner binding about which my patients complain so much. . . . " In the next letter, 12 days later (p. 225), he writes, "Business is hopelessly bad, . . . so I am living only for my 'inner work.' It gets hold of me and hauls me through the past in rapid association of ideas; and my mood changes like the landscape seen by a traveler from the train. . . . " Later, in the same letter (p. 226), he re-emphasizes the strength of the forces opposing insight when he recognizes, "Resistance has thus become an objectively tangible thing for me. . . . "

Both Freud and Kramer stress the frequent sense of failure in active attempts to follow a line of associations against resistance. Insights cannot be forced either in a formal analytic situation or in self-analysis. Every analyst learns to assess the strength of a patient's resistance at a given moment, and when his probing interpretations fail, he waits or focuses on a smaller, more peripheral area that shows signs of weakness. Insight, whether it comes in formal analysis or self-analysis, is achieved slowly by a gradual integration of many pieces of working through akin to the process of creativity. [Beres, 1957].

Active efforts may not bring insight with conviction (Reik, 1937] at the conclusion of a given period of "activity," yet a deliberate effort to use the tools of analysis on oneself opens channels of inner communication and a flow of associations, preconsciously "processed" [Kubie, 1958] until a gestalt can be integrated. When this gestalt meets ego-syntonic requirements, it acquires a cathexis strong enough to break through barriers to consciousness, and it then appears to have been achieved spontaneously. The sense of spontaneity, however, is illusory since it does not happen without effort. An energy drain often accompanies this integrative "work" of the ego.

Knowledge about how resistance feels, and the recognition that it can be overcome are parts of the insight resulting from analysis, although the preconscious operations remain outside conscious control. This experiential knowledge is reinforced by the cognitive appreciation of concepts about conflicts, defenses, and symptom formation. The ego operates "auto-analytically" within a field of forces given cohesion by the insights previously achieved in formal analysis, and theoretical knowledge provides a frame of reference for organizing the dissonant, fleeting signals of psychic activity not usually in the foreground of consciousness.

These self-analytic processes undoubtedly proceed more automatically and with less active effort in an experienced analyst. For a student whosse attitude of self-scrutiny is not yet disciplined by practice, some assistance is required during the period of initiation into the work of analyzing. A natural tendency is to feel that with the shift from patient to analyst he need no longer listen to himself but only to the person on the couch. The difficult task of associating freely is now for someone else to do—or so it may seem to the student. He may tell himself with a sense of triumph, "Now *I* will make the interpretations." Although this description is exaggerated, and students are now told from the beginning of training that analysis is a never-ending process for an analyst, conviction that this is so has to be learned from experience. It is in this area of practicing self-analysis that a supervisor serves as a catalyst for these processes.

In this chapter we have emphasized the role of experiencing

unconscious–preconscious, as well as conscious, knowledge in learning psychoanalysis. We have described different kinds of experiences which contribute to the development of a professional work ego. In learning the clinical science of psychoanalysis the problem does not seem to come under either the first or the second "family of learning theories" [Hilgard, 1948]. Both the stimulus–response association theories and the cognitive-field theories seem to apply. The most successful learning of psychoanalysis results from a cognitive integration of associative patterns into general principles which are then applied to practice, tested for success, and modified into new forms of technical behavior. The essential step in this clinical learning, however it is achieved, lies in the development of the learner as an instrument not only to accomplish learning but also to measure it. To be able to objectify the process and to evaluate degrees of success marks the independent learner who can teach himself and who is invested in maintaining an attitude of inquiry directed toward discovery about his patients, himself, and his field.

In summary, we reiterate our thesis: To make self-analytic functions readily available equipment for working as an analyst is the basic and continuing goal of psychoanalytic training. Each phase of the training program contributes in special ways to this overall goal, and each psychoanalytic teacher can enhance his effectiveness if he orients the content and method of his teaching in this direction.

·2·

FREUD'S CONCEPT
OF SELF-ANALYSIS:
ITS RELEVANCE FOR
PSYCHOANALYTIC TRAINING

In this essay written in 1971, Dr. Fleming shows her appreciation and sensitivity for psychoanalytic history. Dr. Fleming reviews Freud's own analysis as extracted from the important Freud–Fliess correspondence, and notes the changing concepts of the role of the training analysis for the education of an analyst. These changes in viewing the training analysis are identified with different historical periods having different educational philosophies.

Dr. Fleming emphasizes that the training analysis is the essential experience from which learning about theory and acquiring clinical skills proceeds. It is an experience of self-discovery that initiates a self-analytic process, which serves to achieve both therapeutic and professional skills that are basic to analytic work.

It is the need for a successful training analysis for candidates that makes psychoanalytic education so unique, so difficult, and so very rewarding.

Ferenczi (1911), in his paper "On the Organization of the Psychoanalytic Movement," advocated periodic consideration of the successes and failures of psychoanalysis, saying, "Drawing up such balance sheets from time to time is as necessary in scientific workshops as it is in trade and industry" (p. 299). To follow his advice is especially important for psychoanalytic educators, since with expanding knowledge about psychoanalysis, the objectives and methods of educating new generations of analysts need continual review and modification in order to keep pace with the prog-

Reprinted by permission from *Currents in Psychoanalysis*, I. M. Marcus, Ed. New York: International Universities Press, 1971, pp. 14–45.

ress of our science. Today more than yesterday, it is the quality of the education we provide for our students which determines the quality of psychoanalytic contributions to knowledge and its practical applications in the years to come. We must continue to examine where we are in the evolution of our educational philosophy, to identify the areas where we feel dissatisfied, and in open discussion to attempt to find ways to improve our present training programs.

It is in the spirit of Ferenczi that I propose an examination of a persisting question concerning the goal of that cornerstone of psychoanalytic education, the training analysis. A conflict between therapeutic and professional learning goals has been called the "problem of the training analysis" (A. Freud, 1950; Kairys, 1964). Professional goals are seen as reality contaminants of a therapeutic experience, and a training analyst is said to be confronted by an irreconcilable dilemma (Lewin and Ross, 1960): Should he treat or teach?

I believe it is accurate to say this question has troubled every analytic educator, including Freud, at one time or another in his career. Treating and teaching are so often held to be mutually exclusive. Insofar as teaching is seen as intellectual and instructional, for an analyst to give instruction is regarded not only as an overemphasis on cognition at the expense of affective experience, but it is also assumed to include recommending a course of action. Such activity by an analyst is considered to be undesirable manipulation that interferes with the emancipative therapeutic goal of analysis. Therapy, too, has limited definition for many therapists, since it is assumed to involve techniques for relieving symptoms, modifying maladaptive behavior of the environment by one manipulative means or another.

Analytic therapy should avoid manipulative maneuvers of all kinds; of that there is no question. Desirable change is produced not by external manipulation but by reliving a neurotically solved childhood conflict under conditions of the analytic situation which facilitate a different, more mature and adaptive solution to a childhood problem. This transference reproduction of the past is, however, only part of the therapeutic goal of analysis. The individuating, integrative experience of exploring oneself in an analytic situation requires a differentiation of past from present, of analyst from transference image—tasks which call on all of the learning capacities and educative skills which analyst and patient possess.

Solving the problem would seem to consist first in finding the factors common to both therapy and learning. If we look at learning and therapy as developmental processes, there is much that they share together. Increased knowledge, freedom to develop to a more mature level, and motivations more realistically determined are shared goals, and the person who helps, be he educator or analyst, is one who "leads out from" the bonds of ignorance and irrationality that block freedom to develop. Both are striving for the same results. Even many of the techniques of teacher and therapist are similar, attempting as they do to continue to extend along productive lines the developmental, educative process set in motion at birth and initially guided for better or for worse by the child's first educator and first therapist, his mother.

Without question, our positions on these problems today have their origins in past attitudes and practices. The trouble is that old practices are always subtly modified in one direction or another by various influences coming from both events and people. These changes are often accommodations that become popularized and established as policies, without much thought being given to the underlying rationale or the fact that the original accommodation becomes outdated. Earlier policies and procedures may no longer fit the more current situations, yet they continue to be followed or they are changed under influences which often neglect to preserve the best of the old in the service of emphasizing an aspect of the old which seems more imperative at the time. I believe we have become caught by these influences when we forge "to treat or to teach" into such a dichotomy for the training analysis. To follow Ferenczi's stock-taking advice, it becomes necessary to go back into the past, to try to understand what influenced the practices then, what caused the changes that have lead to our present ways of doing things.

With this goal in mind, I reviewed the literature relevant to the evolution of our present-day concept of the training analysis, searching for some clues to "the problem" outlined above. A result of this review was that although I found no satisfactory answers for the causes of change, I was nonetheless impressed with the truth of another statement by Ferenczi (1930), i.e., "We must constantly be prepared to find new veins of gold in temporarily abandoned workings" (p. 120). It is the results of such reworking that I want to present in the current essay with the hope that this effort at stock taking will help to clarify the issues and lead to more effective educational practices.

Today, everyone agrees that the training analysis is the foundation on which the further development of a young analyst is built. Today, analytic educators consider the training analysis to be the essential educational experience from which learning about theory and acquiring clinical skills proceeds. Yet it has not always been this way. Ernest Jones practiced analysis for eight years before he sought a didactic analysis for himself (Oberndorf, 1953). Bernfeld was told by Freud, when he asked about being analyzed, to start with a patient and when he got in trouble they could think about having some analysis for himself (Ekstein, 1953). These two instances bear witness to the fact that in the beginning a training analysis had a purely professional goal, was considered to be a "didactic" (instructional) procedure and was conducted under circumstances which would be labelled "impossible" today. For example, Eitingon went on walks with Freud twice weekly after supper and had his analysis on these walks (Balint, 1954).

When such an analysis was undertaken, it was short and primarily directed toward offering a sample of the activity of the unconscious and a brief opportunity to observe the analytic method. Prior to 1920 there was no formal training program as we know it today. Analysis at that time was more like a game of detection, probing through the wall of infantile amnesia following clues from dreams, symptoms, and slips of the tongue.

It did not take long before the consultations between neophytes and senior colleagues or group discussions about cases revealed how easy it was for a patient to provoke inappropriate responses in the analyst, who seemed unaware of these affective unconsciously motivated reactions. Freud (1912) compared them with transferences and when seen in the analyst called them "countertransferences" which needed "psychoanalytic purification." Since Freud, at that time (1910), considered transference to be an obstacle to analytic work, he felt countertransferences were even more so. A patient's transferences could be resolved with skillful handling, but such was not the case for the analyst himself. Yet

Freud realized the importance of bringing such unconscious motivations under conscious control.

Hence, it was in 1910, in a statement that seems to mark the beginning of a shift from a primarily professional objective for the "didactic" analysis to a therapeutic aim, that Freud correlated the occurrence of "countertransferences" with the need for "self-analysis." In this paper, Freud felt that self-analysis was a remedy and that "Anyone who fails to produce results in a self-analysis of this kind [should] at once give up any idea of being able to treat patients by analysis" [p. 145]. The "countertransferences" were looked upon as symptoms resulting from unconscious conflict and should therefore be treated to "clarify the instrument," to use Isakower's (1963a) more current phrase.

Freud's statement in 1910 well describes the informal attitude toward training which prevailed at that time but also the seriousness with which he made his recommendation. I quote:

> We have become aware of the "countertransference" which arises in him [the analyst] as a result of the patient's influence on his unconscious feelngs, and we are *almost* [italics mine] inclined to insist that he shall recognize this countertransference in himself and overcome it. Since analysts have begun to exchange observations with each other we have noticed no psychoanalyst goes further than his own complexes and internal resistances permit; and we consequently require that he shall begin his activity with a self-analysis and continually carry it deeper while he is making his observations on his patients. (p. 144)

In this recommendation for a "self-analysis" Freud (1887–1902) is referring to his own experience in analyzing himself which he described in his letter to Fliess. The letters which contain the references to his self-analysis cover a portion of this time, the period from the death of his father in October 1896 to the fall of 1900, when there was a rupture in his relationship with Fliess which never healed. I intend to review some of the aspects of Freud's self-analysis discernible in his letters and in the commentaries by Kris (1954), Jones (1953), Buxbaum (1951), and others (Bernfeld, S., 1946; Bernfeld, S. C., 1952; Eissler, 1951) as they bear on the acquisition of self-analytic skills and the necessity for an interminable application of these skills in the professional work of a psychoanalyst.

However, before presenting that material, I should like to review the changing concepts of the role of the training analysis in the education of an analyst as described by Balint (1954). Balint identified five historical periods, each of which emphasized a different educational philosophy.

The first or instructional period stressed learning the theory and technique by reading books or by a kind of practicing on each other. Knowledge of current theory and the ability to recognize evidence of unconscious activity were the primary learning goals. Didactic analysis apparently was not sought by many until around 1909, and then, according to what Freud said to Ferenczi about Eitingon (Balint, 1954), the model approximated Freud's pattern of self-exploration in which a report of dreams, associations, slips, etc., were discussed.

This kind of limited analytic experience involved more than reading books and became the period of education by demonstration, according to Balint's classification. The chief teaching technique was didactic and the expectations were not yet therapeutically direct. In his 1937 paper, Freud described these limited goals in terms of demonstrating intrapsychic processes and techniques of uncovering, stating, however, that "this alone would not suffice for [the student's] instruction" (p. 248).

Even in 1937, however, Freud did not emphasize the "therapeutic need," although he did stress the need for "self-analysis." The 1937 paper assumes a period of analytic work with an experienced analyst, something he recommended as early as 1912. But he also assumes that this period of formal analysis will be "short and incomplete" and that even the "processes of ego transformation" which differentiate the analyzed person are considered to be goals in the service of professional learning. Freud called himself a patient in Letter 67 to Fliess and compared his experiences in his self-analytic work with what he observed in his "other" patients, but, it seems to me, in spite of his depression and confusion, he thought of himself more as a subject of investigation than a patient hoping for relief of suffering. In this sense, he was more like the "normal candidate" of today who resists accepting a need for help even when hurting symptoms are present (Gitelson, 1954).

The normal candidate resists the therapeutic aim of today's training analysis (Greenson, 1967; Bibring, 1954; Kairys, 1964; Fleming, 1969; Greenacre, 1966) and in so doing he recapitulates the "demonstration" phase (Balint, 1954) of early training. In the recommendation to Bernfeld to start with a patient and when he got in trouble to consider analysis for himself, Freud may have been responding to an empathic recognition of the resistance to "being a patient." Consequently, he placed greater emphasis on the professional, rather than the therapeutic value of analysis. For Freud, at that time, analysis was still an intellectual self-discovery, a synthesis of past and present by means of recall of traumatic memories and abreaction of repressed affect. What permitted the recall and freed the repressed in terms of working through the transferences and facilitating the discriminating, integrative functions of the ego had not yet become the focus of investigation.

Balint (1954) comments that no one directed serious thought toward a scientific evaluation of the goals of the training analysis until Ferenczi (1927) began to advocate a "proper analysis"—one as thorough as the therapeutic analysis of a patient, Ferenczi felt that if analysis had beneficial effects on a patient, an analyst deserved the same. He told Clara Thompson (1955) that he sometimes envied his patients who had gained something more from analysis than he did. Balint describes how the opposition to Ferenczi argued that such an analysis, as long and as deep as with the usual patient would involve "tampering" with the character of the analysand. Such tampering was felt to have unforeseen and dangerous consequences. Yet, today, we think of a training analysis as necessarily including the character structure of the candidate. Perhaps Ferenczi's outspokenness offered a displaced target for the resistance latently stirred up by Freud's (1910) statement which advocated self-analysis to overcome the "countertransferences" increasingly visible in consultations about patients and in analytic discussion groups.

Freud wrote little about training as such. Consequently, we are largely in the dark about what he really thought. Yet what appears to be his first published statement (quoted above, 1910) on psychoanalytic training was undoubtedly stimulated by what he felt were manifestations of unconsciously motivated responses from the analyst to his patient—responses which should not be there and which interfered with the mirrorlike neutrality he considered professionally desirable. As far as we know, Freud assumed that all analysts would be motivated as he was to undergo the trials of self-discovery in order to increase their professional skill. Apparently in 1910, Freud's feeling of success in his own self-analytic work made him confident that others could do the same, but it was only two years later that he (1912) more strongly advised prospective analysts to undergo "an analysis by someone with more expert knowledge." In this paper, he compliments the Zurich group which had begun this practice. Pointing out the rewards accruing from self-knowledge and self-control, he says: ". . . we must not underestimate the advantage to be derived from the lasting mental contact that is as a rule established between the student and his guide" (p. 117). Here, Freud acknowledges the personal value of the personal relationship with the analyst, apart from professional advantage. Nevertheless, he again stresses the goal of self-discovery for its own sake when he takes for granted that ". . . when it is over [the student] will continue the analytic examination of his personality in the form of a self-analysis, and be content to realize that, within himself as well as in the internal world, he must always expect to find something new" (p. 117).

With the 1912 recommendation, the institution of training analyst was thus initiated, although the early *Lehranalytiker* and his student were often neophytes together, since there was not much difference in knowledge or experience between them (Benedek, 1969). The newly constituted training analysts had probably not thought of themselves as patients and had not experienced a fully developed transference neurosis as we expect to have happen today. In fact, the term *"Lehranalytiker"* continued to put the emphasis on the didactic goals of the analytic experience for a student. Nevertheless, as clinical experience with patients (students or otherwise) continued and deepened under the inevitable dynamic pressure of transference and the repetition compulsion, beneficial relief of symptoms, anxieties, and inhibitions was observed.

Balint (1954) attributes to Ferenczi the role of chief advocate for the shift to stressing a therapeutic aim for the analysis of a student-analyst. Ferenczi (1928) talked of a "fully-completed analysis" as being something which should be expected of a training analysis. This proposition went beyond his previous position that claimed there should be no difference between a therapeutic and a training analysis (Ferenczi and Rank, 1924). In 1928, Ferenczi stated new goals, saying, ". . . that while every case undertaken for therapeutic purposes need not be carried to the depth we mean when we talk of a complete ending of the analysis, the analyst himself must know, and be in control of, even the most recondite weaknesses of his own character, and this is impossible without a fully completed analysis" (p. 89). Here we see a combination of therapeutic and professional aims for the training analysis: therapy for personal advantage as with any other patient, but carried to a high degree of perfection for professional reasons.

Balint (1954) labels what Ferenczi advocated as the fourth historical period, where the educational philosophy was one of "supertherapy." Other analysts, notably Nunberg and Eitingon, followed Ferenczi's lead to some extent, although their principal objective was to institutionalize the training analysis and make it not an elective procedure but a requirement for becoming an analyst. In 1910 Freud's language was not so strict, but in 1925, Eitingon (1926), half apologetically, said he thought there was "an additional aim that supersedes or goes hand in hand with the therapeutic aim" [p. 132]. Ferenczi in his book with Rank (1924) made this additional aim more specific, i.e., to prepare the student-analyst for the heavy drain on his emotional resources and the strenuous task of strict control of his own responses which treating a patient demanded. In other words, Ferenczi picked up Freud's 1910 statement about self-analysis as a remedy for countertransference, and from 1908 until he died in 1933, Ferenczi (1928) stressed the need to recognize what behavior of his own the patient might be responding to.

Because of his interest in the "personal equation" as a factor in analytic work, Ferenczi (1927) attempted to isolate and to define the elements in the analyst's behavior which might influence a patient's reactions, e.g., the cool aloofness, something which analysts consider a proper attitude but which a patient may feel as a rejection. He described in detail and stressed again and again what the analyst is called upon to do at his end of the interpersonal interaction in the analytic situation. He elaborated on how the analyst "has to let the patient's free associations play upon him; simultaneously, he lets his own fantasy get to work with the associated material; from time to time he compares the new connections that arise with earlier results of the analysis; and not for one moment must he relax his vigilance and criticism made necessary by his own subjective trends" (p. 86).

Ferenczi (1928), Robert Fliess (1942), and Hans Sachs (1947) more than others have tried to describe the process in the analyst's mind—the process of stimulus and response sequences, some conscious, many only half-conscious, and many more outside of awareness altogether, that determine the analyst's empathic understanding and his communications to his patient. In Ferenczi's (1927) words, "One might say that the analyst's mind swings continuously between empathy, self-observation, and making judgments. The latter emerge spontaneously from time to time as mental signals, which at first, have to be assessed only as such; only after the accumulation of further evidence is one entitled to make an interpretation" (p. 86). Ferenczi tries to paint in explanatory terms the elements of the self-analytic process which Freud (1887–1902) described experientially in Letters 72, 74, 75, and 130. Freud did not focus on the process of self-analysis after that, but paid more attention to motivation, the control of attitudes, and countertransferences.

After the period of "supertherapy," the fifth philosophy of training analysis focused neither on therapy nor instruction, but "research" (Balint, 1954). What happened seems to have been a disillusionment with psychoanalysis as a method of treatment. If the super goals seemed unattainable, it was rationalized that the failure was attributable not to the pathology of the patient or to the inadequacy of the analyst, but rather to the method. Thus the reassuring conclusion could be reached that the method was not designed for such achievements, and, therefore, those ambitions could be given up and attention paid to using "the method" for "research" purposes, i.e., to investigate mental processes. Balint (1954) comments that the advent of the "research" period aimed to avoid the problems inherent in the termination phase of a training analysis, with its postanalytic introjection of the idealized analyst. This aspect of continuing transference has been a powerful factor in perpetuating and intensifying the rivalries of the training analysts in the "supertherapy" period. If the "research" emphasis is in the service of carrying on a mutually gratifying self-exploration and discovery that leaves the analyst divested of omniscience and the student-patient free to individuate himself, then "research" in the sense of self-discovery might well become the goals of the training analysis. Freud's self-analytic effort accomplished both. He discovered things in himself which freed him from his dependence on Fliess, and he was able to conceptualize his findings with benefit for general psychology. His attitude of self-inquiry and the courage to struggle with inner resistances in unremitting self-analysis is a most valuable legacy for present and future generations of analysts.

Kurt Eissler (1951) compares the creative process and Freud's self-analysis. He stresses that the urge to create, whether in art or science, must always operate against an inner resistance; new forms, ideas, or demands on the self are opposed by strong forces striving to maintain the status quo in comfort. He describes Freud's self-analysis as "so to speak, against human nature; without prospect of reward, without an inner compulsion or impulsion, the ego seems out of its own resourcefulness to have evolved the firm intuition to withstand an inner revulsion and to bear voluntarily and of its own accord that pain which is for several reasons the most difficult to bear" (p. 322).

Eissler thinks that Freud's heroic effort cannot be repeated. This is true if we think of it as a unique, unassisted struggle across uncharted seas. But now the seas are charted to some extent and the initial avoidance resistances are not dealt with entirely without help. A method for self-discovery has been provided. Its application sets going a self-analytic process and skills in this direction can be developed. The training analysis is the start of that voyage. Other learning experiences continue the process and sharpen the skills. The source of the motivation to continue the effort on one's own is the chief unknown. Some of it apparently comes from neurotic suffering and some from an untraceable thirst for knowledge.[1]

When Freud began his self-analysis he was already using the skills of free association, introspection, and interpretation on his own dreams and with his patients. At that time (prior to 1896) these tasks had a more professional and scientific, rather than a personal goal. He used his skill in introspection to bring into conscious focus peripheral associations, and his skill in interpretation to find links between associations, the symbolic meanings, and the connections between conflict and repressed affect.

1. It is not my intention to recapitulate Freud's self-analysis. The Fliess letters (Freud, 1887-1902), however, contain such valuable information and insights into the process of self-analysis that I will present here significant excerpts in order to make the data readily available. What is reported here should not substitute for rereading the letters.

In 1896 and 1897, however, several events seemed to converge and disturb his inner equilibrium. In his own mind, the most impactful event (Freud, 1900) was the death of his father in October 1896. "Torn up by the roots" (Letter 50), he was grief stricken and began a mourning process which inevitably stirred up old memories, painful ambivalences, and problems of separation and individuation. A second external influence seems to have been his patients, whose preoccupation with their recall of sexual seduction aroused buried affects and impulses in Freud himself which broke through the repression barrier and found an outlet in his dreams and intruding thoughts and feelings (Letters 58–60). A third set of circumstances appears to have been a recurrent sense of failure with patients who interrupted treatment before Freud thought they were through, and the recurrent disappointment over not receiving his professorship. These three experiences, apparently touched off unconscious conflicts with all of their erotic, aggressive, and envious affects which began to be felt in relation to Fliess, as the letters of the spring and early summer of 1897 reveal (Letters 60, 64, 65). His practice was going well and he even had "a real pupil from Berlin" (Letter 62, May 16, 1897) but he felt exhausted by the demands of 10 patients a day (Letter 58). This exhaustion must have decreased his resistance emotionally as well as physically and so played a part in his depression, which became evident in Letter 65 of June 12, 1897.

Three authors, Kris (1954), Jones (1953), and Buxbaum (1951), have given us extensive commentaries on Freud's self-analysis based on the data in his letters to Fliess and the analyses of dreams reported in *The Interpretation of Dreams* (1900). Each of these authors stresses a different aspect of the self-analytic work. Kris focuses on Freud's attempt to reconstruct childhood events occurring chiefly before the age of three; Jones emphasizes the work on his own dreams. From a detailed study of dreams reported in the dream book published in 1900 with the account of the same dreams sent to Fliess in letters containing much other personal material (not published until 1950), Buxbaum stresses the evidence for a symptom neurosis which by June 1897 was disturbing Freud's work. She calls our attention to the transference phenomena in his relationship with Fliess and concludes that we "have to look upon the development of his thoughts and feelings toward Fliess in the light of a transference analysis" (p. 200).

Freud's letters to Fliess began in 1887 and continued until 1902. We are indebted to Whilhelm Fliess for preserving these letters, to a German bookseller for offering them to Marie Bonaparte, and to Mme. Bonaparte herself for recognizing their unique historical value and for resisting Freud's plea that they be destroyed (Jones, 1953). The dramatic story of their rescue from the Nazi persecutions is recounted in Jones's biography of Freud. The letters themselves, with the accompanying drafts of Freud's theoretical thinking at the time, provide us with an awesome view of the vicissitudes of creative work as it begins, unfolds, and progresses against both inner and outer obstacles. These letters and drafts reveal the origins of a vast body of theory which has relevance to all of the behavioral sciences and the world of the arts. Other scientists and artists have given us the story of their lives and insight into the flowering of their creativity, but in these letters Freud, unknowingly, made a unique contribution to our understanding of the psychoanalytic process when he accomplished the monumental task of bringing together what he was experiencing with what he understood his experiences to mean in cognitive conceptual terms. Nor did he stop with this large achievement. He went on to describe his awareness of the process—actually a process of creating, which he called his self-analysis. It is the evidence for this aspect of his analysis of himself that I wish to collate here, since it has significance for our understanding of self-analysis as a goal for the training analysis and other learning experiences in the education of an analyst.

I have already indicated that Freud was using the analytic skills of introspection, association, and interpretation with his patients and on himself prior to the month of July 1897, when Kris and Buxbaum date the beginning of his self-analysis. I have discussed to some extent the precipitating events, and now I would like to discuss further the transference phenomena which seem to have intensified during the spring of 1897 and to have developed into a transference neurosis which caused Freud great anguish during June, July, and August of 1897. Freud's struggle with his transferences and with Fliess's countertransference reactions on this as yet uncharted sea offer psychoanalytic educators today much to think about. Freud's beautiful descriptions of his self-analytic efforts, the experiencing of resistances, the importance of surrender to preconscious working through, and the gradual emergence of insight are most relevant to the implementation of an educational program which must integrate experiental and cognitive learning more deliberately than is necessary in most disciplines (Fleming and Benedek, 1966 [see Chapter One, this volume]).

Before and during June 1896, Freud's (1887–1902) relationship with Fliess was exaggeratedly positive. In this month his father became ill (Letter 48) and in the next published letter, four months later (Letter 49), he announces his father's death. In Letter 50, November 2, 1896, "torn up by the roots," he grieves but his work and practice move on—especially his work on his own dreams and on the mechanisms of hysteria. During this period, from October through April 1897, he is able to keep his grief over his father's death from interfering with either his work or his positive attachment to Fliess. He sends drafts to Fliess on hysterical mechanisms, on his theory of seduction, on the relation between hysteria and perversion. In January 1897, he describes himself as in the "full swing of discovery." In February, he learns that he may be considered for a professorship. Exhausted by his 10 patients, and working some 12 hours a day, he finds it necessary to postpone "all attempts to obtain understanding." Here it would seem that the drain of energy coming from his clinical work prevents him from having any left over to devote to the work of conceptualizing. This circumstance must have produced some conflict and frustration, since Freud had a tremendous investment in this aspect of his creativity. It may have disturbed his equilibrium with Fliess, since he felt their respective scientific discoveries were an important bond between them. Some regression seems to have occurred, undoubtedly reinforced by his mourning for his father.

I base these suppositions on the fact that on April 28, 1897 he introduces a dream of being irritated at Fliess "as if you were always claiming something special for yourself" (p. 194). We do not know whether Fliess may have written something to provoke this thought, although we hear in January that Fliess seems not to feeling well. In the April 28 letter, there is a hint of disagreement about "father-figures." In May, Fliess is refreshed and Freud feels "impelled to start writing about dreams" (p. 200). "Inside me there is a seething ferment, and I am only waiting for the next surge forward" (p. 200). He is proud of having a real pupil from Berlin and feels Fliess approves of the dream project (Letter 62).

In Letter 64, May 31, 1897, Freud sends Fliess Draft N in which he talks of hostile impulses against parents. "It seems as though in sons this death-wish is directed against their father and in daughters against their mother" (p. 207). An editorial footnote identifies this as the "first hint of the Oedipus complex" (p. 207).

Earlier in this letter Freud calls Draft N "a few fragments thrown up on the beach by the last surge" (p. 206). He half apologizes for them, saying, ". . . I know they are only suspicions, but something has come of everything of this kind. . . ." (p. 206). He makes a reference to the concept of the system Pcs [preconscious] which is not elaborated and then adds, "Another presentiment tells me, as if I knew already—though I do not know anything at all—that I am about to discover the source of morality" (p. 206).

He then tells of two dreams. In the first he feels overaffectionately toward Mathilde (his daughter). "The dream, of course, fulfills my wish to pin down a father as the originator of neurosis and to put an end to my persistent doubts" (p. 206). The second is a dream of climbing a staircase not fully clothed; he meets a woman; is paralyzed but erotically excited. (See also Freud, 1900, pp. 238–240.)

In Letter 65, June 12,1897, his professorship is voted on favorably by the medical faculty but his appointment is delayed by the administration (footnote to Letter 62). Freud is depressed. He tells Fliess, "I have never yet imagined anything like my present spell of intellectual paralysis. Every line I write is torture" (p. 210). We note that this month is the anniversary of his father's final illness. About a month later (Letter 66) he says,

> I am a useless correspondent just now. . . . I still do not know what has been happening to me. Something from the deepest depths of my own neurosis has ranged itself against my taking a further step in understanding the neuroses, and you have been somehow involved. My inability to write seems to be aimed at hindering our intercourse. I have no proofs of this, but merely feelings of a very obscure nature. Has anything similar been the case with you? For some days past an emergence from this darkness seems to have been in preparation. I notice meanwhile my work has made some progress, and every now and then I have started having ideas again. No doubt heat and overwork have contributed. (p. 212)

In spite of intense resistance, there is some relief in this letter, and Freud makes some conceptual formulations comparing dreams and neurotic symptoms.

In August (Letter 67) there is no doubt that Freud has accepted himself as a patient he is trying to analyze. But "This analysis is harder than any other. It is also the thing that paralyses the power of writing down and communicating what so far I have learned. But I believe it has got to be done and is a necessary stage in my work" (p. 214). In this letter, recognizing his "little hysteria" and his resistances, he continues to link his self-analytic motivation to scientific discovery and his professional work.

He writes to Fliess of his fears and anxieties (Letter 68), realizing that his fear of a railway accident is associated with some feeling about Fliess. In the letter, Freud backs away from the hostile component and reports that the fear left him when he thought of the fact that Fliess and his wife would be on the train. It is easy to believe, however, that Freud was aware of the full interpretation but just could not put it down on paper for Fliess to read. The basic trust necessary for the expression of such transference wishes was not strong enough. Neither Freud nor Fliess possessed at that time the insight into transference and countertransference phenomena which Freud learned later and passed on to us. In the light of subsequent events in his relationship with Fliess, however, it is possible to speculate that the feelings he describes in this letter represent an aspect of his self-analysis which he could not objectify until later.

After a long vacation, toward the end of September (Letter 69) he feels better, knows he has been through a period of great turmoil and disillusionment but is coming out of it. In the letters of October, Freud is turning more to attempts at recall and to following out associations not necessarily connected with dreams. In Letters 70 and 71 he describes the material of his self-analysis as it took shape out of the analysis of his dreams and the childhood memories which his associations recovered. Apparently, he is less involved with any transferences to Fliess except what is appropriate to a working alliance when the process of synthesis and integration of the past in relation to the present is dominant, and transference reliving is less active as a form of resistance to remembering. His relationship with Fliess is still manifestly positive.

All of this time he also generalizes from his own and his patients' experiences and is able to apply to some of his patients what he learns from his self-analysis, e.g., an idea about resistance. An editorial footnote comments that, "Many of the phenomena of resistance seem to have become intelligible to Freud through his self-analysis" (p. 226). The experience of resistance is more intense in self-analysis than with an external analyst present. When Freud entered upon an analytic pact with himself, he had no way of knowing what lay in store for him. Today, having experienced resistance in an analytic situation and having struggled with it there, we are better prepared for the phenomenon when it occurs during a self-analytic effort. We know it can be overcome with persistent effort and in time. In the analytic relationship there is always assistance available when indicated. In a self-analysis, the assistance comes from an attitude toward one's self, a desire for self-discovery and a willingness to make a persistent effort. When this attitude is coupled with empathy for oneself in the struggle with resistance, an intrapsychic alliance of sorts can operate. It temporarily relaxes conscious effort and relies on a continuation of the analytic process preconsciously. In other words, the process of realignment and reorganization begun in the training analysis can continue on a self-analytic basis provided motivation, knowledge of the analytic process, and introspective skills are there.

Through October and early November 1897 (Letters 73, 74), Freud tells Fliess, "My self-analysis is stagnating again, or rather it trickles on without my understanding its progress" (p. 228). Then, in Letter 75 (November 14, 1897), after describing the birth of a new piece of knowledge, he makes a contradictory statement. He says, "Before the holidays I mentioned my most important patient was myself and after my holiday trip my self-analysis, of which there had previously been no trace began" (p. 231).

It would seem that on the one hand he needed to protect himself from the transference neurosis of the summer months and to take comfort in the professional value of his self-analysis (Letter 67). In addition, Freud found gratification in being able to recall and reconstruct the past—analytic objectives originating in the period of hypnosis and basic to his theory of etiology. That he could demonstrate these theories on himself, including the phenomenon of resistance, restored his self-confidence, shaken by the regressive experience of elements of his own Oedipus complex during the summer of 1897. So far as we know, however, although he felt resistance as tangible (Letter 72) and sensed the significance of his ambivalent feelings toward Fliess, Freud did not correlate his own transference phenomena and his experiencing of Fliess's countertransferences with either the process of his self-analysis or the later conceptualization of the same phenomena observed in others.

After his statement in Letter 75 that there was no trace of his self-analysis before his return from his 1897 holiday, Freud tells Fliess about his latest ideas on repression and remembering. He ends with a paragraph about his self-analysis, saying, "My self-analysis is still interrupted. I have now seen why. I can only analyze myself with objectively acquired knowledge (as if I were a stranger); self-analysis is really impossible, otherwise there would be no illness. As I have come across some puzzles in my own case, it is bound to hold up the self-analysis" (pp. 234–235).

Here Freud describes the objectivity necessary in an analyst, whether it is directed toward his patient or himself. Today we speak of this attitude as belonging to the empathy of the analyst and the development of the self-observing function of the ego. Freud's self-observing function was developed to an extremely high level, something he begins to conceptualize in this letter. Today, the operation of this function of the ego is a part of the self-analytic skills developed in a training analysis without which therapeutic insight and professional objectivity are lacking. Today, we recognize the contribution to the development of this skill made by the objective, uninvolved attitude of the analyst, something Freud defined in Letter 75 as appropriate to a stranger, a bystander in the struggle.

In the fall of 1897, disagreements between Freud and Fliess begin to appear. They have to do with Fliess's theories of left-handedness, bisexuality, and questions of priority. In a letter written by Fliess in 1904 (Freud, 1887–1902, footnote, p. 241), Fliess recalls Freud's resistance to the ideas about bisexuality at their meeting in Breslau and accuses Freud of failing to give him credit for priority, a problem which led to their final estrangement. Here we see more overtly expressed some of the countertransference reactions in Fliess. Freud (Letter 80) tries to treat the disagreements as something that can be scientifically and objectively reconciled. Only much later did he realize that Fliess had a more personal investment in proving himself right and claiming priority for a discovery.

Through January and February (three letters), the subject of Freud's self-analysis is only vaguely mentioned. During this period he seems less dependent on Fliess, working more alone with himself. In March, he reaches out to Fliess a little and sends him what is to be the second chapter of the book on dreams. Freud seems to be trying to appease Fliess by belittling his own work. But Fliess evidently approves the second chapter and Freud feels good (Letter 86). April, May, June, and July continue the work on dreams with feelings of uncertainty and hesitation about sending the chapters to Fliess, "but our intellectual honesty to each other required it" (Letter 92, July 7, 1898) (p. 258). In September Freud makes reference to the problem of psychology versus biology as if Fliess felt they disagreed, which Freud denies (Letter 96). In October, his practice is flourishing and leaves him exhausted. In December, Freud reports he is reading the literature on dreams.

The next reference to his self-analysis is in a letter of January 3, 1899 (Letter 101): " . . . I have accomplished a piece of self-analysis which has confirmed that phantasies are products of later periods which project themselves back from the present into earliest childhood; and I have also found out how it happens, again by verbal association" (pp. 270–271). This work led to the paper on *Screen Memories* (Freud, 1899; Bernfeld, 1946). He feels creative again and attributes it to a meeting with Fliess just before this January letter. But he wonders if this upsurge is due to Fliess's period theory and hopes "the dynamic aspect is not ruled out." In May (Letter 107), he has great confidence in the dream book making a great contribution: "None of my works has been so completely my own as this; it is my own dung-heap, my own seedling, and a nova species mihi (sic!)" (p. 281). He is not bothered by the fact that " . . . the ten analyses have not come off" (p. 282).

In July (Letter 110), Freud is feeling good and recalls an early meeting with Fliess in 1890 or 1891 when "you witnessed one of my very finest attacks of travel-anxiety at the station" (p. 285). Freud seems to feel independent enough of Fliess to report a critical thought at that early meeting about feeling oppressed by his superiority and that Fliess had not yet found his vocation "which later turned out to be shackling life with numbers and formulae" (p. 285). He seems unaware of the not-so-subtle depreciation of Fliess's life work in this remark.

In August (Letter 113), still riding high, Freud turns again to the problem of bisexuality. But here he only mentions it, since the dream book is progressing. His success in nearing its completion intensifies his anticipation of a hostile reception. "When the storm breaks I shall fly to your spare room" (p. 295), he tells Fliess, "You will find something to praise in it anyway, because you are as prejudiced in my favor as the others are against me" (p. 295) (Letter 117).

On September 21, 1899 (Letter 119), Freud mentions that he is astonished at how often Fliess appeared in his dreams. "In the *non vixit* dream I find I am delighted to have survived you; is it not hard to have to hint at such things—to make them obvious, that is, to everyone who understands?" (p. 299).

On October 27, 1899, Freud thanks Fliess for his kind words about the dream book and then goes on to mention five more books he has in mind. The dream book came out in November (Letter 123) and Freud immediately begins on the "choice of neurosis" and its relation to sexual theory (Letter 125).

On March 11, 1900 (Letter 130) Freud remarks about not having heard from Fliess for about a month. He thinks they would both be sorry if their correspondence dried up, yet it seems to be becoming less frequent. The reaction to the dream book was not all Freud expected and he is disappointed. He is more aware of the vicissitudes of the creative process and is better reconciled to its slow pace and to the social isolation which his way of living and his discoveries brought about at this time.

March 23 (Letter 131) introduces a new feeling in Freud's relationship to Fliess. He withdraws from the prospect of meeting him at Easter because of "an accumulation of imponderables" (p. 314) and a fear that with Fliess he might regress into envy and dissatisfaction and again have to go through the depression he feels he has been climbing out of. "No one can help me in what oppresses me" (p. 314), he tells Fliess, but we do not know if this is something uncovered in his self-analysis or if it represents his slowly increasing distance from Fliess.

April 14, 1900 (Letter 133) marks the first report to Fliess concerning transference as it occurs in therapy. Its dynamics and technical handling were not yet understood, although Freud (1905) was working with Dora during this period and formulated a theory of transference on the basis of his frustrating experience with that case.

His disappointment in not being acclaimed for his dream book is still bothering him, and Fliess's praise does not comfort as it used to (Letter 134, May 5, 1900). Depressive discouragement sets in again.

An arrangement was made in July (Letter 138) to meet around the first of August. Apparently, the two men quarreled at this meeting. Fliess says Freud showed an unintelligible violence toward him which seemed to Fliess to be rooted in envy. After this meeting Fliess "quietly withdrew from Freud and dropped our regular correspondence" (ed. ftn., p. 324). The next letter from Freud in the published series was dated October 14 (Letter 139) and the next was January (Letter 140). Neither refers to the meeting in the summer. The first reference is in Letter 142 dated February 15, 1901. He says, ". . . the congresses themselves have become relics of the past; I am doing nothing new, and, as you say, I have become entirely estranged from what you are doing" (p. 328).

What has happened? It would appear that Freud has become increasingly disenchanted with Fliess, both regarding his theories, his claims to priority, and his praise of Freud's dream book. Apart from the reality assessment of Fliess's scientific theories, it would seem likely that Freud grew increasingly distrustful of the ambivalence underneath the praise, as is indicated in Letter 134 written in July before the fateful meeting at Aachensee.

Freud continued to write to Fliess with the usual news, and not until Letter 145 in July 1901 does he explicitly comment on the fact that they have drawn apart. Freud feels hurt and depreciated by Fliess's accusation of "merely reading his own thoughts into other people" (p. 334). He defends himself against the accusation of plagiarism. Then he tells Fliess that his next book will be called *"Bisexuality in Man"* and "it will tackle the root of the problem and say the last word which it will be granted to me to say on the subject—the last and the deepest" (p. 334). This sounds provocative, which Freud must have realized because he goes on to say, "The idea itself is yours . . . So perhaps I shall have to borrow still more from you . . . or even co-author the book" (p. 335). He hopes this "will satisfactorily unite us again in scientific matters" (p. 335).

Then he fulfills his long-cherished desire to go to Rome. After his return from this "overwhelming experience" (Letter 146), he tries to answer complaints from Fliess that Freud is not interested in his work. Freud pleads ignorance of mathematics and tells Fliess of his hurt and his feeling that if an interpretation to a patient makes Fliess feel uncomfortable so that he accuses Freud of projecting, then ". . . you are really no longer my audience, and you must regard the whole technique as just as worthless as the others do" (p. 337).

The complicated transference–countertransference reactions intimated in this letter make the reader sad that this friendship had to end in this way. Neither one fully understood the dynamic forces in operation that generated the transferences from Freud to Fliess in the beginning or the countertransferences from Fliess to Freud in the end. Freud's disillusionment with Fliess and with himself must have been extremely painful and may have left him especially vulnerable to the rivalrous transferences which appeared among his students as time went on. He was able to study the transference phenomena that arose from a patient to his analyst, but he had little to say about countertransferences in an analyst except that they should be overcome by self-analysis.

From this resume of Freud's self-analysis as he reported it in his letters to Fliess, and in the dream book, we can see the dedicated self-discipline with which he devoted himself to the effort to penetrate his resistances. We marvel at the way in which his introspective, associative, and interpretive skills developed and sharpened as his professional and self-analytic work went on. For Freud, the two kinds of analytic situations went hand in hand, each one of benefit to the other. We stand in awe of his ability to grasp the inner processes of this struggle with resistances and to conceptualize the experiences he observed in himself, whether they were available to conscious recall and interpretation or only vague bubblings from within.

Several aspects of Freud's self-analysis have definite bearing on the goal of the training analysis as an educational experience for present-day students of analysis. The record documents the importance of experiencing the phenomena of resistance and of learning through persistent use of the method of free association that new knowledge and new integrations can occur when resistances are overcome. Experiencing the phenomena of transference as a special form of resistance is of paramount importance for a student-analyst. Today, he can read about these things and understand them intellectually, but the vitality of conviction comes only from having lived through the regressed ego state of transference neurosis and worked through the differentiation of what belongs to the past from what is more appropriate to current reality. There is an emancipating value in this therapeutic experience. Ferenczi's aim of "supertherapy" focuses on this point in terms of the "depth" and "completeness" of the affective experience and the insights into the student-patient's personality structure which a training analysis can achieve. During this therapeutic experience any patient, whether he is a student or not, becomes able to develop his own observing and interpreting functions and apply them to himself. These functions in the beginning of an analysis are carried out mainly by the analyst, but as the process goes on, the patient becomes freer and more skillful in making his own interpretations independent of assistance from his analytic mentor.

But there is another kind of experience which is equally valuable, perhaps even more so, in preparing a student to become an analyst of others as well as of himself. I refer to a different level of learning on which the affective experiences are given cognitive and explanatory meaning (Fleming and Benedek, 1966 [see Chapter One, this volume]). When a student is able to objectify his experiences as a patient, and to anchor these fleetingly conscious moments in a cognitive framework, he enlarges the scope of his empathic understanding and knowing, and thereby "a dimension is added to his professional work ego" [p. 11, this volume].

Throughout the record of Freud's self-analysis there is evidence of his constant effort to describe, objectify, and explain what was going on within him. At times he was only painfully aware of feeling but not knowing (Letters 130, 72, 74, 75). The necessity to communicate with Fliess by letter facilitated this process of objectification. It forced Freud to put his experiences into words and to write them down for Fliess to read. There must have been at times a cathartic effect from this procedure as well as a penetrating of the barriers to consciousness. It might have stopped there, but Freud went beyond describing in words what he was experiencing and developed explanatory generalizations. This latter activity was also part of what he communicated to Fliess.

The most significant difference betweenn Freud's self-analysis and that possible today is the analytic work on the transfer ence–countertransference reactions (Benedek, 1969). This latter experience changes the self-analytic situation. Before we are on our own, we have had the assistance of a well-analyzed, well-educated analyst who has himself worked through many of his transference conflicts and has developed his own self-analytic skills. Fliess was not an analyst and therefore could not provide the kind of assistance in preparation for continuing self-analysis that we expect for our students today. He did supply a listening ear, and as the relationship between them grew more intimate, Fliess became an object for Freud's transferences. Neither one understood what was happening as it can be understood today. In Freud's intense dependence, admiration, and idealization, there were all the ingredients for the reproduction of childhood envy, jealousy, and competition, something which did happen and which Freud faithfully recorded. As these negative affects became more clear-cut, and as Freud's success in grasping the emotional and dynamic mechanisms determining behavior became more obvious, Fliess seemed to feel threatened and reacted with a counter hostility which shocked them both. Neither understood this as a reproduction of a childhood rivalry with siblings and a powerful father, although by way of his dreams Freud was able to realize that he was behaving toward Fliess as he had toward objects of rivalry in the past. In being able to do this Freud kept a hold on current reality and experienced a complicated conflict over his current attitudes to Fliess. He expected tolerance, understanding, and scientific objectivity from him. Instead, Fliess began to withdraw without explanation after the angry confrontation at Aachensee in 1900. The experience of Freud's own negative transference shook him deeply, but out of it came a formulation of the Oedipus complex. His experiencing of Fliess's negative countertransference, however, was even more profound and disturbing. Perhaps this explains why Freud said so little about his analytic work with Fliess during his lifetime and why he was so cautious about talking of countertransference among the early analysts as revealed in the 1910 paper. He must have felt that the younger colleagues of the early 1900s would resent being told they needed therapy (just as they do today). Perhaps he was reluctant to stir up the negative reactions toward himself that he had experienced toward Fliess and had not thoroughly worked through. Actually, of course, what he feared did come to pass with a number of "deviationists."[2]

Freud's faith in self-analysis as a means of learning how to be an analyst went through several ups and downs. I have already referred to Freud's recommendation in 1910 for a self-analysis because of countertransference. I have indicated the tentativeness of his recommendation at that time and his firmer statement concerning analysis with an experienced analyst, which he made two years later.

Strachey (1957), in an editorial footnote to Freud's (1914) history of the movement, does us an important service by pulling together several of Freud's references to self-analysis which indicate this oscillation of attitude toward its value. Discouraged in 1897 (Letter 75), Freud feels that genuine self-analysis is impossible. In 1910, he recommended it; in 1912, he felt a more formal analytic relationship was important; in 1914 ". . . I soon saw the necessity of carrying out a self-analysis, and this I did with the help of a series of my own dreams which led me back through all the events of my childhood; and I am still of the opinion today that this kind of analysis may suffice for anyone who is a good dreamer and not too abnormal" (p. 20). In 1916, in the *Introductory Lectures*, Freud said, "One learns psychoanalysis on oneself by studying one's own personality" (1916–1917, Vol. 15, p. 19). This statement could include both kinds of analytic situations. E. Pickworth Farrow (1942) published an account of his self-analysis for which Freud (1926) wrote a preface. He comments on Farrow's "systematic application of the procedure of self-analysis which I myself employed in the past for the analysis of my own dreams" [1926, p. 280].

Near the end of his life, Freud (1935) wrote a short paper on "The Subtleties of a Faulty Action" in which he struggles to explain a slip of the pen in writing an inscription on a gift to a women friend. Having written the word *"bis,"* he then crossed it out as inappropriate attempting to analyze why it should have been written at all. He arrived at an explanation satisfactory to himself which he recounted to his daughter who reminded him

2. See Jones (1953, pp. 315–317) for an account of what appears to be an intense countertransference conflict in relation to Jung. The issue was over priority credit and occurred in 1912.

that the word *"bis"* could also refer to the fact that Freud was repeating a present, since he had given this friend a similar gift once before. Freud analyzes the slip further in this short paper, something not as pertinent to our immediate purpose as his reference to self-analysis. In spite of his pleasure in the solution before he spoke to his daughter, he concludes that "in self-analysis the danger of incompleteness is particularly great. One is too easily satisfied with a part of explanation, behind which resistance can easily keep back something that is more important perhaps" (p. 234). With this I am sure we would all agree, but today a well-educated analyst has learned to take resistance and the partialness of insight into account. Such an analyst expects incompleteness, has learned to respect resistances whether in himself or someone else, and can wait for signs in dreams and other behavior that the "autoanalytic process" is continuing. Here, I use Maria Kramer's (1959) term, accepting her stress on the necessity for preconscious activity to work with resistances before a new integration can add anything to conscious insight.

Stracher'ys (1957) last comment in his editorial footnote refers to Freud's 1912 paper and the advice in *Analysis Terminable and Interminable* (1937) that training analyses should be undertaken with a training analyst. It is interesting that Strachey neglects to comment on the strong recommendation in this last paper for a continuing self-analysis as well as additional periods of formal analysis every five years. It is here that self-analytic skills are described as a part of analyst's professional equipment, albeit often in need of objective assistance from a colleague when transference phenomena appear as resistances too strong to be worked through alone. It is in this paper, one of his greatest, that Freud discusses the effect of analytic work on the patient's ego. He says, "Is it not precisely the claim of our theory that analysis produces a state which never does arise spontaneously in the ego," a state which "constitutes the essential difference between a person who has been analyzed and a person who has not" (p. 227). This state comes about, he says, when analysis of the infantile defenses against instinctual forces enables the ego to revise and strengthen its defenses and achieve freedom from their dominance. In these remarks Freud is expressing what would be an ideal analytic result and what analytic theory postulates as possible. True to his ever-present scientific skepticism and his reliance on clinical experience for evidence to support his theories, Freud recognizes that the hopes of psychoanalysis are not always fulfilled. He cautions against coming to settled conclusions and against the inadvisability of trying to activate dormant conflicts for the sake of the analyst's therapeutic ambition. In other words, a training analysis should terminate, even if it begins again later.

In 1937, as in 1910 when he spoke of countertransference phenomena, Freud counted the analyst's ego of equal significance in influencing the prospects of analytic treatment. He recognized the special conditions of analytic work which "cause the analyst's own defects to interfere with his making a correct assessment of the state of things in his patient and reacting to them in a useful way" (p. 248). He sets high goals for an analyst whose love of truth is paramount, since "it precludes any kind of sham or deceit" (p. 248). Realizing the unachievable ideal which he has just described, with sympathetic humor, he asks, "But where and how is the poor wretch to acquire the ideal qualifications which he will need in his profession?" He answers, ". . . in an analysis of himself, with which his preparation for his future activity begins" (p. 248).

Freud then proceeds to outline what he expected of a training analysis. He says, "Its main object is to enable his [the analyst's] teacher to make a judgment as to whether the candidate can be accepted for further training. It has accomplished its purpose if it gives the learner a firm conviction of the existence of the unconscious, if it enables him, when repressed material emerges, to perceive in himself things which would otherwise be incredible to him, and if it shows him a first sample of the technique which has proved to be the only effective one in his analytic work" (p. 248). This statement may sound superficial to us, since it seems to stress more cognitive aspects of the analytic experience. However, Freud, as late as 1937, was still optimistic about self-analysis and by that time has seen the evidence for alterations in the ego brought about by the analytic method. Because he says it so much better than I can, let me present it to you in his words, which set a course toward a hoped-for goal while at the same time they chart some of the shoals and narrows.

He feels that the analytic experience described above would by itself not be sufficient for a prospective analyst's education.

... but we reckon the stimuli that he has received in his own analysis not ceasing when it ends and on the processes of remodeling the ego continuing spontaneously in the analyzed subject and making use of all subsequent experiences in this newly acquired sense. This does in fact happen, and in so far as it happens it makes the analyzed subject qualified to be an analyst himself.

Unfortunately something else happens as well. In trying to describe this, one can only rely on impressions. Hostility on the one side and partisanship on the other create an atmosphere which is not favorable to objective investigation. It seems that a number of analysts learn to make use of defensive mechanisms which allow them to divert the implications and demands of analysis from themselves (probably by directing them on to other people) so that they themselves remain as they are and are able to withdraw from the critical and corrective influence of analysis." (p. 249).

Freud recognized the hazards of analytic work for an analyst. He saw a danger in the power with which a patient endows his analyst and warned against the temptation to misuse it. He saw a danger to the analyst's impulse control from "a constant preoccupation with all the repressed material which struggles for freedom in the human mind" (p. 249). He compared the effect of this danger on an analyst with the effect of X-rays on technicians who do not take special precautions and advised periodic return to analysis, "without feeling ashamed of taking this step" (p. 249).

I hope I have made the point that in this final statement of Freud's ideas about how to become an analyst, he stressed the need for a therapeutic experience plus a never-ending self-scrutiny in order to manage the inevitable countertransferences which confront an analyst. Freud told Jones (1953) that he devoted the last half-hour of every day to his own analysis. In other words, he consciously continued to employ self-analytic skills in an attempt to make contact with preconscious processes, to widen the horizons of knowledge and to integrate experience with cognitive functioning. (For a late example, the reader is directed to Freud, 1936).

Today we have an opportunity to make explicit this kind of activity as a skill to be taught during the education of a young analyst. The learning experiences of the training analysis and supervision can and do reinforce both the incentive and the know-how. Even the transferences in those situations can contribute to developing this skill if the ongoing nature of the self-analytic effort is focused on as a professional objective by the student's teachers. I stress this because I have seen a tendency among the faculties of Institutes to expect the training analysis to end the need for analytic effort. This tendency is only rarely stated as such, but implicitly carried out in at least two not uncommon instances. The first can be inferred in the practice of prolonging a training analysis. It is as if there is some lack of confidence in the student's being able to work on his own without benefit of his training analyst. Other circumstances and other dynamics in the training analyst may and do influence interminable training analyses, but time does not permit discussion of these variables here. The second instance can be inferred from the taboo on discussing countertransferences in a supervisory situation. Supervisors in turn are sometimes reluctant to deliberately structure the supervisory situation (such as frequency and explicit learning tasks) to encourage a student's assumption of a more independent position (Fleming and Benedek, 1966).

In this essay, one of several devoted to problems of psychoanalytic education (Fleming, 1961 [see Chapter Three, this volume], 1969; Blitzsten and Fleming, 1953), I have attempted to review the following questions: What are the origins of a training analysis; what did Freud have to say about it; what were the first stated objectives; how were they implemented in the early days; how did experience modify these beginnings; and what were Freud's later compared with his earlier ideas? This stock-taking effort is based on the conviction that the thought we give to the education of new generations of psychoanalysts is an investment in the future of psychoanalysis. If the education is good, it will provide experiences that stimulate a spirit of inquiry and a wish to push back the frontiers of knowledge, as well as to acquire the skills to use the analytic method for therapeutic purposes. I believe the problem also concerns the thought we give to the education of the teachers of the new generations of analysts, since it becomes more and more clear that the principal difficulty in learning to conduct an analysis *and* in learning to teach it is the "personal equation," for which an ongoing self-analytic effort is an invaluable corrective.

The therapeutic advantages of a training analysis we tend to take for granted, but the additional aim which Eitingon (1926) mentioned we can today spell out more specifically. It is the aim of assisting a student-analyst to develop the self-analytic skills of introspection, empathy, and interpretation not only for acquiring insight into himself but as a built-in part of his "work ego." A basic attitude toward continuing self-exploration and a beginning development of the basic self-analytic skills are expectable results from a training analysis which has both therapeutic and professional aims.

In other words, the "problem" of a training analysis need not remain such an irreconcilable dilemma if we keep in mind the goal of self-analytic skills to be developed in the service of both therapy and professional work. Today, training analysts have techniques for increasing the depth of personal insight and professional attitudes. To enlarge on these techniques is beyond the scope of this essay, but it is an important task to which analytic educators should attend (Fleming, 1969). The position stated in our book on supervision (Fleming and Benedek, 1966 [see Chapter One, this volume]) stresses the need to make self-analytic skills the principal educational objective for student-analytic training. We need to integrate the aims and techniques of treating and teaching, a philosophy of education for an analyst which includes Freud's original ideas and also makes use of the advances in theory and techniques of both therapy and learning.

·3·

WHAT ANALYTIC WORK
REQUIRES OF AN ANALYST:
A JOB ANALYSIS

This paper, written by Dr. Fleming in 1961, is one of the earliest
attempts to define selection criteria and to emphasize the need for
systematic studies on the selection process.

Dr. Fleming realized the importance of accurate selection decisions for applicants, Institutes, and the science and profession of
psychoanalysis, and she appreciated the need to define in more precise and communicable terms reasons for selection decisions. Dr.
Fleming worked toward educational objectivity and sought to replace
impressionistic criteria that could lead to "convoying" (Greenacre,
1966) and to other transference–countertransference biases.

Dr. Fleming's approach in this paper, unique at the time, is to
define the tasks required of an analyst to conduct a proper analysis
and to explore the ego functions an applicant should possess, at least
in larval form, that should mature and develop within a good educational program and environment. The analyst must acquire through
training an analytic "work ego"; in this paper, Dr. Fleming discusses
the various ego functions that make up this ego structure. Her contribution has been most significant for the study of analytic prediction,
analyzability, and the talents and qualities needed to be a competent
analytic clinician and scholarly analyst. Dr. Fleming's approach as
set forth in this seminal article initiated further studies on formulating criteria for all progression decisions in the psychoanalytic educational program.

Selection of candidates for psychoanalytic training is a constant
task for our training facilities and a constant challenge. Each year
decisions are made to accept some applicants and to reject others.
Much time and effort is spent on coming to these decisions, and

Reprinted by permission from the *Journal of the American Psychoanalytic Association*, 9:719–729, 1961.

since the training program itself is long and costly, mistakes become expensive for all concerned.

To avoid mistakes and their consequent waste would be reason enough to warrant close scrutiny of the problems inherent in selection. But there is another equally cogent reason, namely, to arrive, if possible, at criteria for selection which go beyond the impressionistic "sizing-up" so commonly used as a basis for accepting or rejecting an applicant. We need to define in more precise and more communicable terms our reasons for selection decisions. Systematic studies of the problems which the task of selection presents and of the procedures used to study them need to be undertaken.

The process of selection is a process of prediction. Each selection choice is one which makes a prediction reagarding the eventual success of the applicant as an analyst. This is a judgment that predicts success or failure in a particular task. A systematic study of the process of making such predictions requires a knowledge of what the particular task demands. A necessary step in this direction is an analysis of the activity for which success or failure is being predicted. In the language of the many investigators making predictive studies [Holt and Luborsky, 1958; Horst, 1941; Shouksmith, 1960], it is called a job analysis.

This paper presents an attempt at a job analysis. It tries to answer the question "What are we selecting for?" By examining the tasks which a successful analyst is called upon to do in his work an an analyst, we can formulate more specifically these tasks with reference to identifiable talents and personality qualifications in an applicant for training, so that our yardsticks can be better defined and a foundation laid for a systematic study of selection. The work of analyzing a patient will be examined in relation to the goals of analysis, and the tasks required will be correlated with the skills and tools an analyst must possess in order to perform them.

The effort here is to move away from the long detailed lists containing descriptions of behavior or itemized character traits which could be applied to almost any successful professional person who deals with people in his work. Instead, I shall present an analysis of the job of analyzing emphasizing its specific and unique aspects as they are related to special abilities in the analyst. The demands of the job require the analyst to behave in special ways, and the ability to behave in these ways requires special endowment and ego functions of a high level of integration. My emphasis will be on the tasks required of an analyst and primarily on an exploration of the ego functions a successful analyst must possess.

The first task which the psychoanalyst is called upon to perform is to build a special type of interpersonal relationship in which a special type of experience can take place. This is the analytic situation in which the analytic process can operate toward the analytic goal of therapy for the patient. It calls for certain conditions which facilitate the process and which permit the technical work of the analyst to be carried on. Grotjahn [1949, p. 141] comments relevantly here: "Psychoanalytic treatment is not giving motherly love to a sick child." Rather, it is a method of treatment that uses special instruments and techniques developed over a long period of study. The main instrument is the personality of the analyst, of which his ego is the primary element and which he uses for reaching the therapeutic goals.

In the case of psychoanalysis, this goal is reached by efforts to develop the patient's capacity for communication with himself and with others. The patient needs to learn more about himself, and to do so he must work at being able to relate to and communicate with his analyst more intimately, more totally, and more searchingly than he has been able to do before. It is hoped that insight into himself will provide him with insight into others also and enable him to change the troublesome patterns of adaptation which brought him into therapy. It follows that an analyst must already possess a high level of capacity for this kind of communication if he is to use himself as an instrument in facilitating the communication processes of another person. This statement is, of course, true for many professions and occupations, but in none to the degree required in conducting a psychoanalysis. "Ministers in any religion, counselors, teachers, lawyers belong to such professions. But their tasks are different from analysts'. In general they are confined to a specific area or select which area of the patient's personality to communicate with; their skill lies in limiting the patient's communication with himself to just that area which relates to the problem at hand, and in preventing too many unconscious tributaries from entering the field. The psychoanalyst attempting the analysis of the total personality has to broaden the

area for communication; he must first select the unconscious tributaries which refer to the problem; second, open the door to the
next level of communication; yet, third, gauge the pace and direction of the process according to the patient's ability to deal with
the affect and ideational content involved" [Benedek, personal
communication, 1960]. It is our purpose to examine in what way
the work of analyzing calls for these special capacities for communication for which an analyst requires special equipment if he is to
do a good job.

The importance of the analyst's personality in the therapeutic
process was clearly recognized by Freud when, in 1910, he described how "blind spots" in the analyst could interfere with effective analysis. Since then, the basic notion of the analyst's use of
himself as a therapeutic instrument remains the same. Many
authors have contributed to this idea in the course of the years.
Strachey in 1934 described the way in which the analyst as a good
introject becomes an important factor in the therapeutic process.
Ferenczi before him had attempted to elucidate the role of introjection in the analyst's understanding of the transference of the
patient. Freud in 1938 [see Freud, 1940] compared the analyst
with the educator who can "correct blunders" for which his (the
patient's) parental education was to blame. Freud warned, of
course, against creating the patient in the image of the analyst,
but his recognition of the influence of the analyst's personality is
clearly stated.

The way in which the analyst uses himself as an instrument to
further the therapeutic process is one of the points to be discussed,
for if the analyst's personality is a significant factor in achieving
analytic goals, discrimination between a well-qualified personality and one unfitted for this purpose is essential to the task of
selection.

R. Fliess [1942] attempts to define the way in which the
analyst operates, bringing his personality into dynamic interplay
with the patient's personality. It is through this dynamic interplay
that the analyst gains understanding of the patient and thereby
can be helpful in the reintegrative process of the analytic experience. He describes the empathic identification by which the
analyst, like a tea-taster, understands his patient's strivings and
conflicts going on within him. In metapsychological terms, Fliess
differentiates the process of this empathic experiencing of what

the patient is experiencing from the process of nonempathic understanding. The latter results in reactions in the analyst which produce an acting out of his infantile conflicts, and as such interfere with the goal of insight for either patient or analyst. With such inappropriate behavior, the analyst can hardly be a corrective model of reality.

Most of the articles written on this subject are descriptions of personality characteristics which are desirable in analysts and which, therefore, we look for in analytic applicants. Sachs [1947] listed a number of qualities, such as intelligence, honesty, reliability, etc. But he felt these were not the significant factors for the task of selection because they are not specific for the profession of analyzing. These qualities must be part of the equipment of any professional person. Sachs talks about the need to define "these special qualifications, uniquely different from those of any other profession, which give the promise of the good analyst" [1947, p. 159]. Most of his criteria are related to the degree of pathology and the severity of the neurosis present. He stresses the normal candidate, but aside from one point, he does not relate his qualifications to the work of an analyst. This one point he defines "as the faculty of access to and the will to face his own unconscious" [p. 159]. This job of the analyst to communicate with the deeper recesses of himself in the service of the analytic process will be discussed later.

As was stated above, the analyst must operate within the conditions of the analytic situation, where an atmosphere of trust characterized by extreme intimacy makes possible the analytic process. Ella Sharpe [1930, p. 11] describes the analytic situation as the place where "we can tell all we have never told another, all we have never told ourselves." To create this kind of atmosphere requires, in Sharpe's language, "a technique above the average in ordinary human contacts" [p. 12]. The analyst must build a relationship not only of trust, but one in which the patient has confidence in the ability of someone else to see and understand more than he can himself. This trust and confidence constitute the foundation of the intimacy and openness essential for a successful analysis.

Another characteristic of the special kind of relationship necessary for analysis is the deprivation under which it is conducted. Both analyst and patient deprive themselves of direct libidinal gratification. This condition of abstinence facilitates the regulation of discharge processes and the regression necessary for the reproduction of infantile conflicts within the analytic situation. Under controlled circumstances this regressive reliving in the transference neurosis can lead to new and better-integrated solutions for the patient. The analyst must devote all of his energies to understanding and aiding the patient rather than to achieving gratification of his own impulses on a libidinal level. The only gratifications for the analyst in this special kind of relationship are altruistic, vicarious, and sublimated.

The patient's chief task in the analytic work is the production of free associations. The analyst listening to the patient's communication maintains a "free-floating attention" which Fliess describes as "conditioned daydreaming," since it is not the same kind of freely associating process required of the patient. Conditioned is not the best term here, because what the analyst does is not to be compared with a "conditioned reflex." "Controlled day-dreaming" might be a better term. It is not an automatic and consistent response to an associated stimulus. What Fliess means is that the analyst's associations are largely in response to the patient's communications and reactions. In actual daydreaming, the stimulus is more internal than external. With the patient this is so, but for the analyst the stimulus is more external then internal. As he follows the patient's associations, a channel of communication develops, beginning in the unconscious of the patient, extending through his preconscious, and by way of conscious elaborations reaching the preconscious of the analyst. By means of introspection and empathy so well described by Kohut [1959], the analyst processes the patient's contributions, sensing the form and color of his primary-process thinking. To do this, the analyst must keep his censorship in partial abeyance, allowing free play between his own fantasies and the patient's, a kind of responsive fantasying with the patient. He must, however, remain in a position where the critical eye of the reality-testing function maintains his secondary processes in command, since, if this function is permitted to relax too much, regressive daydreaming takes over and interferes with the introspection necessary for understanding the patient. One might say the analyst experiences the primary process while simultaneously applying the secondary process to his own experiencing. The "good" patient does this also, but to a lesser degree.

Kris [1956a] defines and differentiates these two levels of ego activity when he distinguishes between the ego's observation of itself and the ego's observation of its own functioning. What one part of the ego experiences, another observes, and simultaneously a good analyst also interprets what he is observing in himself. This latter operation produces an empathic integration which enables him to understand his patient. Ferenczi [1919, p. 189] describes this analytic task as follows: "Analytic therapy . . . makes claims on the doctor that seem directly self-contradictory. On the one hand, it requires of him the free play of association and phantasy, the full indulgence of *his own unconscious*; . . . On the other hand, the doctor must subject the material submitted by himself and the patient to a logical scrutiny, and in his dealings and communications may only let himself be guided exclusively by the results of this mental effort. . . . This constant oscillation between the free play of phantasy and critical scrutiny presupposes a freedom and uninhibited motility of psychic excitation on the doctor's part, however, that can hardly be demanded in any other sphere." R. Fliess [1942] comments on this passage from Ferenczi that analysis requires the impossible from the analyst. He must acquire a "work ego" with a special structure in order to perform his job.

Examining the special structure of this "work ego," we can identify a number of ego functions which must be developed to a high level of operation if analytic work is to be successful. The analyst's perceptual apparatus, his system of communication with himself and with others, must be exceptionally open. His integrative and regulatory systems must possess free energy for productive, creative activities not bound to serve defensive purposes only, but freely perceiving and translating the messages which the patient is sending to him. His own associative processes must be maintained for use by the patient rather than by his own process of discharge toward gratification. As the patient succeeds in his work of associating and moves toward regressive states of ego oganization, the analyst must maintain his own hold upon present reality, and his capacity to differentiate and discriminate between symbols and what they represent, between secondary- and primary-process activities. To be able to tolerate the regression of his patient, to follow this regression with his own empathic understanding, and yet to maintain his own integrated nonregressed position is the job for the analyst's "work ego." To recognize simultaneously the behavior of the patient and the behavior which belongs to himself is inherent in the work of understanding the patient's transference. R. Fliess [1942] uses the term "transference dummy" to describe the way in which the patient's transference conflicts become temporarily intrapsychic conflicts in the analyst. Ella Sharpe [1930, p. 25] defines the same operation with the statement, "The analyst must permit and sustain every role thrust upon him. Those roles must be worked through and exhausted via himself." In this process, the analyst identifies with the patient and experiences the correlated striving. Recognizing his subjective responses, observing and experiencing at the same time, he understands by a process of empathy. If his infantile neurosis is not integrated with insight, his subjective responses strive toward gratification of his own infantile longings, and thus interfere with his therapeutic effectiveness. Insight gained from his own analysis permits the recognition of the infantile origins in himself and therefore the infantile quality of his patient's strivings. The analyst himself does not achieve direct gratification, but through a process of sublimation and tolerance of frustration he avoids calling into action old defenses. By empathic responsiveness, he helps the patient to understand the infantile quality of his struggles.

Kris [1956a] in his paper on the vicissitudes of insight, has listed three integrative functions of the ego which are essential for development of the analytic process and the achievement of insight in both patient and analyst. These three integrative functions of the ego summarize the points which I have been attempting to emphasize here: (1) The capacity for self-observation . . . involves the split of the ego into observing and experiencing parts. This split with its resulting introspection is fundamental for the task of perceiving and interpreting communications from the patient as well as simultaneous differentiation of patient behavior from the analyst's behavior; (2) control of the discharge of affect relates to the regulation of the analyst's response and his tolerance of need tension in himself and in the patient with the achievement of effective detour functioning; (3) the capacity to control regression is definitely related in the analyst to the ego operations involved in empathizing with the regressions manifested by the transferences of the patient, and permits the use of himself in empathic understanding without loss of his reality-testing functions or his own identity. Only with these ego functions in operation can the analyst establish successful interpersonal relationships of the special kind, with the special goal which analysis requires, and where he uses himself as the special instrument to permit the patient to relive traumatic conflicts in the therapeutic situation.

So far in our examination of the analyst's "work ego," we have emphasized the ego functions involved in the task of understanding the patient. This is only half of the job the analyst must perform. The other half includes the use of his responsive and expressive functions to help the patient understand himself. This is the process of interpretation. The subject has been investigated by many different authors and from many points of view, such as its place in investigative procedures, its role in understanding meanings, and its use as a tool of psychoanalytic technique [Loewenstein, 1957]. For our purposes, in studying the work of an analyst, we approach interpretation as a step in understanding and as a tool for therapeutic communication. The analyst must make diagnostic interpretations to himself as contrasted with therapeutic interpretations to the patient. Diagnostic interpretations, of course, precede the therapeutic. The essentials for success in this part of the work are the ego operations which I have already described in terms of introspection and empathy. To these must be added a synthesis and integration of the understanding arrived at followed by transmission of this interpretation in a communication to the patient. Loewenstein [1957, p. 145] refers to this activity when he says, "Interpretation is meaningless as a one-sided act and acquires its full significance only through its counterpart, the effects it produces on the patient." Any interpretation must be structured in such a form and communicated in such a way that it produces an effect on the patient in line with the therapeutic goal.

The dynamics and economics of the technique of interpretation are not topics for discussion here. Suffice it to say, that awareness of the level of regression and the state of resistance in the patient—an awareness resulting from good perceptiveness and empathy—is a crucial determinant of the form and manner in which this tool is used. We see that diagnostic understanding is not enough, but that responses must be made in the framework of the analytic relationship. These two operations go hand in hand and are inseparable in analytic work.

Tact, which recognizes the appropriateness of the moment and the limits of what can be made explicit, is the term most often used to describe this aspect of the analyst's interaction with his patient. In addition, his verbal skill, the free use of verbal equivalents to facilitate discriminations between fantasy and reality, between past and present, is an essential element in effective analytic work. When we relate this operation to the work ego of the analyst, we find again the importance of introspection and empathy, of reality testing, and of conflict-free functioning, which can integrate understanding into a creative interpersonal act which is therapeutically oriented. Schafer [1959] distinguishes between empathic understanding and empathic communication, both being stages in the operation of "generative empathy." It is the generative quality of empathy in the empathic experience of the psychoanalytic process which makes possible the structural changes aimed for in the ego of the patient. According to Schafer, good generative empathy produces changes in the ego of the analyst also. Maria Kramer [1959] in her recent article on self-analysis, contributes the idea that the experience of analysis results in the development of a new ego function which is not found in an unanalyzed person. She, too, recognizes that such an ego function is an essential part of an analyst's equipment.

Thus we can see that the analyst's work with a patient becomes deeply and intensely work with himself, work in which he experiences emotionally strong infantile strivings and their frustration, with full knowledge of the strivings and full acceptance of their frustration. In other words, the analyst's work requires living in two worlds—past and present, real and unreal, of himself and someone else simultaneously. He must identify with another person with no loss of reality contact or of his own identity. He must be able to live another person's life by empathic understanding and at the same time maintain himself in a situation of deprivation and frustration. From this experience he is expected to feel pleasure and to perform creative work. R. Fliess [1942] and Freud [1937] comment on this seemingly impossible task demanded by analysis. Their refuge is found in the temporary character of these ego operations; i.e., analyzing is work and as such the ego is required to work in this way only during working hours! Only a mature ego capable of sublimation, with a strong sense of reality and developed insight, can manage such a job.

With a job analysis completed, ways of measuring success or failure in the job must be forumlated, and then the factors in the worker at the job, in this case the analyst, which make for success or failure must be identified. A correlation between these factors in a successfully trained analyst and the characteristics which indicate potential for these factors must be determined. In other words, what are the personality characteristics which indicate potential for successful performance? Answers to these questions lead us into the problems of evaluating students and trying to define what makes a good one. This brings the study into the field of evaluation where criteria for successful performance must be developed by supervisors and other teachers. In correlations of these performance criteria with selection criteria, the latter can be sharpened and refined to increase our skill in recognizing the indicators of good or poor potentials in applicants for psychoanalytic training.

·4·

THE TRAINING ANALYST
AS AN EDUCATOR

This paper, read at the Second Three Institutes Conference on Training Analysis (held in Topeka in 1969) and published in 1973, was an important contribution in the evolving development of psychoanalytic education. Many analytic educators up to that time had concentrated on the adverse influence of the realities of the training organization on the therapeutic alliance and the transference neurosis—on the "syncretistic dilemma" (Lewin and Ross, 1960) brought about by the task of needing both to analyze and to educate. In this paper, Dr. Fleming acknowledges that conducting an analysis within the framework of a specific Institute carries with it the potential for certain problems and complications, but she stresses that they can be utilized, in most cases, constructively within the analytic process.

Dr. Fleming's paper has stimulated many other important contributions on the training analysis and the role of the training analyst in the tripartite psychoanalytic educational program.

For many years there has been a certain pessimistic attitude among analysts about the education of analysts. This has been especially true with reference to the training analysis. David Kairys (1964) comments on the dearth of literature on training analysis. He attributes this partly to the feeling that "the problems of analyzing within a training program are intrinsically insoluble and no longer worth discussing" (p. 485). Many other analytic educators today, however, are more optimistic, perhaps braver, perhaps more stubborn, perhaps more ready to accept the challenge of these seemingly insoluble problems. The First Three Institute Conference on Training Analysis, held in Pittsburgh in 1965 (see Babcock, 1965), and the Pre-Congress Conference on

Reprinted by permission from *The Annual of Psychoanalysis*, 1:280–295. New York: Quadrangle, 1973.

Training Analysis in 1965 are evidence that efforts are being made in this direction.

The Pittsburgh Conference was a unique event; it was an experiment in trying to define the educational role of a training analyst and the complications which confront us in trying to carry it out. That conference was organized to encourage free and open discussion of clinical data in order to learn from actual experiences what the problems are. We did not know if this could be done profitably. Nevertheless, we tried and came away stimulated by new perspectives.

Over the last 30 years, the struggles within and between our Institutes have been based to a large extent on the proprietary power vested in "the right to train." This kind of strife indicates some basic trouble in our educational household. It emphasizes not just the importance of these so-called insoluble problems, but the necessity to keep on discussing them. In this endeavor lies the preservation of what is good from the past and the nurturing of the spirit of inquiry with which Freud began his studies. Both the old and the new are vital to the future of psychoanalysis. Our profession has seen too often the unhappy effects of attempts to take one position and discount the other. The battles over orthodoxy, over what is classical analysis, over neo-Freudian inclusion of cultural and interpersonal factors, actually are manifestations of the ever-recurring anxieties that develop when security and comfort are threatened by the strange and unfamiliar. It is up to us not to be intimidated by the famous "syncretisitc dilemma" (Lewin and Ross, 1960), but to continue to explore the issues in this seemingly irreconcilable situation in which education is mixed with analysis.

The dichotomy "to treat versus to teach," which raises such difficulties for analytic educators, is more apparent in the supervisory situation than in the training analysis, but it presents itself there too. The issue is often seen as jurisdictional. According to this view, treatment is the territory of the training analyst, teaching the responsibility of the supervisor—and neither should trespass on the other's ground. However, since both therapy and learning can be blocked by unconscious conflicts, it behooves us to investigate where the blocks come from and how they can be removed, rather than to argue over who should do it. Analysts should understand these things better than anyone else; yet, in spite of the advances against cultural resistances since Freud shook the tradition-bound medical profession and the Victorian world of the 1890s, the history of psychoanalysis is full of repeated turmoil over these proprietary issues. Interestingly, it is in the area of education and government, Freud's two "impossible professions" (1937, p. 248), that the worst battles have been fought. Freud called psychoanalysis the third "impossible profession. I hesitate to remind you of that because, if it is so, then educators of psychoanalysts (whatever their proprietary jurisdiction) are confronted with educating for the impossible!

Nevertheless, undaunted by pessimism and the impossible, I want to emphasize a point of view concerning psychoanalytic education and then apply it to some special problems of the training analysis. Started briefly, *the overall goal of psychoanalytic training should be to make self-analytic skills readily available for working as an analyst*: "Each phase of the training program contributes in special ways to this overall goal, and each psychoanalytic teacher can enhance his effectiveness if he orients the content and method of his teaching in this direction" (Fleming and Benedek, 1966 [see Chapter One, this volume, p. 20]). This point of view is not new. Freud described it in 1910, and others have followed him. The Pittsburgh Conference report is very explicit about self-analysis as an educational goal and the training analyst as an educator as well as a therapist of an analyst-to-be. In this paper I want to examine in greater depth some of the linkages between learning and therapy, integrating the treatment goals of the training analysis with other educational objectives.

In preparing this paper, I returned to the early history of psychoanalysis, attempting to trace the concept of the analytic experience as an essential part of learning to become an analyst. In 1910, Freud (p. 145) specifically connected the growing evidence of countertransference as the reason for his first recommendation that a prospective analyst begin with a self-analysis. In this recommendation I believe Freud was referring to his own experience in analyzing himself, which he described in his letters to Fliess [1887–1902]. Freud recognized the necessity for analysis with an experienced analyst (1912) and in 1937 made his strongest statement about self-analytic skills and the educational role of the training analyst.

It is tempting to present the evolution of Freud's thinking as revealed in his writings over the years, but I would rather proceed to the more specific problems which a training analyst encounters in his educational role and which make a training analysis different from a nontraining analysis.

In Freud's final statement (1937) about how to become an analyst, he stressed the need for a therapeutic experience and for a never-ending self-scrutiny in order to manage the inevitable countertransferences which confront an analyst. This correlation between countertransference, a training analysis, and an ongoing self-analysis may seem very clear to us today; nevertheless, although countertransference was recognized, its investigation was neglected for over 30 years (Racker, 1968, p. 3), and self-analysis was hardly a term in our vocabulary until after the publication of the letters to Fliess in 1954. Training analysis has become an institution, but its therapeutic role has been emphasized to the exclusion of anything else, and its specific educational contribution and the special problems rooted in its training function have received little scientific attention. This is in spite of the fact that the interfering effect of countertransference on both the therapeutic alliance and the transference neurosis has been generally recognized for some time.

Many of the authors who have written about training analysis have concentrated on the adverse influence of the realities of training on the therapeutic alliance and the transference neurosis (Gitelson, 1948; Kairys, 1964; Greenacre, 1954; A. Freud, 1950). These authors speak of "reality" as a contaminant which prevents the development of an analyzable transference neurosis. They stress the importance of separating education from therapy. Kairys would keep the analysis of a candidate from any involvement with educational and administrative aspects of training. Other authors, notably Bibring (1954), Benedek (1954), Weigert (1952), and Racker (1968), recognize that difficulties are presented by the training situation, but they feel that these difficulties need not prevent a good analysis. They feel the realities cannot be ignored, but may actually be used in working through to an insightful differentiation of transference from the distortions of current reality. Bibring [1954, p. 171] says that "exclusion of the training analyst from official influence on the analysand's career indicates some doubts in the analyst's objectivity, i.e., his mastery of countertransference." Benedek (1954) discusses the so-called neutrality of the training analyst in terms of a conflict over being a good parent. She describes the efforts to remain "outside of the professional reality" [p. 15] of the candidate as important in the development of observable transferences. But she feels that these transferences often stimulate a conflict in the training analyst over the wish to be helpful and protective as against the fear of being overprotective and indulgent. It is her opinion, which Weigert also supports, that efforts to solve this countertransference have resulted in an overemphasis on educational neutrality and the significance of anonymity in a training analysis. In other words, neutrality and anonymity are important in facilitating the development of an analyzable transference neurosis in the usual therapeutic analysis. For a training analysis, however, these attitudes may reflect a countertransference conflict which can have a negative influence on optimal analytic results for a candidate.

I believe we can assume that sometimes such a countertransference conflict does exist. If we look at it objectively, we can see how it might influence the educational role in different ways. For many training analysts with this problem, a strict avoidance of any participation in career progression decisions becomes the essential position. Others seem to feel that their knowledge of the candidate is better than that of any other person and that, therefore, they should be the sole arbiter of progression in training. These two contradictory positions have determined many of the educational procedures established by training facilities, both in America and abroad.

If we examine these attitudes as objectively as possible and in the light of actual experience, it seems clear that although neutrality and anonymity do have a favorable effect on the regressive re-experiencing of a childhood conflict so necessary for a good analysis, they may interfere with the resolution of that conflict. I believe the trouble lies not in the reality of the professional relationship or the lack of objectivity or anonymity, but in the failure to differentiate transference from reality. Reproduction of the past is not usually so difficult in a normally conducted analysis; interpretation by means of reconstruction of childhood events, including fantasies, is not so difficult either. The challenge for both candidate and training analyst is "to differentiate the realistic factors of the training situation from the crosscurrents of transferences and countertransferences" (Weigert, 1952, p. 475). It is the confusion of the present with the past that distorts the perception of current reality. This is a phenomenon which must be worked through in any analysis. The difference between transference and reality must be experienced and then integrated into insight. I believe that in many respects this level of insight is more possible in a training analysis than with the usual patient. A training analysis offers sharper confrontation with the incongruity of transference reproductions, just because of the current actuality of training goals and the educational role of the training analyst in accomplishing them. This confusion and its differentiation can be better focused for interpretation. The therapeutic goals and the training goals may interfere with each other, but I believe that the actualities of the training goals need not be looked upon as "contaminants" in the sense of impurities which spoil or harm the analytic experience. I hope to demonstrate how the educational role of the training analyst can deepen and expand the therapeutic results.

If a candidate in the beginning of his training analysis possesses an aptitude for analytic work, he will be able to permit the regression in time orientation and secondary-process thinking which is necessary for a transference neurosis to develop. If good analytic work has been done on the way, the candidate-patient will tolerate this re-experiencing of a regressed ego state in the service of the analytic goal. Immediate, present-day events, such as the knowledge that he shares his analyst with a fellow candidate, can trigger sibling rivalries and other conflicts in analytically useful ways. Such reality events, in my experience, have enabled the patient to experience the warded-off affects more completely when I have not warded off the reality perception but, instead, encourage associations activated by the reality. The technical problem at this stage in any analysis seems to me to demand that the analyst recognize how the patient may be using reality as a defense against regression by emphasizing the unreasonableness of his feelings about his rival. At this stage in a training analysis, the patient may be even consciously avoiding reporting his thoughts and feelings in this area, on the grounds that such reality events are irrelevant.

For example, seeing a smile on my face as the previous candidate-patient left the office stimulated a flash feeling of anger in an analysand. He reported the flash of anger when he saw me, but at first he could give no explanation and began to talk of an argument he had with his wife for letting their three-year-old son claim her attention during the night. This was a present reality event, too, but since the flash of anger was in relation to me, I interpreted his use of the event with his wife as a displacement from anger directed toward me. But I was told there was no reason for his being angry at me. For some minutes he was not to be diverted from talking about his wife and her indulgence of the three-year-old. Discharge of affect was in full swing in spite of the fact that his anger at her was not really reasonable either. I repeated my interpretation of displacement and suggested, without result, that he try to recall what might have preceded the flash of anger at me. Knowing something of his sibling-rivalry situation, I refrained from giving a genetic interpretation of the transference at home or with me. Affective discharge seemed more important at the moment, but he was resisting the immediate impact of the infantile reliving with reference to me. Consequently, I asked if he ever had any thoughts about the previous patient, B. To his surprise, he suddenly had an image of my smiling face as I opened the door to let B. out and waited for him to come in. The image did not last long, but its recall permitted further recall of thoughts that I preferred B. and would have liked to be with B. longer, that I was not eager to see him next because he was such a difficult patient and would probably never make it at the Institute, that B. would get there first, etc. The anger had gone underground again and he was feeling frustrated and depressed.

I acknowledged his mood and pointed out that he was feeling things he had felt about his older brother in childhood. I let the anger at me remain repressed for the time being. As he recovered his equilibrium, he said that this morning's experience had taught him how important it was to pay attention to little flashes of feeling and to talk about them even when they made no sense. This incident occurred early in this man's analysis. I felt I could wait for further regression and transference development to occur. I did not feel that his integration of the morning's experience on an objective and intellectual level toward the end of the hour was altogether in the service of resistance. I thought of it as his learning an important fact of analytic work which would help him tolerate further regression in himself later and would be useful in his professional work as time went on. My thought was related to the educational goal of his analytic experience and my interest in his success. Perhaps this interest was a countertransference resistance, but, at that moment in his analysis, I felt his intellectual insight was not seriously interfering with his transference reliving but would strengthen his ego for further analytic work; neither did I feel any conflict over my pleasure in his intellectual achievement, which would have actual value for him later. If I had been in conflict over my identification with my patient as a professional student, I might have interpreted his resistance against further transference reproduction of his sibling rivalry and depreciated his compensatory coping ability.

From this example of an incident in analysis which had both therapeutic and educational value, I would like to go on to discuss four problems which appear in a training analysis that are not present in the usual therapeutic situation. I hope to show that the exigencies of training when imbricated with educational realities have a bearing on both the therapeutic transference–countertransference interactions and on the development of self-analytic skills. These four problems are related to, first, the candidate's experience of being a patient; second, his experience in being an analyst also; third, his integration of the simultaneous experience of being a patient and a student-analyst with both a training analyst and a supervisor; and fourth, his experience in terminating his training analysis.

Probably the most important experience for an analyst-to-be is to learn what it is like to be a patient in analysis. This sounds like a simple statement, but as a therapeutic objective and an educational experience it has far-reaching professional implications. It touches on the persistent resistances of a "normal" candidate, on the special problems of a working alliance in a training analysis, and on analysis of career motivations, as well as on narcissistic character defenses. All of these topics bear directly on the development of an analyzable transference neurosis and, therefore, indirectly on the development of self-analytic skills.

To be a patient has different meanings, depending on many factors. Most patients are seeking help in order to achieve relief from suffering. Relief from suffering is also the most powerful motivation for cooperating in an analytic working alliance. Only a few candidates fall into this category at the beginning of the training analysis. More frequently, the ego-syntonic motivation is to accept the role of patient, admitting a need for help because they are "not living up to their potential." These candidates lack self-confidence but often resist a working alliance for a long time because the inevitable exposure of infantile conflicts threatens an already vulnerable self-esteem. Many candidates, however, fall into a third group. They do not suffer or lack self-confidence, at least on the surface. Their choice of medicine as a career is often determined by an idealization of the image of a doctor and even a defensive identification with the "aggressor" in childhood illnesses (Simmel, 1949). This group has a stronger defensive system than the second group. Their defenses are buttressed by the gratification of being the recipient of admiration and other omnipotent fantasies from patients whom they have helped. Consequently, it is easy to understand their resistance to the analytic pact. They experience it as "being put down" by the establishment which requires them to behave like patients when "this is really for training."

For them, being a patient is associated with a weak, depreciated image which, in spite of conscious ideas to the contrary, touches the deepest core of narcissistic investment in the self. Understanding the roots of this transference resistance does not make analysis of it easy. It is especially difficult because this resistance manifests itself in the early stages of analysis and interferes with the development of what Greenson wisely calls a "working" alliance (1965) rather than a "therapeutic" alliance. The goal of the alliance is the same whatever term is used, but the connotation of mutual cooperation is more accessible in the word "working." The word "therapeutic" implies passivity and manipulation and conjures up a sense of shame in being a patient. Unfortunately, this problem is more prevalent in psychiatry than in other branches of medicine, where a patient who actually hurts physically is willing to be passively manipulated if it will help. Even with these patients, however, the factor of shame and the feelings of humiliation must very often be considered and occasionally even become a life-saving matter, e.g., in the treatment of a patient with a coronary occlusion (Lewis, [personal communication, 1964]).

So far I have talked about the phenomenon of the narcissistic resistance which complicates the initial stages of a training analysis. If this resistance is understood by the training analyst and if his own self-esteem does not need to be supported by a candidate's "submission" to a mutually projected image of a patient as being a depreciated object, then by his attitude and technique in enlisting cooperation on a partnership basis, he can gradually help the candidate overcome his resistance. When this happens, a very significant piece of analytic work will have been accomplished and a step toward restructuring a more effective work ego in the student-patient will have been taken.

For psychoanalytic educators, the importance of understanding this problem cannot be overemphasized. It manifests itself in both parties to the analytic situation, and where it is not part of the training analyst's self-insight or accessible to his self-analytic work, it may interfere irreparably with development of an analyzable transference neurosis. This outcome blocks not only the therapeutic goal of a training analysis, but also the firsthand experience of regression and working through which analysis of a transference neurosis provides.

Such a derailment of an optimal experience for a student-analyst may not even be seen as such in a first round of training analysis. There are many circumstances which contribute to such a state of affairs. The evidence often does not appear until a test of empathy and self-analytic skills occurs in the supervised analysis. The supervisor may be the first to observe the blind spot or defensive reaction to the patient's regression, which can be presumptive evidence of a deficit in the experiential learning to be expected from a training analysis. Such evidence is presumptive, of course, until the student's self-analytic skills are tested further by the supervisor. But if the supervisor encounters resistance against this self-examination, he can assume that a fundamental attitude toward being an analytic patient, i.e., an object of continuing self-analysis, has not been accomplished in the student's training analysis.

Partial awareness of this problem is seen in the selection criterion which puts a plus value on an applicant's insight into the fact that he has difficulties that need analytic help. This insight is assessed as a measure of his ability to become a patient, which Greenson (1967, p. 360) rates as a prime measure of analyzability. It may be a part of his conscious motivation for seeking analytic training. More often it is not. Other valuable information is obtained on admission by inquiry into an applicant's response to failure and experiences of shame and humiliation. Such an evaluation gives valuable clues to whether or not the task of "being a patient" will be a serious obstacle in his analysis.

Two clinical vignettes will illustrate the two sides of this problem from an analytic educator's point of view. In the first one, a countertransference in the training analyst probably contributed to a prolonged resistance against a working alliance and blinded the analyst to an early narcissistic defense transference. The analysand was just finishing his residency. A top performer in his group, but with a long-standing sense of inferiority well covered up, he was given instructor's rank several months before graduation. At about the same time he applied for analytic training and was deferred. The reasons for deferment are not as important here as his reaction to rejection and the way in which his manifest attitude to analysis aroused a counterreaction in myself, his training analyst. He responded to the feeling of failure and shame with a sour-grapes attitude on the one hand and, on the other hand, a compensatory struggle with me to prove there was nothing wrong with him. In other words, he was not sure he wanted to be an analyst anyway, and, if I thought he needed to be analyzed, he would prove how wrong I was and frustrate me just as he had been frustrated by the Admissions Committee. The first thing I became aware of was a feeling of annoyance and the thought that the patient was wasting my time. I had accepted him for analysis under pressure from both outside and inside. To some extent, I was staking my *Menschenkentnis* on this case, for I had been willing to accept him at admission and here he was rejecting and defeating me. Not all of this recognition of my wounded self-esteem or my narcissistic motivations for trying to analyze this patient came into awareness at once or easily. But, by the time they did, the patient felt rejected by me, too, and was experiencing his relationship with me as being all too similar to fantasied rejection in childhood. For a long time, all I could see were the defenses which he had used on many occasions when a current incident reactivated the childhood disappointment. Gradually, as I gained command of myself, it was possible to establish a working alliance and to interpret the transference neurosis which developed. I considered transferring him to another analyst, but it seemed as though that would only compound the difficulties.

The second vignette illustrates how deep-seated and unconscious the negative attitude toward being a patient can be. In this case the patient was an experienced analyst, in a second analysis, who worked hard and whom I considered an ideal analytic patient. The working alliance was good and the analysis moved along well. Imagine my surprise when one day he said, "You know, the funny thing about this analysis is I feel like a patient." With a shock I wondered to myself what else he had been feeling like, and realized we both needed to do some work on "What's a patient?!"

Once the initial hurdles are overcome and the candidate accepts himself as a patient, the usual analytic work proceeds. If all goes well, the candidate experiences things that he has heard about and observed in patients during his residency training, such as resistance, regression, transference, etc. During this stage of his own analysis, however, he is usually too busy with being a patient to call his experiences by any conceptual name. It is during this phase that he learns to associate against resistance, to introspect, to tolerate himself differently, to objectify his own experiencing, and to assimilate painful truth on the road to self-discovery. These are the experiences that result in freedom from neurotic conflicts and in insight and structural change. They also provide experimental learning about the basic elements of the analytic method, learning which has a bearing on self-analytic skills but which will become more cognitive in later phases of training.

As the working alliance is established and the transference neurosis develops, the infantile roots of career motivations appear. It is in relation to the candidate's wish to progress in training that the training analyst's sensitivity to his patient's shifts in ego motivation must be very keen and his countertransference responses (to use Racker's concept) must be conflict-free and reality-oriented. Such wishes from the patient may be seen as competitive resistance, as an acting out of infantile fantasies of taking father's place, or they may be more oriented to professional reality goals.

The analysis, and especially the training analyst, is put to a second crucial test when the candidate-patient becomes ready to move into a position of student-analyst. We must be able to assume that the training analyst can assess how ready his patient is to start analyzing his own patient. What belongs to infantile carryovers and what belongs to current career goals on a realistic basis

needs to be explored and differentiated. The Pittsburgh Conference report (Babcock, 1965, p. 37) describes discussion of these
issues and states as a conclusion that "the best the training analyst
can do is to learn how to assess the growth of the candidate's
capacities for empathy and self-analysis, in order to help the candidate assess himself and come to a decision about his career." My
remarks are aimed at a deeper exploration of some of the points to
be considered by the training analyst in learning how to do this.
For the training analyst to abdicate his responsibility for making
this diagnostic differentiation and for participating in the necessary interpretive work is to abandon his candidate-patient in a
crucial phase of his analysis—a phase that includes not only the resolution of his Oedipal conflict, but also the re-solution of his
adolescent conflict and the development of a mature ego capable of
reality-oriented self-assessment—a basic attitude and skill for the
self-analytic tasks of his professional work ego.

When a candidate poses questions of career progression (matriculation, termination, supervisory conflicts, or even a return to
analysis), he confronts his analyst with a problem of double vision.
In an Oedipal transference, one image is that of a child caught in
the web of Oedipal fantasies which protect him against the narcissistic injury of recognizing his real limitations at that level of
development. The other image is that of a chronological adult who
presents himself as a younger colleague with or without demonstrated potentials for analytic work. Both images must be looked
at and perceived in the perspective of the transference neurosis
and in the frame of adult reality assessments. This is the analytic
task of the training analyst, keeping this third eye and ear on his
own responses in each of these frames of reference.

If the training analyst backs away from taking a reality
stand, the analytic situation is likely to become a replica of parental failure to help a growing child learn to assess the reality of his
ambitions in the frame of his abilities and limitations. The evaluating analyst may be seen as a hostile, judging parent, but let us
remember that the parent who does not evaluate his child's behavior, who cannot say no, set limits, or express disapproval, may very
often not be helpful or understanding. Such a parent is not providing a good framework of reality, both physical and social, against
which the child's knowledge of danger and limitations can grow so
that he can survive physically and can develop coping mechanisms

that permit behavior in tune with environmental and social expectations. The nonjudging parent may identify with his child and in his overpermissiveness actually do harm by failing to confront him with the realities of life, allowing childhood delusions of omnipotence to persist. The neutral parent may even have a destructive effect. No child believes in neutrality. Such parental behavior is felt as indifference, or even, "If you are not on my side, you are against me." Many a patient repeats this childhood stance and complains, "You don't understand me," meaning "You don't agree with me and see it my way." Experiences with an honestly evaluating parent assist a child's ego to develop a good sense of reality; tolerance for frustration; and skills for balancing pleasure and pain, frustration and gratification, and for integrating id, superego, and social pressures.

The candidate who is always expecting hostile frustration from his analyst, whether it be in the area of immediate gratification of an expected, even demanded, response or in the area of more distant career progression, is suffering from a transference resistance which distorts the whole meaning of analysis; he is reproducing a situation from the past which needs to be differentiated from the present or is projecting childhood fantasies which he has not outgrown or integrated into a reality-oriented ego structure. Unfortunately, there are immature, hostile parents who do envy and compete with their children, who, like Laius, are afraid of being displaced or surpassed by the baby Oedipus.

Unfortunately, there are some analysts whose narcissistic needs and other childhood conflicts have remained unintegrated and unmodified by insight. But, on the whole, analysts struggle with these conflicts and, in my experience, succeed in being fair most of the time. In assessing questions involving the candidate's career progression, the danger, as I see it, is in the analyst's not being able to say no when he recognizes interfering pathology or lack of aptitude. If the analyst stays "neutral" and "uninvolved," saying nothing either to the candidate or the Education Committee, he is shirking his educational responsibilities. Such analysts permit a candidate to progress when he should be stopped. They rationalize their silence not only with a cloak of neutrality but by a persisting countertransference hope that the candidate will "get away with it," or "get by," or change, or go back to analysis with someone else, etc. In my experience, the more an analyst's doubts, questions, and positive evaluations can be shared with an objective, like-minded group of colleagues, the better he can understand the problem, clarify the issues, and arrive at a decision with more confidence. Objectivity in these situations increases in the evaluating training analyst and in the group who listens and assesses all of the evidence as to a candidate's readiness for analyzing a patient under supervision. It is a learning experience for all concerned, which, according to Grete Bibring, provides the training analyst with "helpful perspectives on his candidates" (1954, p. 171).

To my mind, a candidate's experience of how his training analyst participates in such professional moves makes a big difference in his attitude toward analysis in general and toward his future use of self-analytic skills. An honest, "I don't know if you are ready to start with a patient," or, "I don't think you are ready," or, "Yes, I think so," followed by, "And what is your reaction to what I say?" provide more productive analytic work than a dead silence or an interpretation which does not include the realistic elements of current professional ambition, or a statement such as, "You know I have nothing to do with your training."

At this point in a training analysis, the defensive countertransference of the training analyst is on the scales, since the patient will respond with elements of transference reactions regardless of what the analyst does. The technical problem is to keep the lines open for observation and to keep the training analyst's responses as conflict-free and reality-oriented as possible. Children are very sensitive to the hypocrisy that is evident when their parents ignore, or keep quiet about, or identify with something that seems to bring secondary gain. Patients are like children in this respect and can sense the hypocrisy in a training analyst who protests a pseudoneutrality on this subject. For, regardless of protest, I have yet to see a training analyst who is not interested in the professional progress of his candidate-patient. It would not be natural or human. The line should not be drawn on such a basis, but rather on the demonstration of differentiation between transference and reality for both patient and analyst. It is not important whether the training analyst writes a letter to the Education Committee. The important thing is the way he handles reality while simultaneously keeping the analytic process moving ahead. For the candidate who is not only a patient but about to become an analyst, too, the attitude of his training analyst toward the meaning of this shift in his identity can determine the candidate's own attitude toward the never-ending process of making himself the object of analytic exploration of transference distortions and reintegrating them in the light of current reality.

Let me refer you to Greenson's example of the disastrous effect of an analyst's inhuman ignoring of a reality crisis in the life of his patient (1967, p. 219). This student-analyst failed even to acknowledge his patient's absorbing concern and anxiety for her sick child. He was unable to recognize the validity of Greenson's questioning of his attitude until the third supervisory hour. In this example, not only his readiness to analyze a patient can be questioned, but also the quality of his training analysis. If he had had any aptitude for analytic work, his lack of ability to assess immediate reality and to observe his own behavior in relation to the totality of the analytic process would at best suggest a poor prognosis for the development of self-analytic skills. Something in his experience as a patient had gone awry. Since, in Greenson's report, the student-analyst did not seem to accept the confrontation except with some defensive counterreaction of his own, one wonders if he would even bring it up in his training analysis. It might not occur to him in the analytic situation, or he might succeed in isolating or withholding the incident, supported by a rationalization that his experiences with patients or supervisors did not belong in analysis.

I have heard this rationalization used, after a candidate becomes a student-analyst, to explain why he seldom talks about his patients or his supervisors. These two sets of experiences are normally laden with emotion and conflict and, therefore, should appear in his associations. I consider it a serious resistance if they do not appear directly. If I cannot identify any disguised clues, I begin to wonder about something in my countertransference. On one occasion, my student-patient had begun a new case with a new supervisor. Early in the situation he talked about his patient and who the supervisor was, but he omitted anything about the supervisory relationship. When I realized this and asked him about it, he said with too naive sincerity, "I thought you did not want me to learn anything from him." As we worked on this, he went on to say, "I knew you did not like him and would resent my talking about all he has been teaching me." Needless to say, there was plenty of analysis and self-analysis to be done here. It was true; I did not like the supervisor, which I acknowledged, but went on to point out how he was using this bit of reality to perpetuate a feeling he had had about his mother, both before and after she and his father were divorced when he was about 12 years old.

This example illustrates an important point for our discussion here: A patient's knowledge about his analyst can be used to support transference resistances, and the manifest way in which the resistance is expressed can fit so easily into the analyst's economic and dynamic state of mind that the patient's resistance is not felt as such. A countertransference blind spot can allow what in this instance was an important transference to go unanalyzed. I think the way in which a student-patient brings his supervisory experiences into his own analysis depends a great deal on his analyst's countertransference rivalries. In direct correlation, it influences the student's attitude toward the self-analysis of his countertransferences when he is on his own.

So far, I have tried to indicate the educational objectives which are inherent in the beginning phase of a training analysis. Learning to be a patient and being a patient teach a candidate the fundamentals of what he needs to know experimentally about himself and the analytic method. Many training analysts think that a candidate should have experienced at least the beginning of his transference neurosis before he is considered ready to begin theoretical courses or to analyze a patient under supervision. They argue that both of these progressive steps tend to distract from an optimal concentration on his work as a patient. But equally important are the experiences of being a patient and an analyst in rapid succession, if not simultaneously. For this reason a training analysis should not stop prior to beginning a first case. On the other hand, there are educational advantages to its coming to a termination before graduation. I will elaborate further on these two points.

Being in analysis and supervision at the same time is a third major educational experience which needs analyzing. It provides situations of triadic relationships which are very helpful in activating conflicts of loyalty and competition in the student-patient that take him deeper into Oedipal and adolescent transferences. The multiple triangles offered by these new situations stir up countertransferences as well as tranference conflicts. Unfortunately, they are supported by the patriarchal organization of our professional relationships, especially in their educational aspects, I have already referred to several. I will mention, however, a very significant contribution which the training analyst makes to his student-patient's self-analytic skills. By way of his own attitude toward countertransference and by freeing his candidate to learn from someone else, the ground is prepared for the student to tolerate the confrontations of countertransferences necessary in supervision. Such confrontations can be accepted by a student-analyst when he has learned from his training analyst to look into himself with curiosity, to examine his own reactions, and to build not only insight for himself but understanding of the analytic process on the basis of his self-analytic efforts.

Termination of his training analysis is the fourth major experience as a patient which contributes to development of a candidate's self-analytic skills. After all, the whole training program is geared toward educating analysts who can independently treat patients by the analytic method. Therefore, it seems logical that his teachers will be interested in knowing how a student is able to analyze on his own—without the support of a training analyst and with decreasing frequency of official supervision. In this respect it can be stated that evidence of self-analytic skills is the most significant measure of a student's qualification for graduation.

Interminable as analysis is for an analyst, the maturational value to be achieved in a termination experience cannot be provided in any other way. But working through to emancipation from childhood conflicts and renunciation of childhood ties is a phase of every good analysis. Is there something more in a training analysis? I belive there is. Specifically, this something more involves the opportunity for a continuing relationship between a candidate and his training analyst, but on a different basis than in the analytic situation. Having worked so hard at being a patient, the student-analyst must now work equally hard at shifting to another level, that of colleague and friend. There are some analysts who say this cannot happen and some who say it should not. Both groups seem to me to sell analysis short. Their attitude says, "Once a child, always a child, never a grown-up to a parent." If so, the reality principle is negated by both parties, and I believe the responsibility for the failure to accept the adult status of his "child" would belong to the training analyst.

The problem is a matter not simply of analyzing through to a good analytic termination, but of being able to develop a new and different relationship, should circumstances permit. If the trouble lies with the candidate, the analysis has failed in some way to reach an optimal end point. If the analyst is unable to make the differentiation, but tends to perpetuate a patriarchal culture in the profession, it will be that much more difficult for his former patient to consolidate the self-analytic skills so essential for both the science and art of the profession. He will inevitably identify with the patriarchal image and all its burden of defensive counter-transference. Questions about who has the "right to train" will continue to sidetrack the more vital questions of what an analytic student needs to learn, how we can help him learn, and how we know he has learned.

In conclusion, let me say that I feel it is essential to continue an exploration of eductional goals and teaching methods, as well as research into theory and technique. The two fields of investigation are more closely interrelated in psychoanalysis than in other professional fields, but, so far, the latter has absorbed most of the scientific energies of psychoanalysis. The scientific study of educational problems has only just begun. I say this in spite of the complaint heard in the late 1950s and early 1960s that "education" was taking too much of the time, interest, and financial resources of the members of the American Psychoanalytic Association, to the detriment of "science." It seemed to me then, as it does now, that such complaints were shortsighted and failed to realize that good psychoanalytic education for new generations of analysts is the best insurance for a steady scientific advance.

·5·

ASSESSMENT OF PROGRESS IN A TRAINING ANALYSIS

(*with Stanley S. Weiss*)

Dr. Fleming always emphasized the need for evaluation in psychoanalytic education, both for assessing competence and for use as an educational tool, important for the advancement of both faculty and students. This paper reports one method for evaluating the extent to which the preparatory and therapeutic goals of the training analysis have been reached, so that the candidate is ready to work effectively in class and with patients.

The paper acknowledges that psychoanalytic educators appreciate the uniqueness of each candidate's talent, ability, and rate of development, but states that this fundamental analytic knowledge is not sufficiently taken into account in structuring the educational program, especially in deciding when a candidate is ready to proceed after a period of time in the training analysis to the next step in training. It is noted that the training analysis is perceived and even labeled as preparatory, but that objectives and criteria are not spelled out except in terms of an expectation that psychopathology observed at selection will change.

The paper stresses that a candidate's progress should be part of the analytic work, but that in many instances it is not. Evaluation of progress in a training analysis by outside evaluators is said to be important for evaluating the training analyst, as well as the process and the product of the training analysis; it is also described as an important means for integrating that phase of the educational program with the other two phases.

Dr. Fleming was gratified that some form of assessing progress had become an increasing activity of analytic educators, although she believed that this was not the case for the training analysis. Dr. Flem-

Reprinted by permission from the *International Review of Psycho-Analysis*, 5:33–43, 1978. Spelling and punctuation in the original have been changed to conform with American usage.

ing was one of the first psychoanalytic educators to focus on matriculation criteria and formulate a procedure for evaluating the training analysis at this important point in progression.

Dr. Fleming hoped that this paper would stimulate discussions of all the pros and cons of the matriculation procedure at ongoing workshops. She believed that this is the only effective way to bring the subject and problem of evaluation to the level of the individual training analyst.

In most Institutes, acceptance by the admission interviewers is tentative, pending a successful training analysis. But what is a successful training analysis? By far the majority of candidates begin courses and start a patient in analysis under supervision before they finish their personal analysis. When should this step occur? How does the Institute know the candidate is ready to take this step in progression? What criteria are used to determine this important decision? Stone (1974) emphasizes the importance of an "adequate analysis," but he finds it difficult to be more specific about how one determines its adequacy. Stone refers to the problem of "syncretism" (Lewin and Ross, 1960), something which is undoubtedly present in psychoanalytic education but which has been used, in our opinion, to avoid the difficult task of differentiating and still integrating the therapeutic role of the training analyst from and with his role as a participant in an educational process (Fleming, 1973 [see Chapter Four, this volume]). Stone (1974, p. 308) feels that "the operational principle of 'syncretism' . . . in many directions uniquely productive, should be carefully reevaluated in terms of its optional and purposive applications." In the same paragraph, Stone says that syncretism "so permeates our training system that therapy threatens to crowd out the art and obligation of teaching as well as the objective extra therapeutic assessment of candidates." If this trend should continue, we feel that much gain in both professional and educational knowledge and skills would be lost. Furthermore, much that we could learn from trying to solve the problem of syncretism and to use evaluation consciously and explicitly for educational purposes will be kept on an implicit, intuitive, impressionistic level of operation. We feel that active study should be given by analytic faculties to defining what we expect from a training analysis, what constitutes success or failure, and what procedures can be used to measure a candidate's professional progress.

This paper is one of a series on assessment of progress in psychoanalytic education. A previous paper (Weiss and Fleming, 1975 [see Chapter Six, this volume]) dealt with criteria for assessing progress in supervision and the problems involved in making an educational diagnosis of the learning difficulties manifesting themselves at the point of evaluation. In that paper a number of examples were given describing the process the supervisor went through as he made his assessment.

Our intent in this paper is to make more explicit the contribution which a training analysis should be expected to make to a professional "work ego" (R. Fliess, 1942; Fleming, 1961 [see Chapter Three, this volume]) and to propose a procedure for correlating the experiential learning of a training analysis with the next phase of training.

At the point of selection, acceptance is based on a prediction that a successful applicant is analyzable and that he has the potential to develop the ego skills necessary to achieve competence as an analyst. Selection predictions are tested in the training analysis and at some point in this experience the successful candidate is judged ready to matriculate,[1] meaning to move on in the educational program.

In order to assess whether or not a candidate has come far enough in his analysis, a criterion for matriculation should be formulated and a procedure devised for evaluating his progress. This requires an educational assessment which estimates the candidate's ability to enter classroom and supervisory learning situations at a point when this step will further the analytic work as it stimulates the candidate's academic work. In this paper we attempt to present a point of view about when, how, and by whom this educational decision should be made.

The preparatory purpose of a training analysis, whether it is called "didactic," "therapeutic," or both, has been implicitly recognized since 1910 when the appearance of "countertransference" stirred Freud to recommend that a student of psychoanalysis should "begin with a self-analysis and continually carry it deeper while he is making his observations on his patients" (Freud, 1910, p. 144). Eitingon, addressing the International Training Commission in 1925, supported this double goal when he stated: "The point

---

1. To matriculate means to enroll or register in a group, such as a college or university where further development takes place.

in which instructional analysis or didactic analysis differs from therapeutic analysis . . . is not in having a special technique . . . in having an additional aim, that supersedes or goes hand in hand with the therapeutic aim" (Eitingon, 1926 [, p. 132]). Gradually, the growing body of psychoanalysts has recognized that a personal analysis is an indispensable part of their learning (Balint, 1954). Moreover, in the last 15 years a number of Institutes have become involved in trying to define the professional objectives, specific contributions, and therapeutic goal of the training analysis in order to define its place in the totality of the education of an analyst (Freud, 1937; Fleming and Benedek, 1966 [see Chapter One]; Benedek, 1969; Fleming, 1971 [see Chapter Two]).

Evaluation is an ongoing process in any educational venture and occurs at many levels, each of which may have a different purpose. It may be used to assess achievement of the overall objectives of a program. Final examinations in all of their various forms are an example of the use of evaluation to measure adequacy and to certify competence at the end point of educational work. Evaluation is also used to assess progress at different points along the way and to measure readiness to proceed to the next phase of training (COPER, 1974, p. 4; Stone, 1974).

The educational value of assessing progress has been generally neglected or actively resisted by psychoanalytic educators. We are well aware that some form of assessing progress has now become an increasing activity of analytic educators, although this activity has not involved the training analysis and has not led to explicit and communicable results. Evaluation inevitably makes judgments and certain kinds of judgmental attitudes do not belong in analysis. However, these moral and punitive connotations should not be confused with the evaluations which do belong to analysis and are intrinsic to any diagnostic and interpretive work. Evaluation, in this context, is made during every analytic, classroom, and supervisory hour. What is being evaluated varies according to the different purposes for making an assessment, whether it be a patient's resistance or depth of regression, a candidate's sensitivity to unconscious meanings, his interpretive skill, or his understanding of theoretical concepts (Weiss and Fleming, 1975 [see Chapter Six]).

Actually, decisions about progression have been made in all Institutes for many years, but the basis for the decisions has varied considerably in terms of its explicit relevance to educational objectives and to a definite effort to assess preparatory goals. A brief review of the criteria serving as a base for these decisions is indicated at this point.

1. An "undefined and hidden" criterion. The first of these criteria is relatively indefined, since progress has been implicitly evaluated by the training analyst, who might or might not communicate his opinion to his candidate-patient or to the Institute administration. Under this procedure the criterion which a training analyst uses has been unavailable, since what he said to his candidate was not reported and what he said to the Institute was limited in most instances to the simple statement: "I consider Dr. B. ready to begin courses. His analysis is progressing." Implicit in this statement is the assumption that reading psychoanalytic literature in a critical and insightful manner and listening to lectures will not interfere with the analysis, that the candidate has aptitude for becoming an analyst, and that he is ready to matriculate in courses. But, from the training analyst's statement, one cannot assume that he is also ready to start analyzing a patient with supervision. Progression to clinical experience is often not planned for with specific criteria and procedures of assessment, either by the training analyst or by the Education Committee. Unless someone takes responsibility for this decision, the less vociferous candidate may be left in limbo without a patient for several years.

2. A "time criterion" for progression to classes. In many Institutes, the candidate progresses automatically, enrolling (matriculating) in courses after a period of time in his training analysis. This period of time varies from six months to a year or more and may operate entirely independently of any evaluative procedure. To us, it seems that this "time criterion" ignores the concept of the preparatory goal of a training analysis. It bypasses the educational advantages of assessing whether or not the changes in pathology and in ego skills to be expected from an analytic experience have occurred. Also, it omits recognition of individual variations in the rate of progression. This automatic time criterion is described by some as protecting the training analysis from contamination with professional reality goals. It seems to us that such an educational attitude does more to isolate the experiences

that should not be isolated but should be integrated in a total educational program (Fleming and Benedek, 1966 [see Chapter One]; COPER, 1974).

3. A "time criterion" for progression from classes to cases. Another form of a "time criterion" is observable in the custom in many Institutes which determines progression from classes to clinical work after a candidate has spent so much time in "courses" or has completed certain basic theoretical work, plus a course on technique. Such a criterion seems to us to prolong an already long period of training and to postpone the vital experience of beginning clinical work with a patient while the candidate is still with his training analyst (Fleming, 1973 [see Chapter Four]). This kind of learning sequence can put a premium on intellectual knowledge separated from the experience of correlating behavior in the analytic situation with explanatory theoretical concepts.

In most Institutes the criterion for progression from the training analysis has been a candidate's readiness for beginning formal theoretical study and progression to clinical work is made automatically. Explicit assessment may not be made if automatic time criteria are used. However, in some Institutes (Ferber, 1974, p. 86), evaluative interviews are set up to measure progress before beginning courses. These Institutes recognize the educational need for an evaluation of the changes resulting from analysis, but the main reason for having an interview procedure at this point is to relieve the training analyst of the sole responsibility of making such a decision. This kind of criterion and evaluative interview done by analysts other than the training analyst can be a *pro forma* gesture, or it can provide very valuable data on what persisting unconscious conflicts might interfere with theoretical learning and what behavioural evidence indicates their solution. These data offer an excellent opportunity for analytic educators to increase their own diagnostic skills and their ability to assess changes in ego structure aimed for in any analysis.

4. An "educational criterion" for matriculation. If we accept that the primary goal of a training analysis is to prepare the candidate for being ready intrapsychically to begin to analyze a patient, then the criterion for matriculation should express this objective. It could be formulated as follows: "The candidate is considered ready to begin analysis of a patient with supervision."

This criterion makes progression to the clinical phase of training the primary measure, and readiness for progression to theoretical courses something to be assumed. Time is involved here also, since the date for the assignment of the first case varies according to how much theoretical and formal technical knowledge is thought to be needed to prepare a candidate for beginning an analysis. We feel that careful evaluation along both of these lines will prevent difficulties that are frequently encountered when a candidate begins analyzing a supervised case before he has had an adequate analytic experience.

If this criterion is accepted as the basis for making a decision about progressing to the second phase of training, i.e., matriculating, then the problem becomes one of identifying the evidence upon which a yes or no decision is made. This involves an investigation of several subcriteria as matriculation interviewers attempt to evaluate the structural change that has taken place in the candidate since selection and to assess whether or not the preparatory goals of the training analysis have been achieved.

The following statements are an attempt to define specific areas in which a training analysis can contribute to the professional learning of a candidate and for which evidence should be observable in evaluative interviews (COPER, 1974, p. 18):

1. The training analysis will have developed the candidate's potential for empathic understanding and communication with himself and others (Sachs, 1947; Fleming, 1961 [see Chapter Three]).

2. The training analysis will have provided a firsthand and very personal experience in learning about unconscious conflict, anxiety, resistance, defence, symptomatic behavior (such as learning blocks), genetic determinants, dreams, regression, and transference.

3. The training analysis will have developed some skill in introspecting, associating, and interpreting latent meanings (prerequisites for skill in self-analysis).

4. The training analysis will have developed some insight with conviction into the conflicts that have played a major role in determining the candidate's character structure and neurotic symptoms.

5. The training analysis will have developed some insight into the Oedipus conflict in particular and how the candidate solved it for himself.

These subcriteria involve a combination of educational and therapeutic skills and the ego functions that should be more observable and assessable in a matriculation interview than at the time of selection. For such a procedure, matriculation interviewers should go beyond the kind of general assessment made at selection to questions about the nature and progress of the analytic experience itself and the stage of transference development. In fact, the candidate's analytic experience should be the main focus of the matriculation interview as compared to the focus of selection interview. For instance: "Tell me about yourself; let me get to know you" may be the initial question of a selection interview, whereas: "Tell me about your analysis; what have you learned about yourself in analysis?" might be the initial question in a matriculation interview. At selection, a suitable applicant should be able to respond to the interviewer, relax the social façade, and present as clear a picture as possible of the feelings, thinking, and functioning of his inner self. If the applicant has had psychotherapy or psychoanalysis, he should be able to describe clearly some part of his treatment or his analyzability and suitability might be in question. A suitable candidate for matriculation should be able to present a clear picture of the analysis, make some important connexions between past and present, speak of some of his conflicts, describe the relationship and the interaction between himself and the analyst, especially about the analytic work involving the meaning of matriculation. Some thoughts, fantasies, anxieties about becoming an analyst, analyzing a patient, supervision, courses, etc., should be meaningfully presented.

A topic profitably explored at selection and matriculation is the area of object relations. At selection this area is tapped with questions about family, past and present friends, ability to love, etc. The selection interviewer obtains information not only about object relations but also about reality testing, sense of identity, and self-image. The same questions may give clues that pertain to fantasy life, secondary-process thinking, and creativity. At matriculation these questions take a different path by focusing on the candidate's view of his analytic experience. Evidence for increased openness; access to his unconscious; awareness of the purpose of a training analysis; objectivity toward self, patients, and analyst; insight into his defenses; motivation for a commitment to the science of analysis; etc., comes easily from this line of inquiry.

In selection interviews a common topic is the motivation for entering medicine, psychiatry, and psychoanalysis. At matriculation a more important area for investigation is the candidate's motivation for matriculation: his understanding of what it means to him to enter courses, to begin to analyze a patient, his anxieties about success [and] failure, etc. The topic of motivation and its transference roots can be inquired about directly.

Selection interviewers find it helpful to have an applicant briefly discuss a patient treated in psychotherapy. How the applicant conducts therapy and understands the patient can give many clues to the ego functions that a selection interviewer looks for in a potential analyst. During the presentation of the case, the applicant's empathy, sensitivity, psychological-mindedness, understanding of the unconscious, healthy curiosity about people, healthy passivity, etc., can be readily observed. Often at selection, when an applicant describes a patient, it is one who is very much like himself. The applicant may or may not have insight into this.

At matriculation we are also interested in how a candidate works with and understands a patient in a clinical encounter as we look for evidence of change and growth in clinical skill. Usually, at the time of matriculation, the candidate has a wider range of patients to choose from and he will usually choose a patient that shows his growing diagnostic and therapeutic skills.

At selection, if an applicant presents a dream, it will often be interpreted by him at the level of the manifest content, and the interpretation will usually not show a sophisticated ability to work with dreams. At matriculation, however, we would expect a suitable candidate to handle a dream with growing clinical skill and with knowledge of the importance of the day residue. The candidate might readily connect the dream to thoughts and fantasies about matriculation.

At selection, interviewers have to assess if the candidate can be successfully analyzed in an Institute setting. Matriculation interviewers need to assess whether matriculation will interfere with further analytic work and progress. Evaluation of what might interfere with further analytic work is difficult to accomplish in a single interview. This is an area, it seems to us, which needs further study. To investigate this area would ideally require the cooperation of the training analyst and the candidate as well as matriculation interviewers, supervisors, and teachers. It is our impression that premature matriculation stirs up counterresistances in supervision that would not offer the same kind of learning problem if the candidate had worked through his conflicts more extensively in analysis. We also feel that the candidate's first patient should not have to bear the brunt of iatrogenic obstacles which could be avoided by more analysis. This does not mean that the training analysis should be terminated before matriculation. On the contrary, it should go on, since supervision always stirs up unconscious activity which can deepen and extend the insights to be gained from continuing analysis (Fleming and Benedek, 1966).

We have described the lines of inquiry which we feel are contributory to making a matriculation decision. These data need to be organized in a well-documented report that includes behavioral data describing clearly the interaction between the candidate and interviewer and reveals the candidate's ability to talk about the meaning of his analytic experience.

Obviously, a good selection report will also highlight the interaction between candidate and interviewer. Some selection and matriculation interviewers regrettably leave out this kind of data. The most valuable matriculation reports will sum up observational data and evidence in the candidate for a growing ability to observe himself, increasing empathy, impulse control, sublimation, healthy narcissistic balance, and a growing ability to read critically and with pleasure.

The matriculation procedure can be divided into two evaluative situations, the intra-analytic and the extra-analytic (Ferber, 1974).

The intra-analytic evaluation has been the subject of much controversy on two points. The first objection deals with the training analyst making any kind of evaluative judgment. We have already touched on this in this paper to some extent. The second objection has to do with whether the training analyst communicates anything to the candidate or Institute. Several papers have been written on the controversy about reporting or not reporting to the Institute (Kairys, 1964; F. McLaughlin, 1967; J. McLaughlin, 1973; Calef and Weinshel, 1973; Stone, 1974). In this paper we will not enter into this debate, partly because we feel reporting to the Institute by the training analyst is not as important as his making an assessment of his candidate's preparation for analyzing a patient and making this evaluation a part of the analytic process. The motivation for the wish to matriculate is multidetermined, as will be demonstrated in our examples. When this motivation becomes a part of the analytic process, its roots and determinants in childhood conflicts are an essential part of the intraanalytic work and should be evaluated by the candidate himself as well as by the training analyst.

We realize that certain analytic educators conducting a training analysis feel it is absolutely necessary for them never to let their candidates know how they feel about the candidate's progress or lack of progress in becoming an analyst, and they do not wish to play any part in the progress of their analysand within the Institute program. In fact, some of these analysts feel that to do otherwise interferes in a significant way with the personal analysis. Other analysts feel they can speak more freely to an Education Committee and to their candidates at the proper time and in a proper analytic way without interfering with the analytic process. Much needs to be written and discussed about the complex and subtle relationships between analysts and candidates and the mutual identification processes between the two (Shapiro, 1974a, 1974b).

When there is a criterion for readiness to analyze a patient and a procedure for evaluative interviews, reporting to the Education Committee is often of more scientific value than it is significant for a matriculation decision (Fleming, 1973 [see Chapter Four]; Ferber, 1974).

However, if the training analyst accepts the responsibility for evaluating his candidate's progress and his readiness to analyze a patient, then the following guidelines might be found useful:

1. Is there a firm working alliance? Will it continue against the distraction of courses and cases? Or, will these possible distractions serve as resistances against further progress in the candidate's analysis?

2. Is the candidate able to associate freely? If so, this usually accompanies a good working alliance and demonstrates some ability to regress.

3. What is the stage of transference development? Is the transference neurosis still being resisted? If so, this form of regression can be interfered with by matriculation. The responsibilities and conflicts associated with courses and cases can very easily be used to avoid the transference neurosis by mobilizing a flight into health and/or success. Is the transference itself so entrenched as an erotized resistance in defence against narcissistic injury that the analysis appears stalemated or in danger if matriculation occurs? If so, it may be that the candidate is not analyzable or not analyzable by his present analyst. Has the candidate experienced negative transference? Has triadic transference material appeared or is it still dyadic? This bears on the strength of the narcissistic core, the level of object relatability achieved, and the solution a given candidate found for his Oedipal conflict.

4. Has the transference meaning of matriculation been worked on in the analysis?

5. How strong a defence is acting out with resistance against analyzing it?

6. How likely is the presence of a supervisor to interfere with analyzing?

These guidelines can help the training analyst in making up his mind whether he thinks the candidate is realy to begin with a patient and a supervisor. A statement of the analyst's assessment of the positives and negatives in the answers to these questions can be very helpful when combined with data from matriculation interviewers in order for the Institute to arrive at a confident decision on the candidate's progress. The training analyst's letter need not reveal the material on which the analyst bases his decision but, if something along the above lines is given, the decision makers have information not obtainable at selection as to the way the candidate adapts to the tasks of associating, regressing in the service of the ego, observing himself, gaining insight, and modifying behavior.

The extra-analytic evaluation would be done by analysts other than the training analyst. These interviewers might never have seen the candidate before or might have seen him at selection. There are advantages to having one interviewer who has not seen the candidate before and one who saw him at selection. For the latter interviewer, comparisons should be obvious and progress visible. However, recognition of changes involving insight and pathology can be misleading if the matriculation interviewer does not focus on the growth and maturation of ego functions necessary for becoming an analyst. These skills should be in evidence at both selection and matriculation, but it is imperative that they show development and maturation at matriculation, especially the candidate's ability to introspect and associate about himself. The interviewer who has not seen the candidate before has to assess those aptitudes, too, and evaluate their adequacy for analyzing a patient.

We wish to stress, since there may be some misunderstanding of our thesis, that matriculation work between training analyst and candidate is never done in an intellectual manner with an unanalytic discussion or dialogue regarding matriculation. The work should be done with analytic tact and sensitivity, and within the analytic process. Like a termination decision or any other important decision during analysis, it should be a mutually acceptable decision, following working through and based on analytic insight and ego growth.

Three clinical vignettes will illustrate how associations regarding matriculation (1) might appear in the analysis; (2) can become part of the analytic process; and (3) be accurately assessed and evaluated by sensitive interviewers. Moreover, these vignettes show that matriculation can facilitate the training analysis and help the candidate to objectify this experience, thus stimulating self-evaluation which can be most important for the candidate.

In an Institute without a matriculation procedure, the candidate might not have the opportunity to objectify his analytic experience and therefore would not necessarily be involved in the evaluation of his own analytic progress. This skill begins the integration of a self-analytic process in the candidate's work ego. Matriculation evaluations can also be important for the education of the entire analytic faculty and serve as a source of data regarding personality structure, analytic process, therapeutic outcome, and the relevance of a training analysis for the educational development of an analyst.

CASE 1

A candidate who was strongly motivated to become an analyst was involved in working through a speaking and reading inhibition.

At selection it was felt that this symptom was analyzable and that the candidate had the attributes and aptitude to complete the Institute's educational program successfully.

During one analytic session in the third year of his analysis, he associated to a traumatic childhood incident in which he was suddenly attacked and bitten by a vicious dog. This painful trauma requiring surgical repair occurred at the height of his Oedipus. While associating about the trauma, he spontaneously stated: "I am thinking of starting classes in the Institute. I've thought about it several times but forgot to tell you." He had briefly and fleetingly associated a wish to enter classes and commence analyzing a patient under supervision several times during the second year of analysis, but had not pursued the associations, and the analyst also had decided not to focus on them. The analyst had felt at that time that an attempt to focus on matriculation would interfere with a transference neurosis that had not been worked through far enough. This time, however, the candidate continued:

> I'm not sure you'll allow me to become an analyst. You'll probably say no. [Why do you think I'll say no?] I don't feel you consider me well enough analyzed or bright enough to become an analyst. I think you'll cut me up when the Institute asks for your opinion. I'd hate to see the letter. It would probably be a biting angry note aimed at hurting me. You just want me to remain a child forever.

The analyst was able to show him that he was viewing the analyst as a vicious dog who would attack and bite because of his wishes to enter the Institute. The attack by the dog during the height of his Oedipal strivings had now shifted to a fear that he would be attacked for his professional strivings. The candidate was now ready to deepen his insight about his Oedipal conflict, to gain more understanding and conviction about the transference, and to understand the genetic roots of his anxiety about entering classes and analyzing patients.

The analyst interpreted that earlier the candidate had not been able to pursue his associations about his wish to matriculate because he was so frightened of what he expected would be the analyst's angry response. It was clear to the analyst and he was able to demonstrate that the candidate at this later point in the analysis must feel more secure and more convinced that the analyst would not attack him for his desire to matriculate. The candidate could now begin to accept that the analyst was different from the vicious dog of his childhood or his insecure and angry father who would humiliate and attack whenever his son showed manly wishes or actions.

When this man was interviewed several months later for matriculation, he was able to speak meaningfully of this incident in his analysis. As he described the transference to the interviewers, he could clearly show them that the current event of matriculation had been connected meaningfully to its infantile roots and that they were now experienced as not the same. The candidate could also with conviction tie his castration anxiety to his writing and speaking inhibitions and show that he understood the interplay between fantasy and reality during his Oedipus and during the analysis.

The matriculation interviewers could see that the candidate's ego was undergoing a structural change involving detachment from an infantile self-representation and progressing towards a more mature identity. He was pleased with the progress he had made in analysis, and it was obvious that he was involved in a transference neurosis and that good analytic work was taking place. Matriculation, it was thought, would not interfere with the analysis. A clear picture of the analytic process had been presented to the interviewers, and the candidate's aptitude and attributes for becoming an analyst that were seen at selection were once again recognized at matriculation, and, after this analytic experience, their growth could be documented.

CASE 2

A candidate entered analysis because of depressive episodes and a sincere wish to become an analyst. Like many candidates, he had put off treatment for his neurotic difficulties for several years since to enter therapy outside of an Institute was viewed by him as a narcissistic wound. However, it was completely acceptable to be a patient in a training program. The candidate had always been outwardly successful in his academic and social life but had always been aware of a low-grade depression and an inability to fall in love. His parents were divorced when he was eight years of age.

After approximately eight months of analysis, the analyst announced the dates of the summer break. In the next session the candidate began by stating:

> I'm planning to call the Director and let him know that I wish to matriculate. I've been thinking of that since yesterday. I'm really excited about it. You and I will be together in the Institute and at Society meetings. It's going to be great! I didn't sleep too well last night. I kept thinking about it. [Did you have any other thoughts that interfered with your sleep?] What do you mean? No! Oh, I did think about your announcing the summer vacation. I was a little angry and a little sad. It's several months off. Why did you tell me now? We have plenty of time. I'd say that was a premature statement.

The analyst was able to show the candidate that his difficulty in sleeping as well as his anger and sadness was a reaction to the announcement of the vacation. The candidate handled the depressive and angry feelings about losing the analyst by mobilizing a wish to join the Institute. His affects could be connected to the trauma of the parent's divorce when he was eight years old. At the time of the divorce, the candidate struggled to remain with his father and now he wished to remain with his analyst. His sudden desire to matriculate was really the premature statement. He appeared to understand this and could give confirming evidence. However, several months later, during a two-day interruption when the analyst had to be away for scientific meetings, the candidate impulsively applied for matriculation. He did not report this to the analyst until two weeks later. The analyst interpreted the acting out as containing rage at the analyst for the missed sessions as well as a secret wish to remain with him. Once again, the candidate appeared to accept this interpretation.

The analyst was fully aware of the acting out of the candidate and the persistent negative transference, but decided not to interfere with the patient's wish to matriculate. He felt that prohibiting the candidate at this point in the analysis would have interfered with the analytic work and forced the analyst and candidate into an unanalytic confrontation. The analyst was counting on sensitive matriculation interviewers to be able to see the resistance against analyzing that was being acted out by the candidate's sudden plan to matriculate. Here we have a good example of how matriculation interviewers can relieve the training analyst of a need to enter into Institute administrative decisions regarding his candidate.

As the analyst had hoped, it was evident to the matriculation interviewers that the candidate was motivated to apply for matriculation because of separation anxiety and rage at the analyst, whom in the transference he felt was the father who deserted him by divorcing the candidate's depressed and aggressive mother. In the interviews he could not clearly describe his motivation for applying for matriculation at this time and he attacked the analyst for "repeated leavings." He told one of the interviewers that he had discussed matriculation several months ago and did not feel there was any reason to discuss it again. It was evident to the interviewers that this man was acting out a negative transference reaction and had at present little distance from his transference feelings. He could not connect any of his present feelings to his past. He could only talk bitterly of his anger at the analyst. The candidate was obviously more interested in attacking his analyst than continuing his training to become an analyst.

This candidate was turned down for matriculation. However, the following year he was able to reapply successfully. He had gained insight into his separation anxiety, his narcissistic vulnerability, and the effect of the divorce on his identifications and development. He could also, during the interviews, discuss the reason why he had been turned down the first time he applied for matriculation. He felt the rejection had spurred his analysis forward by making him face his overwhelming anger at his analyst. Eventually he was able to bring out the love he felt for his analyst and for his father. The analyst was also pleased with the analytic movement his candidate had made. He decided to respond to a letter from the Education Committee of the Institute requesting his impression about his candidate's readiness to matriculate. He wrote a brief positive letter that was shared with the candidate.

CASE 3

This candidate entered analysis during psychiatric residency for episodes of diffuse anxiety and some inhibitions in his social, sexual, and professional life. He applied and was accepted to the Institute after a year of analysis. At selection it was felt that he was analyzable, in contact with his inner life, psychologically minded, sincerely interested in his patients, and motivated to become an analyst. He applied for matriculation after another year of analysis.

The analyst did not send a letter to the Education Committee of the Institute, and the candidate stated to both matriculation interviewers that his analyst would not play any part in his matriculation but said: "We will analyze whatever happens."

The candidate was very anxious during the interviews. He was aware of this and very embarrassed by it. With one interviewer he kept looking at the analyst's chair and was initially unable to associate to the anxiety or to the meaning of matriculation, except to anxiously and without elaboration say that matriculation [meant] "I will soon be doing what my analyst does." He felt that one of the interviewers who asked him to describe a patient he was treating wanted him to show off his therapeutic prowess. The case he described was a patient he had in psychotherapy who needed analysis but refused to leave him for analysis.

The candidate, in trying to understand, master, and explain his undue anxiety and difficulties about the wish to matriculate, reported that his father left home when the candidate was six years of age to enter a tuberculosis sanatorium where he stayed for one year. The candidate remained with a seductive, hysterical mother who expected him to be the man of the house and take the father's place. He then made a slip that he had been in analysis for six years instead of two. He did not recognize that the slip referred to the severe conflicts concerning his father's illness and hospitalization. The interviewer noted the slip and felt it indicated a deep transference neurosis and decided not to pursue it further.

It was clear to both matriculation interviewers that the candidate was deeply involved in his personal analysis. There were many fleeting and meaningful references to his analyst that showed this, but the candidate was not able to objectify his experience. He was asked how the question of matriculation arose in the analysis and how it was handled by his analyst. With embarrassment, the candidate mentioned something about matriculation being viewed as entering his mother's bedroom. He quickly added that he was not quite sure that he was ready to sit all day in an analytic chair.

It was clear to the interviewers that the wish to matriculate had reactived his Oedipal trauma and that matriculation and the Oedipus were not well differentiated. To matriculate was obviously instinctualized, and it was evident that transference reactions were not limited to the analysis but easily spilled over to the matriculation interviewers and would also probably involve supervisors and teachers. It was therefore decided that to matriculate at that time would interfere with resolving the candidate's developmental Oedipal trauma and would be experienced as a fantasied Oedipal success. He did show some capacity to observe himself, although what he was experiencing was not objectified and integrated into insight. To approve him for matriculation would be to repeat the past without insight and growth that another year of analysis might provide.

At the end of the faculty discussion, the candidate's training analyst who did not take any part in the matriculation discussion, except to listen with interest, stated he was quite surprised that the faculty could learn so much about his analysand and about the analysis from two matriculation interviews.

DISCUSSION

Many analytic educators consider the training analysis to be the core experience of the educational program. Analytic candidates in training analysis, more than other patients in analysis, should achieve some degree of lasting insight with conviction and a lifetime wish to practice self-analysis. In addition, if neurotic conflicts reappear or if countertransference difficulties cannot be resolved, the analyst should, without shame or hesitation, be able to return for more analytic work (Freud, 1937). In spite of the marked importance of the training analysis, there has been resistance among psychoanalytic educators against defining its educational goals and evaluating its effectiveness. We agree with Balint (1948) that this resistance operative for many years stems primarily from subtle narcissistic sources in the training analysts.

In this paper we highlight the importance of defining and evaluating the preparatory goal of a training analysis. We feel the candidate's readiness to conduct an analysis under supervision should be the measure for determining progression to clinical training. The amount of personal analytic work completed before the next phase of the educational program is undertaken would often not be accomplished by many candidates for two or three years. Therefore, we consider the six months or one year of training analysis that is now most commonly used as an automatic time criterion for progression to classes to be insufficient. In addition, we take the position that preparation for the clinical phase requires more careful evaluation, both within the analytic situation and administratively.

During a matriculation procedure, the validity of the selection predictions is evaluated, in addition to the candidate's achievement, the training analyst's effectiveness, and the adequacy of the training analysis. We believe that an assessment of the training analysis can be done without violating principles of confidentiality. When a candidate applies for admission to an Institute, he knows that certain information is necessary to evaluate him properly. The appropriate candidate has no real problem with them. He has a basic trust in the integrity of the interviewers and knows that the material will be treated with dignity and tact, and used for scientific and educational purposes. The appropriate candidate realizes that the Institute faculty is not interested in secrets and gossip (Calef and Weinshel, 1973) and can identify with the Institute's wish to use assessment as an educational tool. What should be assessed is the growth and development of certain ego functions necessary for analytic competence and scholarship.

SUMMARY

We offer a point of view which we feel merits attention and discussion by psychoanalytic edcuators about when, how, and by whom the evaluation of the preparatory goal of the training analysis should be done. This evaluation should occur when the candidate and his training analyst feel he is ready to analyze a patient. It should consist of interviews by others than the training analyst and should precede the beginning of theoretical courses.

We propose that this progression be called matriculation. We have (1) contrasted the suggested matriculation interviews with those at selection, including specific statements of what to look for at matriculation; (2) offered guidelines for the training analyst to use as he reflects on his candidate's progress and readiness to analyze a patient under supervision; and (3) presented three vignettes to illustrate how the analytic work involving matriculation can enter the analytic process and can be evaluated by sensitive interviewers for the benefit of the candidate, the training analyst, and the entire analytic program.

·6·

EVALUATION OF PROGRESS IN SUPERVISION

(*with Stanley S. Weiss*)

Dr. Fleming believed that psychoanalytic educators need to learn to use evaluation skillfully and in the best interests of everyone concerned in psychoanalytic education. Dr. Fleming considered assessment as a developmental process where the estimates of potential aptitude and of rate of development need to be balanced. The achievements to be evaluated by both teacher and student should be defined specifically, in order to make teaching and learning a goal-directed process. When objectives are defined, the student can know what is expected of him and can orient his efforts to learn accordingly. The student can also assess for himself and with the teacher whether or not he has reached his goal, what his difficulties are, and what he needs to try for next. Defined objectives also help the teacher, who then has something to go by in measuring his student's progress and assessing his own competence.

In this paper, five learning objectives are formulated as relevant to evaluating competence in analyzing; these objectives can be used by both supervisors and candidates for assessment of progress during each session and throughout supervision. Well-written reports by supervisors are most important for assessing clinical competence. The paper also emphasizes that an evaluation of a candidate's clinical competence should take into account information from all of the various learning situations before an educational diagnosis and a progression decision are made.

The total educational process is beginning to come under the scrutiny of periodical evaluations in all branches of medicine, including psychoanalysis. The task of evaluating and being evalu-

Reprinted by permission from *Psychoanalytic Quarterly*, 44:191–205, 1975.

ated is now reaching even beyond graduation and certification and is understood to be important throughout the life of a professional person.

There is no doubt that evaluation helps maintain professional standards. If properly used, however, evaluation can also be an important instrument for teaching and learning. In the past when educators spoke of evaluation, they were referring for the most part to a grading system that compared one student with a group or attempted to compare him with some absolute standard. This was done to alert students and faculty to the issues of how well the student was learning the subject matter and how the student stood in relation to his peers. This type of evaluation is still very much in use in educational institutions to measure the effectiveness of teaching as well as learning.

In psychoanalytic education, the evaluation process begins with selection interviews and goes on most actively during supervised clinical teaching. Evaluation actually occurs at every level of the psychoanalytic educational experience. DeBell (1963, p. 547) notes that all supervisors and students must work with the knowledge that there is a constant evaluation. In many instances, however, it is so implicit that it can be easily overlooked; therefore its significance in teaching and learning can remain outside of awareness. Neither the teacher nor the student recognizes its value as a means of measuring progress toward the goals of each of the three phases of training and toward the certification of professional competence. The misuse of the technique of evaluation can certainly interfere with the analytic and supervisory work, just as it can interfere with successful classroom teaching and learning. But we should find ways to use evaluation skillfully in the framework of analytic goals and in the best interests of everyone who is concerned with psychoanalytic education.

If we can define our learning objectives, evaluation of progress becomes easier and more than an impressionistic, often personally prejudiced assessment. Defined objectives are communicable goals and, as such, permit more conscious striving toward a known end point than is possible when aims of the total program and its component learning experiences are unformulated.

Perhaps psychoanalytic education has tended to avoid evaluation because of the necessity in our science to develop a specific analytic attitude and technique. We try to form and maintain an objective, neutral, nonjudging attitude, and we use an open-ended exploratory approach to the study and treatment of patients. Unfortunately, these ideal analytic attitudes may at times be used as a resistance against review of our work. This resistance seems to operate in spite of the fact that we know that if the progress of an analysis is evaluated from time to time (as in supervision or case conferences), significant material and subtle resistances of the patient and blind spots in the analyst which might have gone unnoticed come into focus for analysis.

Supervision is one of the learning situations in which we teach candidates the technique of analysis in its investigative and therapeutic aspects. In the supervisory situation, we can observe whether the candidate is able to integrate the experiential learning gained in the training analysis with the cognitive learning of the theoretical phase. Consequently, psychoanalytic educators rely heavily on the supervisor's evaluative reports. These reports are given more weight than any other communication when education and progression committees assess a student's analytic progress and clinical competence. However, very little discussion has taken place in Institutes or in the literature about what we would expect to find in a supervisory report, and also how to use the report for the benefit of the student.

Since evaluation is an ongoing process occurring in every supervisory hour, and since the periodic supervisory report is actually a summary of the day-to-day assessment of learning problems and of increasing analytic competence, we would like to make some general remarks about a supervisor's task and then attempt to define specific learning objectives. These learning objectives can be looked upon as indicators of a student's growing skill in analyzing or as areas which present special difficulty for him and therefore need more active teaching and learning effort. They can serve as yardsticks to measure progress and as guidelines for formulating a diagnosis of areas of competence and/or deficiency. The resulting educational diagnosis, accompanied by remedial recommendations and incorporated in the periodic supervisory reports, becomes useful information for administrative progression decisions. It can also be useful as a focus for discussion with a student to involve him actively in his own self-assessment and educational development.

Evaluation is often done intuitively and awareness may remain subliminal. What we will focus on in this paper is known by supervisors but usually not clearly formulated or used optimally. Some supervisors, hopefully not many, feel that evaluation interferes with thier teaching function. DeBell (1963) states, however, that "it is unrealistic to expect that the supervising analyst would not form an opinion of the student's competence, and that this should not be conveyed to the accrediting agency" (p. 548). It seems to us also that teaching and evaluation cannot be separated, but are interrelated components of the supervisory work.

The following is a formulation of five learning objectives, relevant to evaluating competence in analyzing, that can be used by both supervisor and student as yardsticks for assessment of progress during each session and throughout supervision (cf. Fleming, 1969): (1) sensitivity to unconscious meanings; (2) interpretive skill; (3) capacity for self-analysis; (4) understanding of the analytic situation and process; (5) ability to discuss the case in theoretical terms. This is a simplification of the many complex factors that supervisors are aware of and might express in different terms. Nevertheless, we offer this formulation as a way of orienting both supervisor and student to the skills and knowledge that the student needs in learning how to conduct a proper analysis. Inherent in each factor are short-term and long-term objectives. Successive evaluations should demonstrate progress in learning depending on many variables, such as the type of patient, the phase of the analysis, the learning alliance, the student's experience in analyzing, etc.[1]

Elaboration of these five learning objectives follows:

1. *Sensitivity.* Does the student have the capacity to listen and to associate to the patient's material? It is important to know if proper analytic distance and stance are attained. Can he use his empathy and not sympathetically identify with the patient (cf. Greenson, 1960)? Too much distance, coldness, and lack of humanness or too little objective observation should be noted by the supervisor. Can the student assess resistance and understand dy-

---

1. These variables, which are not dealt with in this paper, have been formulated and discussed in some detail in two books of relatively recent publication (cf. Fleming and Benedek, 1966; Ekstein and Wallerstein, 1958).

namic significance, latent meaning of dreams, transference reactions, and affect, as well as ideational content?

2. *Interpretive skill.* Does the student possess "generative empathy" (cf. Schafer, 1959) and analytic tact? Is he able to show evidence of proper wording and timing of interventions and interpretations? Can the student perceive the effect of an interpretation and assess it in relation to his aims? Do his interpretations facilitate the analytic process?

3. *Self-analysis.* Can the candidate perceive his own associations and affects, and assess their meaning? When countertransference or blind spots are evident, can the student trace the unconscious roots and discuss errors, difficulties, and countertransference problems with the supervisor without undue defensiveness? Does the learning alliance remain intact during discussions or problems?

4. *Psychoanalytic situation and process.* Does the student understand the uniqueness and importance of the analytic situation as differentiated from analytically oriented psychotherapy? Does he understand how the analytic situation facilitates the analytic process? Does he understand the concepts of the therapeutic alliance, free association, resistance, acting out, regression, and transference? Does the student present his material vividly, honestly, and clearly? Is the student able to understand and work with dreams? Does he recognize dynamic lines in the development of a transference neurosis? Can he recognize and understand the shifting intensities of conflict or defense maneuvers, of changes in relation to intrapsychic stimuli and/or to stimuli inside or outside the analytic situation? Does the student understand the meaning of working through to resolution of old conflicts? Can the student perceive indications of growth and structural change, integration, and differentiation of past from present and future? Can he identify and describe the long-range analytic changes from one phase of the analysis to another, as well as short-term movement from hour to hour?

5. *Theoretical grasp.* Can the student recognize, and discuss with clarity, the theoretical and clinical concepts and literature that are pertinent to his patient? Can he move with ease from the clinical material to theory, and vice versa?

Of these objectives, sensitivity is the most basic, since all of the other factors are developed to a higher skill from this foundation of aptitude. Interpretive skill and self-analysis also stem from innate endowment and belong to the instrumental qualities of the analyst, although the candidate has been "trained" to some extent in these two factors by the experience of being a patient in a training analysis. Understanding of the psychoanalytic process and a theoretical grasp of the case are factors that combine more purely cognitive learning with the experience of analyzing; thus a high level of competence in these skills might take longer to achieve. Progress in all of these areas, indicating increasing competence and an integration of experiential and cognitive learning, should be observable at the point of graduation.

Three vignettes taken from supervision will illustrate how evaluation can help pinpoint learning difficulties and make an educational diagnosis which can be used at the proper time to help a candidate learn more about analyzing.

EXAMPLE I

Early in the analysis of his second case, a candidate showed his lack of understanding and appreciation of the psychoanalytic process, in that the behavioral evidence of transference phenomena appeared foreign to him. Since this occurred early in supervision, it was not clear at the time how much of a problem it would be. Its full significance could only be evaluated at a later date. However, evaluation of the material at this point alerted the supervisor to a useful focus for his teaching.

The patient was a 30-year-old school teacher with one child. Following a bitter divorce, she entered analysis in an attempt to understand her difficulties with men. She also wished to learn why she was having trouble accepting an important administrative promotion at school which she had wanted and conscientiously worked for. The patient's father had divorced her mother when she was 10 and played a very minor role in her life thereafter. He literally disappeared from the scene.

In the supervisory hour to be presented, the supervisor did not know until after the material had been reported that the candidate had told the patient two weeks ahead of time that he would have to miss a session. The following is taken from the analytic hour before the missed session.

The candidate stated that the patient opened the hour by

saying she had decided to give her dog away. The dog could not be trained and she felt it was too aggressive and destructive to be kept in the house. She decided this rather impulsively (she had only recently obtained the dog) and made the arrangements prior to coming to the hour. She cried during the session, saying she felt her daughter and possibly she herself would miss the dog. She then spoke of recent arguments that had been going on for several days with her mother and other members of the family. She spoke of how lonely she felt at age six when her father had left for the first time and age seven when her mother had returned to work. She mentioned many memories of being alone and of how she felt furious, depressed, and anxious. She had also felt lonely in her marriage because her husband traveled so much of the time. In an angry tomboy voice she shrieked, "I'll take him to court for the money." (They had been fighting over finances.)

All of this material was presented clearly and vividly by the candidate. Nevertheless, he said he did nothing with it except to sympathize with her about how difficult it must have been during her growing-up years to be alone so much of the time. He then mentioned, almost as an afterthought, that at the end of the hour he reminded the patient on her way to the door that they would not be meeting the following day. The patient nodded, said "I know," and left. It was at this point that he mentioned to the supervisor that he had told the patient he would have to miss a session two weeks ahead of time.

The remainder of the supervisory hour was devoted to this last exchange and to the candidate's apparent lack of appreciation of the meaning of the missed apppointment and his apparent inability to connect it with the poignant material of the session, even though he seemed to appreciate the patient's extreme loneliness in the past.

The candidate seemed surprised, hurt, and somewhat defensive about the supervisor's comments. He stated that he was "put off" concerning the importance of the missed session because he did not realize "that a transference reaction like this could take place so early in an analysis."

The following is a review of the supervisor's thinking as he assessed the candidate's learning problem using the yardsticks we have listed.

The candidate appeared to possess a lack of sensitivity. He

could not understand the dynamic significance of the patient's associations, nor could he see that the affect of the hour was a transference reaction to missing a session with him. The transference roots of this reaction were also missed. He showed a lack of capacity to use his empathy and sensitivity analytically. His interpretive skill was impaired by his lack of understanding. This led him to make an awkward intervention at the end of the session, thinking he was being helpful and kind to the patient by reminding her that she should not come in the following day. His defensiveness when this error was pointed out appeared to disturb the learning alliance (cf. Fleming and Benedek, 1966, Chapter IV), and he seemed, at least initially, unable to recognize that this behavior was unanalytical or that it revealed a learning difficulty. The supervisor therefore concluded that there might be an impairment of self-analytic capacity. There appeared to be deficient intellectual knowledge regarding the concept of transference. He did not understand the importance of the missed session as a stimulus for the activation of transference phenomena and responded to the patient at the end of the hour as one might do in psychotherapy. The discussion of the supervisory hour was confined to assessment of the first three factors. There was little time for discussion of his theoretical grasp of the concept of transference.

In trying to understand further the possible roots of this learning problem, we might ask the following questions which are fundamental for making an educational diagnosis: Was this a fundamental lack of aptitude for analytic work (a mistake in selection)? Was this simply a reflection of his inexperience in doing analysis (this was his second case)? Was this an indication of a deficient intellectual knowledge of the concept of transference (he had completed courses on beginning technique and basic theoretical concepts)? Was this a blind spot in the traditional sense, a sign of unresolved personal conflict carried over to analytic work with patients (the candidate had finished his training analysis)?

The evidence as it was evaluated at this time pointed in the direction of a personality problem of the candidate which was interfering with his analytic competence and his ability to learn in supervision. This might be a problem not amenable to supervisory teaching, something that might require further analysis. Arlow (1963, p. 593) believes that in the supervisory situation only the surface of the therapist's reaction to his patient is laid bare. Because it lacks depth and genetic dimension, supervision does not lend itself to being used for real structural change in the therapist. On the other hand, we feel it is possible that with supervision focused on learning objectives and good self-analytic work, this kind of blind spot and defensiveness might gradually change.

The evaluation at this point was not discussed with the candidate and possibly would not play a prominent role in later evaluation or in the periodic supervisory report to the Institute, if the problem presented did not persist.

EXAMPLE II

After a year of supervision on his first case, a candidate was able to show a marked change in one session in his understanding and technical handling of a difficult patient.

The analysis had moved very slowly for a year and at times seemed to be at a standstill. The patient was a 28-year-old graduate student with a borderline ego organization. His mother had died during his midadolescence after a long and tragic bout with cancer. The patient had entered analysis because of homosexual thoughts, and fears and difficulty in breaking away from his dependency on his father and his home.

The candidate relied heavily on notes for most of his supervisory hours, and it was obvious that he was distant, formal, and correct with the patient, a pattern carried out by the patient as well.

During this supervisory session, the candidate was much more at ease and felt he had made an advance in the analysis, which was also observed by the supervisor.

The patient had opened the hour by stating, "I am going to leave you since I am no longer going to remain in this city. I have decided to go to another city for my Ph.D." His university had not accepted him for the Ph.D. program in literature after he had received his Master's Degree. His marks were good, but somehow he never felt part of the department and the faculty never felt close to him. This, of course, was a problem in all his relationships, including the analytic one.

The patient then spoke of seeing the candidate in the lobby

waiting for the elevator while they were both going to the office for the hour. The patient thought of approaching his analyst to say hello, but did not do this. Instead, he reamined "quiet and frozen." As luck would have it, the analyst had not seen the patient and they entered different elevators. In the analytic session that followed, the patient spoke of this episode and stated that when he entered the elevator, "I erased you completely from my mind. I always erase people and unpleasant things from my mind in a way similar to an elevator door closing. People and memories can just as easily be made to disappear." He said that the night before he was "driven" to speak his thoughts freely into a tape recorder without knowing exactly why he was doing this. He then "had a few beers" and called a friend he had not been in contact with for several years, someone who lived in another part of the country. They "spoke for about 45 minutes" (the duration of his analytic session). He also stated he had received a letter from his father and had given it angrily back to the mailman after writing "reject" across it.

The candidate told the patient, with feeling, "You seem to be desperately trying to get away from me, to erase me completely from your mind and replace me with a tape recorder and a telephone call to a distant friend." The patient responded by saying that he felt very "upset" about the possibility of leaving analysis, since the analyst and the analytic work had come to mean so much to him.

The supervisor up to this point had been presented with a difficult teaching problem. Both patient and candidate had kept a very formal distance from each other. The supervisor had pointed out and even predicted that the patient might leave. It seemed that the candidate's need for positive feedback and the patient's need for reassuring acceptance had interfered with the development of a working alliance. But something had happened to produce a marked change in this hour. Supervisory teaching and the candidate's self-analysis were showing results: The candidate was able to understand the patient and to respond sensitively. He was obviously pleased with his newly found freedom to respond empathically to the patient. He could assess his own change and, in discussion with the supervisor, evaluate what had been the problem in the past and how he felt it had now been resolved.

In the supervisor's evaluative thinking, this candidate's capacity for sensitive understanding had developed so that his own need to keep a distance from his patient no longer interfered with his helping the patient to understand the same defense. The patient no longer needed to run away and the analysis continued. In this hour after a year of supervision, the candidate's interpretive skill was on a much higher level than previously. His capacity for self-observation and self-analysis had also developed to a higher level. For the purposes of evaluation at this time, yardsticks four and five—understanding the analytic process and theoretical grasp—did not contribute much.

Was this earlier problem of defensive distance a sign of lack of aptitude? Was it due to inexperience (it was the candidate's first case)? Was it due to lack of knowledge (he had good classroom reports)? Probably this was a personality problem which was influenced positively the the affectual experience of recently terminating his training analysis and by a deepening supervisory alliance.

In this case, progress was made explicit to the candidate in relation to the goals of learning, and he was able to become aware of his own progress by comparing it with previous difficulties.

EXAMPLE III

In this example, an advanced candidate demonstrated his ability to evaluate his role in the patient's difficulty, to do self-analysis, and to conceptualize the analytic process.

The patient was a 28-year-old married woman who entered analysis because of increasing anxiety and depression following the birth of a male child. Her father, a successful businessman, had established a close companionship with her during latency, which was interrupted by his sudden death when she was 12 years old.

In the supervisory hour to be reported here, the patient was entering her third year of analysis. The Oedipal conflict had been relived in a rich and deep manner. Many important memories were recalled, revealing a "seductive" father who treated the patient more as a wife than as a small daughter. During the second year of analysis, after working through some aspects of this experience in the transference, the patient presented many of the problems associated with the adolescent phase of development. She was eager to expand her horizons but afraid of failure. Analytic work enabled her to maintain her gains and everything seemed to be going well. The patient was moving forward in her life and in analysis. Strong anxiety and depression seemed to be a thing of the past.

After returning from the summer vacation, however, she found out through a friend who also knew the analyst that he was a single man; up to this point, she had always thought of him as married. She could easily have corrected this bit of transference fantasy long before but had obviously avoided learning any "facts" about her analyst until the third year of treatment. When she realized he was a bachelor, she suddenly regressed and became aggressive and hostile to the analyst. "You've humiliated me, you've tricked me, you've betrayed me, you've treated me cruelly like my father did when he died." She now felt that she could not do her housework, care for her child, or function in any way as a mature woman, except in one area: She felt her sexual life had not been affected by the news.

The candidate felt anxious and puzzled by the aggression and regression in the sudden turn of events and, for the moment, had a difficult time understanding the rage. During supervision he reminded the supervisor that the patient's regression had begun when she found out that he was *not* single. At first the candidate was not aware of his slip of the tongue. When the supervisor brought this interesting slip to his attention, he showed his growing ability to do self-analysis and reported being aware of a vague feeling of guilt in response to his patient's anger. He stated he now knew why he was having so much difficulty comprehending the patient's material. "My own father had been sick when I was a child and died when I was quite young." He had known but had had difficulty facing the reality of the fact that his feeling of Oedipal triumph was only a partial victory; he had experienced strong feelings of humiliation, shame, and inadequacy over not being able to replace his lost father. He said that now he could understand one important aspect of the patient's rage: She was feeling helpless and anxious because she was terrified that she might be inadequate as a woman now that the analyst was supposedly eligible. He felt he could now show her in a meaningful manner that the helplessness and shame she felt as a child about her body in comparison with her mother was being acted out in the present, but in reverse. As a child, she had been a pseudoadult and had acted as father's wife in fantasy and in many activities, except for the sexual. Suddenly, in the present she felt helpless as a woman in all areas except the sexual, in which she had demonstrated adequacy and confidence with her husband.

Before the patient's period of regression, the candidate had been able to interpret skillfully the sexual and aggressive wishes and the guilt the patient had experienced toward her parents during her Oedipal period and adolescence. But he could not help his patient face her feelings of shame, humiliation, and inadequacy until he was confronted with her rage and then with his slip of the tongue which recalled the painful affects of his own Oedipal conflict.

A supervisory evaluation of the candidate in this third example began at a level of assessment different from the other two. He was an advanced candidate possessed of a high degree of sensitivity and able to make skillful interpretations which facilitated the analytic process. The analysis had been going well and there did not seem to be any obvious learning problems or countertransferences. Then came the patient's sudden regression and intense negative transference. Up to this point, the candidate had handled negative transference with understanding and appropriate interpretations. The initial clue to a possible blind spot lay in the candidate's awareness of a little anxiety and his inability to grasp the meaning of the rage. He did not report the vague sense of guilt until after the slip of the tongue was made conscious. Without the slip, analysis of these symptoms of conflict might not have taken place for some time, since the anxiety and lack of understanding did not seem to the supervisor to be serious obstacles. The slip, however, was a loud signal, and his failure to hear it by himself reinforced the supervisor's recognition of conflict in the candidate.

Confrontation with the behavioral cue was all that was necessary to start a chain of associations that recalled the feeling of guilt and some childhood memories belonging to his own Oedipal period. He was able to see how his identification with his patient had made him blind to the way her rage defended her against the narcissistic injury of helplessness and humiliation which the facts about the analyst's marital state had triggered. For the candidate, the immediate affects were different from the patient's, but the "fact" of his slip of the tongue enabled him to do a piece of self-analysis in the supervisory hour which enhanced his own learning and the analysis of his patient. Without the slip, self-analytic work would have been slower, but the capacity to introspect and to associate to what he was experiencing was there and was obviously developed to a high level.

This kind of event in supervision reassures a supervisor that the candidate has learned a great deal from his analysis and from supervisory teaching. This candidate had learned that self-analytic skill is an important learning objective for an analyst, and he was able to demonstrate that he could use his analytic tools on himself (cf. Kohut, 1959; Fleming, 1971 [see Chapter Two, this volume]). His aptitude, his understanding of the analytic process, and his ability to learn from experience were all observable in the episode described. In addition, he demonstrated competence in the area of self-analysis and was able to do some integration of theory and behavioral observation. The unsolved elements of his own Oedipal conflict were worked through a little further, deepening his personal insight and expanding his professional skill.

SUMMARY

A view of evaluation as an ongoing process in psychoanalytic education that is useful as a tool in supervisory teaching and learning is presented. A general principle of education has been applied: that defined objectives shared by student and teacher can facilitate learning and intensify the student's involvement in assessing his own progress. Five factors that are important components of good analytic work are defined as learning objectives for clinical training and applied as yardsticks to the evaluative thinking that a supervisor goes through. This process of evaluation is illustrated with three examples of supervisory hours. These continuing evaluations become the core material for long-range periodic progression reports.

·7·

THE TEACHING AND LEARNING
OF THE SELECTION PROCESS:
ONE ASPECT OF FACULTY
DEVELOPMENT

(*with Stanley S. Weiss*)

Dr. Fleming always stressed the need of Institutes to provide opportunities for young graduates and faculty members to develop skills in teaching, administration, and other aspects of Institute functioning. The development of the faculty into a cohesive, scholarly group—a faculty responsible and dedicated to the education of a group of students—takes time, planning, and creative leadership. In Dr. Fleming's judgment, one of the core functions of a good educational program is a program of continuing education for the faculty. Faculty development offers opportunities for analytic clinicians to truly become analytic educators.

This paper deals with one aspect of faculty development: the teaching and learning of the selection process.

INTRODUCTION

The future of psychoanalysis is intimately tied to the caliber of candidates accepted for training, and therefore selection is considered by most psychoanalytic educators to be one of the important core functions necessary for the successful operation of an Institute's educational program. In spite of the importance attached to selection, it is somewhat surprising that the formal teaching and learning of the selection process is often neglected by psychoanalytic faculties. It seems to be assumed that a graduate analyst who

Reprinted by permission from *The Annual of Psychoanalysis*, 7:87–109. New York: International Universities Press, 1979.

has gained clinical competence can carry out the complex task required of psychoanalytic educators without further learning. For example, it seems to be assumed that the analytic clinician has learned and mastered the assessment of pathology, ego structure, analyzability, and·the potential for doing analytic work.

In fact, the selection interviewer has to be able to do even more than this. First, the selection interviewer has to have in mind the criteria demonstrating aptitude for becoming an analyst. Having assessed aptitude, the selection interviewer can predict whether the applicant will or will not successfully complete the educational program and become a competent analyst. Other selection tasks involve knowing how to conduct a good selection interview (Benedek, 1976) and how to prepare an informative report and assessment of the interview experience which will guide other analysts who will also participate in making selection decisions. Good reports will enable the selection committee to integrate the interview information with their own analytic knowledge and experience and to arrive at a good predictive judgment.

Learning how to do the varied selection tasks takes time. The learning process must be repeated and deepened until the ego skills for correctly assessing criteria for analyzability, acceptance, and rejection, and for making accurate developmental and structural diagnoses, become firmly established. The task of making selection decisions is undoubtedly related to the task of analyzing, but it is also different; the analyst involved in selection interviewing must be able to shift easily, back and forth, from the professional image of a clinician to that of evaluator and selector.

It is our impression that very few analysts initially possess the talent and skill for selection interviewing—especially for the assessing and predicting of an applicant's potential for developing the ego functions required of a competent analyst, and for the writing of reports that will be valuable for the committee that makes the final selection decision. Such skills must be part of a program for faculty development; they can be taught and learned, especially by practice and by repeated exposure to good selection conferences. Good selection-committee meetings refine the selection instrument and are helpful even to experienced selectors.

Institutes need to provide an opportunity for faculty members involved in making selection decisions to teach this skill to younger faculty members. The organizational structure should permit selection committees to communicate with the rest of the faculty about their work. When scientific debate about selection issues and actions is part of faculty activity, the development of the faculty as a cohesive, scholarly group will be facilitated. When selection policies, procedures, and decisions are delegated and are not reviewed by the whole faculty, responsibility for analytic education is neglected, and a most valuable aspect of the teaching experience is missing. We feel that selection interviewing, assessing, and integrating of data can enrich and expand the psychoanalyst's clinical skills and also add to psychoanalytic theory and knowledge.

Mistakes at selection are difficult for the candidate, for the Institute, and for the science of psychoanalysis. A wrongly selected candidate, after an investment of much time, energy, and money, may leave or be asked to leave. Another problem candidate may stay with us for a long time and even graduate and become a colleague. A talented applicant *not* accepted due to a selection error is often lost completely to the science of psychoanalysis, because he will not necessarily reapply.

A systematic study of the process of making selection predictions requires a knowledge of what the particular task demands (Fleming, 1961 [see Chapter Three, this volume]; R. Fliess, 1942). After the "job analysis" is considered and the "work ego" of the analyst understood, criteria for acceptance should be formulated. Stated in terms of the personality attributes necessary for becoming an analyst, these criteria serve as guidelines for the interviewer and give clues as to aptitudes for analytic work that will be developed further in the educational program. Following the formulation of criteria, selection interviewers must gain experience in correlating the criteria with the behavioral and clinical material obtained in a well-conducted selection interview.

This paper will describe an effort to implement such a teaching plan and will be divided into three sections. In Section I we will describe the philosophy, policies, and procedures of the Selection Committee of the Denver Institute for Psychoanalysis. We are using the Denver Institute experiences to illustrate general principles of selection, teaching, and learning, since we feel they are applicable to other Psychoanalytic Institutes as well. We will discuss what was done at the Denver Institute to train selectors as examples of what can be done.

Since the Denver Institute for Psychoanalysis is relatively new, early in our history we were confronted with the task of teaching the work of selection to analysts who had had very little experience as psychoanalytic educators and who were not yet training or supervising analysts. This situation came about when several new graduates and a growing group of younger analysts became faculty members. We found that younger analysts require ongoing instruction in selection psychology until the basics of evaluation and assessment of the potential to become a competent analyst are mastered and have become part of the work ego. This process takes time and requires carefully planned teaching. It involves not only interviewing and informative reporting, but also repeated exposure to discussion of selection issues in committee conferences. We believe that even experienced training analysts who intuitively understand selection criteria can gain from good discussions about selection decisions.

Although the literature on selection is increasing, the paucity of shared data which could lead to better knowledge is striking. Some of the impulsive, impressionistic ways in which selection decisions have been made can be found in a report by Console (1963). This extremely valuable study of 100 consecutive applications at the Institute of the Downstate Medical Center noted "some curious statistical facts" (pp. 10–11). Console called attention to "patterns of selecting" which tended to be repeated but were unexplained. Some interviewers never accepted a candidate and never wrote a favorable report. Others would accept everyone and found it most difficult to make an adverse decision. Console noted that the latter group of interviewers either did not elicit unfavorable material, or they minimized it and emphasized the applicant's favorable traits. A third group of rather consistent interviewers recommended neither acceptance nor rejection but chose a middle position. On the basis of these findings, Console saw the advantage of having an admission committee, or at least an admission chairman, who would remain in office long enough for his knowledge to be used in assigning interviewers more efficiently. Console's findings graphically illustrate how important it is to provide an opportunity for selectors to learn more about this most important Institute function.

In Section II we will review selection criteria and discuss the process of evaluation and assessment of the potential to become an analyst. This approach follows an emphasis in two previous papers, in which we discussed the evaluation and assessment of candidates during supervision (Weiss and Fleming, 1975 [see Chapter Six, this volume]) and the evaluation of the training analysis to determine a candidate's readiness to analyze a patient under supervision (Fleming and Weiss, 1978 [see Chapter Five, this volume]).

In Section III we will discuss three selection interviews of three different applicants. These reports by experienced interviewers show the analytic thinking about the clinical and behavioral data that goes on in the selection interviewer's mind as he prepares a well-thought-out recommendation. This recommendation may or may not agree with the final decision arrived at by the full committee.

I. ON THE FUNCTIONING OF
A SELECTION COMMITTEE

Our psychoanalytic educational philosophy at the Denver Institute for Psychoanalysis has always included a wish for ongoing faculty development. Our policy has been to teach the selection process to members of the faculty and to keep the entire faculty involved in selection issues, deliberations, and decisions. It is in the selection committee that this learning can be accomplished while administrative decisions regarding selection are being made. Good Institute organizational structure requires open communication between the members of the faculty and the selection committee.

When we first set up our selection committee and as new members were added, we set aside time to review the literature on selection. For example, a "xeroxed literature package" was given to each member to read and make notes on for discussion. Enclosed in the package were basic papers on selection by Benedek (1976), Console (1963), Eisendorfer (1959), Fleming (1961 [see Chapter Three], 1976a, 1976b), Greenacre (1961), and Pollock (1961). Other papers—A. Freud (1971), Gitelson (1954), Klein (1965), Lewin and Ross (1960), and Panel (1961)— were assigned as the group became more sophisticated in selection work. It is important for members of a well-functioning selection committee to be conversant with the literature on selection. Time should be set aside for the literature to be discussed as the group becomes more deeply immersed in interviewing, evaluating, learning about criteria, and making important selection decisions.

Initial seminars with new selection-committee members focused on the following topics:

1. The differences between an analytic session and a selection interview. Like an analytic session, a selection interview requires the analytic model of passivity and free-floating attention, but the selection interviewer who must arrive at a decision about the applicant in one or two sessions must oscillate comfortably between an active and a passive stance. Important areas not spontaneously brought in by the applicant should be inquired about. This, of course, should be done with tact and sensitivity, as in all analytic work. We believe a good applicant has the responsibility to present a clear picture of himself to the interviewer and usually will do so, but the interviewer has the need to "ferret out" what is necessary for a fair and honest assessment if the material and clinical data are not given spontaneously. This can be done with respect for the applicant's personality and character defenses.

2. Examples of good and bad selection reports. As selection interviews are read and evaluated during the ongoing selection-committee conferences, the attributes of good reporting become clear.

3. The correlating and connecting of the psychological data with the criteria for selection with which the committee members are becoming familiar. This is the most important task for selectors to master, and in the ongoing work of the committee it continues to occupy a prominent place in the learning process.

All selection interviewers who were not members of the selection committee were invited to attend the selection-committee meetings when the candidate they had interviewed was being discussed. They were encouraged to participate actively in the discussions.

The procedure in Denver is for each applicant to be interviewed by three interviewers. One of the interviewers is usually an experienced senior interviewer, another might be learning the selection tasks, and the third is a member of the selection committee. The chairperson selects the interviewers and tries to rotate assignments so that every faculty member has a chance to learn by actively participating in the selection work and deliberations.

Prior to each meeting, the three selection reports are circulated to all members of the selection committee and guests, so that everyone is familiar with the reports before the meeting. This saves much precious time and makes for a more sophisticated discussion.

At the meeting, the chairperson briefly summarizes the application, the letters of recommendation, the transcript, and any other pertinent material, but the emphasis for the discussion is placed on the three reports. At the Denver Institute we believe that properly conducted selection interviews are the most reliable method for obtaining data upon which accurate selection decisions can be made. We are aware that other Institutes might do their selection work differently, but usually such differences involve the instruments used to collect data. For instance, in Denver, we have not used psychodiagnostic tests, autobiographical essays, group interviews, or other selection instruments and procedures, although we realize other techniques besides our own should be studied.

The selection-committee discussions continue until everyone has obtained a clear picture of the applicant and is satisfied that an intelligent and informative decision can be made. All guests contribute, but only the committee members vote. It is our contention that the decision maker should be a member of the committee and should have been immersed in selection work before voting. The member who is just learning about selection or who comes to an occasional meeting is probably not in the best position to cast a responsible vote. All committee members are required to give reasons for their vote as they cast it. The chairperson votes last, since we are anxious to minimize as best we can the influence of a senior selector on the final vote. A simple majority is required for acceptance. In-depth minutes of the meetings are kept. These are useful for future research and teaching purposes.

Three interviewers are necessary because it might take several interviews with different selectors to get a clear and complete picture of the applicant. When possible, we try to include an interviewer of a different sex. What one interviewer might miss or might not ask about, another interviewer might pick up. It is important that each applicant be given a full opportunity to reveal his latent potentialities. Usually, at least one of the interviewers asks about a patient the applicant has treated in psychotherapy, and the last interviewer might ask about the applicant's reactions to the previous interviews (Fleming, 1976b).

We have found that it is not unusual for an interviewer to change his recommendation as more information is brought forward during the discussion and as the understanding of the applicant deepens. At good selection conferences, the discussions lead to higher levels of insight and conceptualization about each applicant. The conferences in fact become research seminars in which ego psychology, advanced psychopathology, analyzability, and selection process come into focus. At times an applicant might be accepted by two or even three interviewers and rejected by the full committee; occasionally, although two or even three interviewers might reject an applicant prior to the selection conference, the meeting discussion finally leads to acceptance. This unpredictability of outcome dramatically proves the importance of the selection process and the value of having experienced analysts look together at complex clinical data.

Rotation on all institute committees, including rotation of the chairperson, is essential. We do believe, however, as did Console (1963), that when a selection committee is newly established it is helpful to have an experienced chairperson serve more than one term. Rotation should be staggered so a nucleus of well-trained committee members is always available to help in teaching new members. Rotation of committee chairpersons and members often leads to meaningful review of policies and procedures and to new creative activity.

We have found that with well-run selection conferences the level of good selection inteviews and reports rapidly improves. Most selection interviewers find the work rewarding and enriching. A common observation made by selectors is that one becomes a better clinical analyst as one is developing and maturing as an evaluator and selector.

II. ON CRITERIA FOR SELECTION

Selection committees wish to provide Psychoanalytic Institutes with candidates who (1) can be successfully analyzed in an Institute setting; (2) can successfully complete the educational program and gain clinical competence; and (3) following graduation, will remain analytic clinicians and analytic scholars and continue their interest in psychoanalytic practice and research.

Early in the history of psychoanalysis, selection was done on a highly personal and impressionistic basis; emphasis was placed primarily on pathology, and the motivation leading to self-selection was frequently a primary factor (Pollock, 1961). At the present time, emphasis is being placed on specific criteria for acceptance and rejection, on assessing certain ego functions that are necessary for becoming a successful analyst—ego functions that should be present at least in larval form at selection (Fleming, 1976a). At regular points in the educational program, selection predictions should be checked, and the growth and development of those ego functions that are considered vital and necessary for a candidate to possess at selection should be monitored.

Selection decisions are primarily based on the applicant's analyzability and on the recognition and appreciation of certain potentials in the personality. Committee members must learn how to differentiate criteria which signify aptitude for success in psychoanalysis from criteria which are nonanalyzable character defenses that would make it impossible for an applicant to function well as an analyst. With a focus on criteria and analyzability, the earlier tendency toward personal impressionistic decisions or "all or none" decisions (Console, 1963) can be replaced with decisions based on definite criteria. Selection committees can then accept candidates who seem capable of successfully completing the educational program. The criteria we look for are relatively rare, even among the group of bright young psychiatrists from whom we draw our applicants, psychiatrists who have completed many years of education and have undergone much screening during the process. Since the emphasis at selection has shifted away from pathology to questions of analyzability and potentials for psychoanalytic work, selection committees can evaluate their applicants in depth. No candidate should be accepted or turned down until a full understanding of the ego–superego organization, and especially the defensive structure, is clearly understood. An important question that needs to be evaluated and answered by the selection committee is the capacity of the applicant to change as a result of the therapeutic process of the training analysis—i.e., prognosis must become an important concern of selectors. Predictions made at selection can be assessed after a period of time in a training analysis and before the candidate moves on to doing analysis under supervision and entering classes (Fleming and Weiss, 1978 [see Chapter Five]). Therefore, though the selection committee may be uncertain about some applicants, it is our belief that they should be given the benefit of the doubt and accepted for a training analysis.

Certain character traits and innate abilities, such as good intelligence, honesty, reliability, and high energy level, are prerequisities for a career in all professions, including psychoanalysis. However, selection committees must evaluate much more than these basic traits in an attempt to assess certain skills which are uniquely required for success in psychoanalytic training (Fleming, 1961 [see Chapter Three]).

These signs of innate character structure should be supplemented by psychological-mindedness, capacity for introspection, contact with inner life, and an ability to be aware of and to express feelings. The applicant should be willing to demonstrate to interviewers how he thinks and relates to people. He should possess good verbal ability and be without excessive guilt, shame, humiliation, or anxiety.

Selectors must assess talent and potential for understanding and working with unconscious meanings. If an applicant has had previous therapy or analysis, he should evidence some insight into aspects of his neurotic difficulties and be able to present at least a partial picture of the treatment and clinical encounters between himself and his therapist. Otherwise, his analyzability might be in doubt.

Selectors should also place emphasis on cultural interests and capacities for assimilating knowledge from others, especially through reading. The committee wishes to know if the applicant is empathic, imaginative, and tolerant of uncertainty. He should be able to demonstrate some tolerance for passivity, a capacity for good object relations, and an ability to love.

Selectors try to examine carefully motivation to become an analyst. It is important to know if the motivation to enter the study of psychoanalysis is based on narcisstic needs or instinctualized wishes, or on genuine interest and healthy curiosity in human behavior, including, most importantly, the applicant's own. The primary motivation which includes all factors should be an investment in psychological truth itself.

The presence of an analyzable neurosis is not a hindrance for psychoanalytic training. Selection committees look with favor on the applicant who wishes a personal analysis to solve problems of which he is aware, problems which would lead him to seek analysis even if he were rejected by the Institute. Some of the so-called normal applicants who really do not believe they have any problems, who wish to pursue analytic training only to learn the theory and method of analysis so they can treat others, are successful narcissists who do not make the best candidates because they defend themselves against the regression and anxiety aroused in the analytic experience. In fact, because of a rigid defensive organization, this type of person might be impossible to analyze within a reasonable period of time and might not, even after analysis, possess the sensitivity and empathy for psychoanalytic work. Our science is inextricably involved with therapeutic considerations, and it follows, therefore, that applicants who are not interested in understanding the inner lives of patients and themselves and who do not possess a therapeutic wish for growth and change might not become good analysts (Gitelson, 1954). However, many of the "normal applicants" who are initially motivated for analysis only to fulfill a scholastic achievement present this as a feeble defense easily handled by an experienced training analyst. Such candidates soon become aware of emotional problems and enter easily into a true analytic process. It is therefore important for selectors to gain experience in differentiating between the so-called normal applicant who can easily become a sensitive student-analyst and the one who has to remain rigidly "normal" at all costs in order to preserve his psychic equilibrium.

In general, the applicant's psychopathology is considered in terms of character structure and rigidity of defenses. Emphasis at selection should be based not as much on specific pathology as on certain ego functions and an understanding of the totality of the ego organization. Some psychoanalytic educators tend to define suitability for psychoanalytic work only in terms of absence or degree of psychopathology. This approach is not without some merit, but in the light of our increasing knowledge of ego and developmental psychology it appears to us to be incomplete. However, from analytic educational experience and understanding of the qualities which we wish to see in successful candidates, we might say that strongly narcissistic, overly dependent, or extremely sadomasochistic individuals would usually not be suitable candidates and that psychotic characters, borderlines, overt perverts, serious depressives, or serious psychosomatic or medically ill individuals would usually be considered too great a risk. However, each applicant has to be carefully and fully evaluated, and until a clear picture of the ego and self organization emerges and an accurate structural and developmental diagnosis is reached, a final decision should not be made.

III. CLINICAL MATERIAL

We agree with Anna Freud (1971), who believes that psychoanalytic educators have underrated and neglected the psychoanalyst's potential ability to draw accurate diagnostic conclusions from the manifest picture of a personality—a skill which is an important attribute for selectors. Much time is spent in our selection conferences on developing an understanding of the behavioral and psychological data observed in a properly conducted selection interview and making sure that it is properly recorded so that interview behavior can be meaningfully related to the criteria for acceptance and rejection.

In the following three clinical examples, we will present the clinical data, plus the analytic thinking that the selector went through as he listened and processed the analytic material.[1]

1. Though such a statement should be taken for granted, we have decided to state that we have disguised or omitted certain biographical facts and altered some material in our serious attempt to protect the identities of our three clinical examples.

Analysts have always attempted to do this with their patients. Questions of confidentiality and deep respect for privacy, as well as a wish and need to share scientific data, have always been an important part of psychoanalytic tradition. Freud [1905], from the very beginnings of psychoanalysis, took many precautions to prevent his patients from being identified and spoke of "guarantees of secrecy" (p. 9) against a "species" he deplored—those who love to play what we call the "detective game," i.e., those who are more interested in identifying the subject than in wishing to learn from the clinical material. . . .

Our culture, at present, is extremely involved, and rightly so, with

Case I

This applicant was a 26-year-old man, engaged to be married. He had sufficient interest and motivation in becoming an analyst to apply early in his first year of residency. He responded well to a request to talk about himself so that the interviewer could get to know him and understand him. He presented his history in a comfortable, sincere, honest, open manner with vignettes that possessed color and richness.

The applicant described being reared in a peaceful and loving home. The large family was devout, and even its social life revolved around church activities. The interviewer thought to himself that he would listen carefully for the reverberations of this religious upbringing, since we know that an unusually strict religious background might lead to serious superego problems that could prove difficult to analyze. It was soon obvious to the interviewer that this applicant did not appear to have the guilt, anxiety, or rigidity one would expect to see in an applicant from such a strict religious background.

The applicant stated that his father had been away from the family for one year when he was five years of age. He had been working in another country, helping to set up an overseas plant for a large engineering company. During the father's absence, according to family stories, the applicant "was the man of the house." The applicant stated that he "doesn't remember much of that," but he knows that he and his mother "have always had a close and special bond." She once said that she wished her son would become a doctor instead of a businessman like her husband, since doctors do not usually have to be away from their families. The applicant always remembered this and stated that he, too, felt this way and did not wish to choose his father's type of work which meant traveling and many separations from the family. He also men-

---

matters of confidentiality, since so much privacy has been invaded and lost due to governmental and institutional growth and to regulations and sophisticated technological advances. However, this cultural pressure toward an increase in privacy and confidentiality can result, if we are not extremely careful, in handicapping psychoanalytic education. It could interfere with the collection, storing, and dissemination of scientific data and thereby interfere with the development of new scientific knowledge and theoretical concepts.

tioned that although his father did not like being away, his job was most interesting and paid very well. As he spoke, it was clear that both the applicant and the mother had respect and understanding for the father, even though they did not like the frequent separations.

The interviewer thought this was an unusual family. They lived in a close-knit religious atmosphere and yet they seemed to be worldly people as well as loving and tolerant.

Rather early in the interview, the applicant stated that he wished analysis to solve the difficulty he experienced separating from family and friends. He spoke of anxiety and depression, especially on Sunday or following vacations when he had to leave friends and return to work. He revealed some insight that his symptoms had something to do with his father's work and absences, but he stated that this awareness had not been curative. He took his residency in Colorado, not only because of the analytic Institute here but because he did want to get some distance from the close family ties and to try to overcome the "pull" he feels toward his family. He clearly described the "pull" as coming from himself as well as from the entire family. The interviewer was impressed with this applicant's wish for analysis and for his struggle to gain independence.

During adolescence the applicant seriously questioned religious teaching and, after much reading, study, and soul-searching, he left the church. This action was accepted by the family, who have remained close and tolerant of each other's beliefs. The interviewer thought positively of this applicant's adolescent struggle and the apparently successful resolution of his religious conflict. He wondered to himself what had set off this adolescent conflict, but the cause did not become clear during this interview.

During high school and college, the applicant read many novels and wrote some psychological papers. He obviously read with ease, pleasure, and understanding. He told the interviewer of a paper he wrote in high school on Beethoven which stressed the death of Beethoven's mother during adolescence and the loss of Beethoven's hearing. The applicant had tried to understand the connection between these losses and Beethoven's immortal music. The interviewer was impressed with the applicant's psychological-mindedness. He considered this interest in reading and writing as a positive sign of analytic potential.

His motivation was long-standing in that he went to medical school to become an analyst. This wish had been present since his adolescent struggle, when he had read Freud's "The Future of an Illusion" and readily understood Freud's insights into the formation of religion. The applicant, the selector thought, was obviously quite sophisticated in his appreciation of the unconscious.

The applicant was engaged to be married to a schoolteacher. He described his fiancée clearly. He was in love with her, and they shared many interests in music and literature. He reported that she was in favor of his wish for analytic training.

The applicant was asked to describe a patient he had treated. He chose the parent of a child who was dying of leukemia and impressed the interviewer with his sensitivity to this tragedy. He was sad and empathic, but it was obvious to the interviewer that he could keep a healthy distance from the patient's sorrow. The applicant wondered how a parent could ever get over the death of a child. The interviewer thought to himself that this man appeared to be unusually sensitive to issues of object loss.

Summary

The interviewer felt that this applicant was basically a healthy person with a good ego who appeared to have an analyzable neurosis with an Oedipal conflict and with ego alien problems around separation. He showed a sincere wish to be analyzed, was empathic, was genuinely interested in self-scrutiny and introspection, and showed a sustained curiosity about psychological matters in himself and others. He comprehended and integrated what he had read and seemed capable of clear description and assessment of himself and his object relationships.

This interviewer recommended acceptance with enthusiasm, and the other two interviewers concurred.

Committee Discussion and Recommendation

The committee reviewed the very positive criteria for analytic training and potential that this applicant clearly demonstrated to all three interviewers.

The applicant's honesty, maturity, and sincere wish for analysis for what appeared to be an analyzable neurosis were stressed.

It was underlined by the committee how clearly the applicant described the important objects in his life and how sensitively he was attuned to his own inner life.

One committee member was impressed with how well the applicant understood some of the psychological forces that had motivated his long-standing wish to become an analyst. Another member commented on the applicant's unusually deep appreciation for and sensitivity to the unconscious, which the committee, unfortunately, had not seen demonstrated by the majority of applicants. A third member was impressed with the mature level of his object relations.

The chairman commented that a long-standing interest in reading was a very positive sign for a potential candidate, and he complimented the interviewer on obtaining this data and putting it into his report. It was noted that psychoanalysis is a science that requires much reading and that a history of reading with pleasure and comprehension is especially important for analysts.

It was predicted that this applicant would do well, and that following a good analysis and clinical training he should become a very sensitive and competent analyst and possibly do creative and scholarly work.

The applicant was unanimously accepted.

Case II

This applicant was 34 years of age and married. He had practiced internal medicine for several years before deciding to become a psychiatrist. During his second year of psychiatric residency, he applied to the Institute.

The interviewer began by asking the applicant why he wished to become an analyst. "That's easy. It's the number one of psychiatry. The analysts are the best." The applicant stated this with awe and excitement, but showed no ability to enlarge on this topic even when invited to pursue his thoughts about analytic training. All that he could further state was that "I experience a strong and exciting feeling when I think of becoming a psychoanalyst."

Even at this very early point in the interview, the interviewer concluded that the applicant seemed to have questionable motivation for psychoanalytic training. His motivation appeared to have a narcissistic basis. He seemed to have overidealized psychoanalysis.

The applicant was asked about his personal history. At this point he became anxious, and actually, for a moment, he even appeared offended by the question. The interviewer noted that the applicant then "caught himself" and recounted his history in a factual, biographical manner as if he were reciting a curriculum vitae. All this was given without any side comments, spontaneity, reflection, or depth. The applicant focused on the places where he had lived while growing up, the ages of his parents and siblings, his high grades in all schools, and his successful medical practice before deciding to become a psychiatrist. The interviewer noted to himself that the applicant did not appear able to talk about his inner life and that he could only stay on the surface when describing self, people, and events.

He was the oldest of three children, the son of a busy surgeon who "doesn't believe in psychiatry and psychoanalysis but looks down on psychiatrists and does not believe they are real doctors." The interviewer thought to himself about the applicant's initial remark that "the analysts are the best."

The applicant noted that although his father had wanted him to become a doctor he initially went to law school, dropped out after his freshman year, traveled, worked at odd jobs, and then "I finally decided on medical school, where I should have gone right after college." He was asked what he thought of his circuitous route to medical school, to internal medicine, and now to psychiatry and psychoanalysis. Following this question, he once again became anxious and could not go into any depth or make any significant connections. The interviewer thought that the applicant was most likely engaged in a struggle with his father and that the initial choice of law, traveling, and odd jobs, then medicine, and now psychiatry and psychoanalysis represented the ongoing struggle with the father, but he seemed to show no insight into this and the interviewer did not probe. The interviewer considered an applicant who could not make any spontaneous connections about these data and showed little capacity for introspection and self-observation as unlikely to make a successful candidate.

It was also evident that the applicant would become very

anxious when questioned about his inner life, his personal thoughts, or his fantasies. It was clear that he was comfortable only on the surface. The interviewer thought that this active and anxious man might experience a most difficult time adapting to an analytic stance, and feeling comfortable as a patient in the analytic situation.

The applicant was asked why he left internal medicine to become a psychiatrist. He answered that he made the decision when he realized that so many of his patients were "sick in the head, not in the body." He spoke of a wish to learn more about "psychopharmacology and other techniques." Here, again, the interviewer noted a lack of curiosity or interest in the inner life of his patients; it was reminiscent of his own difficulties in communicating with his own inner life. The interviewer believed that the applicant's desire to learn about "drugs and other techniques" was tied to a wish to cure patients actively, to become a "real doctor" like his surgeon father. At no time during the interview did he show any appreciation of the unconscious or any knowledge of psychoanalysis as a procedure to reveal the unconscious and to solve psychic conflict.

The applicant was asked why he would want a training analysis. He stated, "if that's what is required to become an analyst, I'm ready." The interviewer thought to himself that this rather unusual response probably represented a counterphobic attitude. It also appeared that the applicant had some fantasy about a "rite of passage" before becoming the "idealized analyst." He was asked if he had any problems that could be helped by analysis. "Yes . . . I do get nervous at times . . . but nothing of any real consequence . . . I just go out and do something such as skiing and I feel good again." The interviewer thought that such a pattern underlined the applicant's need to appear normal. It seemed that he had to rigidly hide any problems, not only from the interviewer but from himself. The interviewer thought that this applicant must have a most rigid defensive structure, and he had serious doubts as to his analyzability. He conceptualized this man as a successful narcissist who would not do well in analytic work. Possibly an acceptance would even strengthen his narcissistic pathology and make a successful therapeutic analysis more difficult. The interviewer wondered if a man like this would ever seek analysis if rejected by the Institute. Probably not, he thought, but he decided not to discuss this. The thought that he could be turned down did not seem to enter the applicant's mind. The interviewer noted that during the interview neither the patient's mother nor wife was touched upon, and he wondered to himself about problems that this narcissistic applicant might have with women. He did not pursue this, since he had enough information on which to base a recommendation.

Summary

The interviewer concluded that this applicant had narcissistic pathology and questionable motivation for analysis. He was not in touch with his inner life, not introspective, not sensitive. He had shown no drive to seek psychic truth and presented no talent or potential for working with the unconscious. The interviewer questioned his analyzability, which he believed should be tested in a therapeutic analysis outside of an Institute setting. He felt that a training analysis would not be in the best interest of the candidate or the Institute.

This interviewer recommended rejection. At the selection committee, two other interviewers confirmed and deepened this impression.

Committee Discussion and Recommendation

The committee agreed that this applicant had demonstrated no potential or healthy motivation for analytic training to any of the three interviewers.

The chairman noted that although problems of narcissism are not always easy to assess during selection interviews, it was apparent that this applicant had significant narcissistic pathology.

One member expressed the hope that an Institute rejection might be experienced as a narcissistic wound that might push this man to seek analysis. The majority doubted that this was true and thought it more likely that he would probably turn away from analysis in anger after a rejection. Another member saw grandiosity as a defense that had been threatened by the interviewers' questioning. His impaired object relations alone would make him an unlikely candidate for analytic training. One interviewer who had probed somewhat into the area of object relations had noted that the applicant had little empathy for his wife, actually perceived all females as degraded, and seemed to be envious of and competitive toward all males.

The chairman emphasized that this applicant's rigid need to stay on the surface, which was well documented by all three interviewers, would make it most difficult for him to experience the necessary regression needed to undergo analysis. Almost all the committee considered the applicant to be in need of treatment but not necessarily analyzable.

One member noted that the profession of analysis would be very difficult for such a driving individual who showed little tolerance for passivity and reflection, two essential characteristics.

Another member noted that the applicant's great problem in making connections and his lack of curiosity about himself and others showed a lack of psychological-mindedness that was indeed striking. This would explain his repeated focus on psychopharmacology. The unconscious appeared to be a dark continent for this man.

The applicant was unanimously rejected.

Case III

This applicant was a 29-year-old, single, third-year resident who called for an appointment for a selection interview early on a Sunday morning. He called the interviewer's answering service first and a few hours later, after no response, called the interviewer's home to set up a time. The selection interviewer wondered if this rather unusual timing and apparent urgency to set up the interview might mean that the applicant possessed poor judgment and somewhat impaired tact and sensitivity. He also thought to himself that the applicant probably would show strong dependency needs, possibly triggered by some weekend anxiety and depression.

When the applicant appeared for the interview, he presented a rather rigid posture and a staring, expressionless face. He seemed very much on guard, appeared very frightened, almost terrified. The interviewer noted all of this and asked the applicant right away if he was aware of how stiff, tense, and frightened he appeared. The applicant stated that he was unaware of his physical and affectual state upon entering the room, but he relaxed remarkably with the question and the ease of the interviewer. The interviewer thought to himself that this applicant must have been undergoing a strong transference reaction. He was obviously not in touch with his inner life and was apparently overwhelmed by certain fantasies and feelings. The interviewer decided at the outset that the Sunday morning telephone call, the anxious, almost frozen, panicked demeanor upon entering the office—feelings of which the applicant was not aware—did not augur well for analytic potential and perhaps analyzability.

The interviewer asked the applicant to tell him about his medical and psychiatric education. The applicant said that he "had wanted to become a doctor since he was nine years of age," but he initially could not connect this to any event in his life at the time. His parents had had a stormy marriage and were divorced when he was nine years old, but he surprisingly could not make connections between the family trouble and the wish to become a doctor. After the divorce, the applicant was "shuffled back and forth" between the homes of his parents and relatives. He stated he "never had a home and that he always missed the security of a home and family." The interviewer thought of the urgent telephone call but decided not to say anything. Another interviewer might have questioned him more aggressively to see how he would react and how he could work with the confrontation. This interviewer did ask if the applicant's wish to become a doctor was in some way tied to the divorce. The applicant then said that a family doctor and friend who was respected by both parents was often consulted by the family during the marital difficulties. He stated, "Maybe that did have something to do with my wish to become a doctor," and he had diligently pursued, and eventually achieved that goal. The interviewer thought that here the applicant did show some ability for synthetic functioning; yet his overall psychological-mindedness appeared quite impaired.

In medical school, during anatomy dissection, he had had a brief memory of hitting his father. This frightened him so much that he entered psychotherapy. At this point, the interviewer thought of the extreme anxiety the applicant showed at the beginning of the interview and wondered to himself if this applicant had not perceived the interviewer as the hated father and if he had not been flooded with a murderous rage that he continued to defend against with significant regression.

The applicant stopped psychotherapy "rather suddenly" after two years. He stated that he did not wish to leave therapy; in fact, he had wanted to see the psychiatrist more often but the psychiatrist believed they should stop since they "had accomplished quite a bit." The applicant stated that he had felt at the time "pushed out and criticized by the psychiatrist" but that his interest in becoming a psychiatrist did have a lot to do with the psychotherapy he received in medical school. In spite of the difficulties at the end of treatment, he had received much help and felt much better, but he was not clear about how this came about.

The interviewer wondered to himself if the treatment came to an end because of aggressive feelings toward the therapist which were overwhelming to the patient and which caused the therapist to decide that it was better not to continue therapy.

The applicant had done very little reading. He stated that he did read all the required assignments during his residency, but had difficulty remembering any of those articles or books.

He stated that he had little social life and felt uncomfortable whenever he got "too close to too many people at one time." He did say that he would like to enter analysis to learn more about himself and how to overcome his difficulties, especially around people or in feeling close to people. He stated that if he did not work that out it would be difficult for him to marry. The interviewer thought to himself that the applicant surely did need treatment for these problems.

When asked to tell the interviewer about a patient he was treating, the applicant mentioned "an angry psychotic young man of 23 years of age" whom he was "mothering and for whom he was reality testing" and who was feeling so much better since commencing treatment. The applicant had a difficult time conceptualizing the case and giving a dynamic formulation.

Summary

The interviewer concluded that this applicant suffered from an ego defect and a borderline condition. He could become flooded by aggressive impulses that at times overwhelmed his ego, as was the case when he initially appeared for the selection interview.

The interviewer thought that the applicant's need for object supplies seemed to be so great that he could not do much independent work in the field and that he needed much more maturity and a sense of identity before he could ever be considered for analytic training. The interviewer questioned the applicant's analyzability but believed in any case the analysis would be long, difficult, and complicated. At the present time the applicant showed no real potential or talent for analytic work. He recommended rejection but expected that this man would seek treatment for himself. One other interviewer arrived at a similar conclusion, whereas a third recommended acceptance.

Committee Discussion and Recommendation

The committee noted how flooded this man became during two of his interviews and recognized that at this time he was not in touch with the extreme anxiety. He required the empathy, sensitivity, and reality testing of the interviewers to reverse the severe regression.

The chairman predicted that this applicant would easily undergo strong transference reactions and that the two interviewers were apparently perceived as the hated father. The applicant projected his rage onto them and then became anxious and furious in their presence.

It was noted that this could also explain the applicant's discomfort around people, especially groups. He must be in almost constant fear of being attacked and of attacking in return.

One member observed that it was a good sign that he had some awareness of his problem and sincerely wished analysis to solve the difficulty with object relations. This member believed that a trial of analysis was surely indicated and that, with a sensitive analyst, much could be accomplished with this borderline man.

Though the applicant believed he had received help from his previous psychotherapy, he could not state, in any way, how this came about. One member saw this as an indication that the applicant was unanalyzable and that the improvement was some form of transference cure. Another member commented that his inability to objectify or remember what occurred during previous therapy might point to a problem in introjecting the therapist, his function, or the therapy as a helpful process. His lack of memories would be seen as evidence of an inability to introject and separate.

Another member noted that this inability to remember his own therapy might also be related to an inability to conceptualize the therapeutic process in the patient he was treating in psychotherapy. His patient was improving, but it was impossible for the applicant to say how this improvement had come about.

A member noted that the patient the applicant chose to discuss was very similar to himself and that such a choice was not unusual. It would be considered more of a positive sign, however, if the applicant were aware of the similarities between himself and the patient. This applicant was not.

The members saw some potential for introspection and for making psychological connections, but the applicant's problems of ego regression, difficulties with aggression, primitive defenses, and strong transference reactions with many different people pointed toward rejection.

The one interviewer who had recommended acceptance had not seen the borderline pathology. The applicant had apparently not presented the extreme anxiety and regressive behavior to this interviewer, but appeared to be a neurotic man. This interviewer stated that he had known the applicant for six months from a course he had given residents and that somehow the applicant had felt very comfortable with him, even though he had not participated too often during class. This interviewer was surprised when he read the other two reports. A member commented that such a personal or social relationship between applicant and selectors might interfere with obtaining a clear picture of the applicant due to some countertransference pressures. The applicant did appear much more comfortable with this particular interviewer—probably, it was thought, by some form of fusion—and he did not show the marked anxiety he had clearly demonstrated to the others. Possibly, a more skilled interviewer might still have identified the borderline ego organization.

Following the discussion, which gave him a new appreciation of this applicant's ego difficulties, the interviewer who had initially recommended acceptance also voted for rejection, and the committee's negative decision was unanimous.

COMMENTARY

It is our aim in this paper to call attention to an important aspect of psychoanalytic education, that of faculty development. Faculty development, we believe, should be an ongoing activity of every Institute. Institutes should provide the organizational structure and opportunity for the education of faculty members for the multiple tasks required of psychoanalytic educators.

In this paper we have discussed one aspect of faculty development, i.e., the training and education of selectors. The teaching and learning of the selection process can become an enriching experience for the entire faculty and can lessen the chances of selection errors which can be detrimental to the candidates involved, to the institute, and to the science of psychoanalysis. It is an important responsibility that can never be taken lightly.

The method of educating selectors at Denver Institute selection-committee conferences can be summarized as follows:

1. We reviewed and discussed the psychoanalytic literature on selection.
2. We worked with the committee members to extract from the literature the various criteria used in the selection process by other analytic educators and then began to discuss and formulate the criteria we ourselves were looking for in a potential analyst. Some of the criteria are complex ego–superego configurations that require much discussion if they are to be evaluated wisely and if sound predictions of success or failure are to be made.
3. As selection interviews were studied at the committee conferences, all members gained experience with connecting the criteria to the clinical and behavioral data obtained from selection interviews. Selection-committee members learned to conceptualize the clinical behavior and observational data from the selection interviews at higher levels of abstraction (Waelder, 1962), which led to deeper insights and understanding about each applicant and about the relation between selection, therapeutic, and educational processes.
4. Selection-committee members and all interviewers learned to write, evaluate, and appreciate the importance and value of good selection case reports. Younger members, once they learned

what selection committees were looking for, began to submit more informative reports. Even experienced analysts began to write more valuable reports with well-thought-out impressions and recommendations once they became actively involved in the selection process by attending selection-committee meetings at which the applicant they had interviewed was being discussed.

An important but purely serendipitous finding was that many selectors experienced an increase in clinical acumen. Many reported to us that they became better clinicians.

We have reviewed and briefly discussed what can be done, what was done in one Institute, and what we think should be done to educate competent selectors. We have presented our experiences with one selection committee which made administrative decisions about selection in an atmosphere of teaching and learning. We have thought that our Denver Institute experience should be reported because of its broad applicability, especially to the growing number of newer Institutes.

As illustrations of our procedures, we offered three examples of applicants, presenting the interview material as it was reported and discussed by committee members, using their knowledge of selection criteria to arrive at a recommendation based on an understanding of the character structure and potentials for doing analytic work in each applicant.

For selectors, as we hope we have demonstrated, diagnosis is not a simple label or category but a metapsychological statement. When one interviewer's impressions and recommendations are put together with those of his colleagues, the selection committee's deliberations can begin. These deliberations should lead to an important administrative decision for Institute and applicant and to scientific understanding and insight for committee members. The tasks of data collection, diagnosis, and decision making are inseparable.

In conclusion, we wish to emphasize again that good selection conferences offer a scientific forum for the integration of newer knowledge regarding structural and developmental concepts which can lead to advances in psychoanalytic theory regarding personality development. A well-functioning selection committee becomes a research seminar dealing with questions of analyzability, advanced psychopathology, ego–superego functioning, and important questions about what a training analysis can and cannot accomplish. Faculty members who participate in such learning and such administrative experiences inevitably widen and deepen their psychoanalytic knowledge and skills.

·8·

THE EDUCATION OF
A SUPERVISOR

This paper was presented in 1979 at the Chicago Symposium on Supervision, but was not published. In it, Dr. Fleming emphasizes her philosophy concerning the need to educate and train supervisors and teachers so that they can be more effective and creative in engaging candidates in the exercise of the synthesizing and integrating ego functions that make empathic understanding and interpretive action possible. The paper stresses that all too often this cognitive part of the teaching dialogue is absent and that supervision or teaching do not reach objectification, a level of more complex generalization. Dr. Fleming also believed that objectification of the personal analytic experience and gradual application of theoretical concepts to the experience are important parts of psychoanalytic education. She expresses the belief here that the pedagogic task of the clinical teacher is to facilitate this active learning.

What I have to say about the education of a supervisor will not be news to most of you here this weekend. You have worked with me as residents, student-analysts, supervisees, beginning teachers of psychoanalysis, beginning supervisors, and now psychoanalytic educators yourselves, writing papers on supervision. Such is the relay nature of education in general, and it is that aspect of clinical teaching, where the clinical baton is passed on from one generation to the next, that I want to talk about today.

    Unlike a competitive relay race, the educational relay goes on and on. There are no winners or losers, only runners who pass batons. The baton is passed in different ways as each teacher contributes to the totality of a student's development. This is something we must never lose sight of. The danger in my metaphor of a relay appears when an individual teacher has a secret idea that

Paper read at the Chicago Symposium on Supervision, Chicago, November 9–11, 1979.

the relay stops with himself. History belies this grandiose view of one's omnipotence and immortality. The race may be slower, the course longer, the track heavier, but the relay continues in any educational process. So it should be that we who are on the educational track in any given generation must insure opportunities for the development of new knowledge and skill and for passing it on beyond our personal range of vision. Today, I want to put before you some general thoughts and some specific suggestions about insuring those opportunities for the next generations of supervisors.

A supervisor is a teacher, a clinical teacher. As such, his task is very complex. He is called upon for creative, growth-promoting work that involves both treating and learning. A supervisor treats as he analyzes the patient's problems, and he teaches as he evaluates his student's competence and assists him in mastering the obstacles to learning the skills of his profession (Fleming and Benedek, 1966). Helen Ross, at a Chicago Training Analysts' Seminar in March of 1956, emphasized the Janus job of teacher and therapist with which a supervisor is confronted. Miss Ross said, "It is very difficult to remain a teacher when he [the supervisor] sees the emotional flounderings, not just of the patient, but of the student as well. How to keep the balance so that the supervisor can continue to be a teacher; to help the patient and to help the student deal with his own emotional problems is the most difficult task I know" [p. 10].

Miss Ross turned to the metaphor of Janus, the god who looked in two directions at once—toward the year just ended and the new year about to begin. A supervisor looks to healing and learning. Both are interrelated through goals and processes that lead toward skills and wholeness. The problems inherent in each may interfere with each other, and so, as we analytic supervisors learn the methods for this special kind of teaching, we are faced with a special opportunity to integrate in new ways the hard-won skills of treating and healing with the often neglected goals of growth and development in the teaching–learning process.

Many of us think of supervision as "didactic," meaning instructional, but it is more than instructional. A supervisor does much more than pour knowledge into a student, like milk from a jug into a mug. A supervisor is also corrective, but he does more than call attention to errors, prescribe remedies, or try to change a student's bad habits into good ones. A supervisor and his student enter into an active teaching–learning experience where, without doubt, information is exchanged, mistakes corrected, old habits reshaped, and new skills established; but there is a more creative aspect of the teaching–learning relationship that needs to be cultivated. There is an expanded level of teaching that goes beyond demonstrations which can be imitated or advice which can be followed. What is missing in much supervision is the active engagement of the student by the supervisor in the exercise of the synthesizing and integrative ego functions that make empathic understanding and interpretive interaction possible.

Here I use the term "exercise" in the sense of use that builds strength and skill. Ego functions need exercise as much as a biceps. A supervisor is expected to be a competent, skilled analyst who has learned to use his integrating ego functions in the practice of psychoanalysis, but my thesis today is that analytic competence does not insure his being a skilled and creative teacher. He may be able to give instruction and describe how he would handle a therapeutic situation, but can he explain why some technical response was wrong and why something else was good or would have been better? All too often this cognitive part of the teaching dialogue is absent. Student and supervisor take a very passive stance toward conceptualizing technique. No questions are asked by either, and, once a teaching intervention has been made, the focus of the learning process turns away from a dialogue between supervisor and analyst and shifts back to the therapeutic process operating around the patient. It is hard to tell if any learning has taken place.

You do not need any examples of the first level of teaching tactics, that of jug–mug information giving (Fleming, 1967). But what if a student is more actively involved and asks questions? The following anecdote was reported in a seminar on how to teach in supervision. The supervisor told of a situation where she felt the patient was talking about negative feelings for the therapist which the therapist had missed. She gave him her interpretation of the negative feelings. At that point she rested on her oars. To her surprise, he asked, "How did you arrive at that?" The supervisor could not give him an immediate answer and felt chagrined. For a moment or two she did some introspecting and recalled a series of associations to the patient's material and the therapeutic interaction. Following the meanings of these preconscious but accessible associations, she realized they had led her to make the interpretation to the student. The sudden insight into the interpretive process excited the supervisor. She felt she had just learned something about learning, a discovery of some importance which enabled her to answer the student's question. She felt the most valuable aspect of this experience was not the interpretation, which was the outcome of her preconscious empathic listening. Instead, the most important result was her discovery that she could trace back the process of interpretation to the analytic evidence and then report her introspective work to her student. She did not stop there. The student was included in her explanation and was able to follow her line of associations. Both of them discussed this as an activity that should go on all of the time in a good analysis and in a good supervision—this process of integrating associations until a meaningful interpretation could be formulated. All too often it goes on outside of awareness. This supervisor had taught her student something which is usually left to chance or an extra dose of aptitude and self-teaching. He gained some information and a guideline, but I think he learned something which is characteristic of good teaching. I will discuss this later.

In this anecdote the student set the process of integration in motion in the supervisor by his question, "How did you arrive at that interpretation?" It can also be initiated in the student by the supervisor. When that happens, a different level of cognitive fit between experience, technique, and unconscious meaning becomes operative, and the student gains insight into what therapeutic work involves. In one instance, I asked the student-analyst that same question, "How did you arrive at that interpretation?" She was at first nonplussed, but was able to free-associate from her preconscious and to her patient's material, which she had tended to bypass. When it all came together, she looked at me with joyful pride. "Now I am an analyst," she said. The teaching tactic here was to give the student the opportunity to actively practice associating and introspecting—an essential task for an analyst, but a skill often taken for granted.

Other related but less fortuitous stories have come to my ears repeatedly from students who complained about classroom teachers or supervisors. "They are marvelous at understanding dreams, but they can't explain how they do it or teach us to do it," they said. Clearly, the level of teaching strategy here was not even explanatory instruction. It focused on establishing a situation in which practicing of functions already partially learned could take place. Should not the supervisor do more than demonstrate his own associative processes (sometimes more oriented to showing off his own skill than to exercising his student's capacities)? Should there not be a way to catalyze the student's associations, bring his marginal awareness within range of conscious meaning, and make the analytic process more explicit? I believe there is, but it requires objectifying the teaching–learning experience and needs more effort directed to educating the educators in how to teach.

Before expanding further on some suggestions for implementing the effort to make better teachers out of our supervisors, I want to look back at the earlier educational philosophy, which leaned on the system of novice–master–craftsman apprenticeship to provide the teaching and learning for the clinical applications of the new science of psychoanalysis.

Our thinking about supervision as a teaching process has had a slow evolution and has made even slower progress toward the idea that the principal learning objective for any psychoanalytic student is the development of his self-awareness and his skills as an instrument in the psychoanalytic process. Freud and his writings were once the only sources of the new knowledge. The experiential nature of learning psychoanalysis and its unconscious derivatives was recognized early by Freud, since in 1910 he spoke of how countertransference can interfere with work with patients and indicates a need for "self-analysis" (Fleming, 1971 [see Chapter Two, this volume]). In 1912, Freud was recommending a personal analysis very strongly, but it was not until 1918 that Nunberg advocated the requirement of a therapeutic analysis for those who wanted to become analysts. In 1922, this analytic experience was still considered "didactic" or "instructional" but was required for the authority to practice as an analyst (Fleming and Benedek, 1966).

With the establishment of the Berlin Institute in 1920, Eitingon recognized the need for "practical training," which he named "*Kontroll*-analysis" (Fleming and Benedek, 1966, p. 8). Gradually, there has been a consolidation of an educational philosophy away from the apprentice–master–craftsman system as more persons took up the new profession, formed faculties of Institutes, and claimed group responsibility for the conduct of education in what had become known as the tripartite system of psychoanalytic education.

Discussions in the International Training Commission (formed in 1925 with Eitingon as chairman) and in the Four Countries Conferences (Austria, Hungary, Czechoslovakia, and Italy) involved educational standards and to some extent teaching methods. Edward Bibring read a paper in Budapest in May 1937, titled "Methods and Technique of Control Analysis." He was probably the first "to formulate the concept that the supervisor not only instructs the student but is also in a position to evaluate his ability to grasp problems, make decisions about dealing with them, and apply what he learned to new situations" (Fleming and Benedek, 1966, p. 14). This was an early and a good beginning on developing an educational philosophy and study of teaching methods.

But World War II interfered with this development in many ways. One wonders whether the Four Countries Conferences might have made progress in solving the "syncretistic dilemma" if there had been no war. This dilemma so cogently described by Lewin and Ross (1960) and persisting into our current debates began to take center stage in the International Training Commission and the Four Countries Conferences. Eitingon is quoted as saying the training analysis has more than a therapeutic goal (Fleming and Benedek, 1966, p. 11). He also said, "there is more to supervision than analyzing the countertransferences" (Fleming and Benedek, 1966, p. 13). Insecurity promoted by the war intensified rivalries and self-esteem needs. Tremendous contributions were made by refugees from Europe in America and elsewhere. But there was an overidealizing tendency which failed to modify an inherent omniscience and elitism among psychoanalysts. Both the insecurity and overidealization converted the controversy over the respective roles of training analyst and supervisor into one of territoriality and personally narcissistic investments. Such a focus has prevented an objective study of educational issues uncontaminated by transferences. The situation was understandable but not interpretable. It is time for new developments.

As Benedek has said about the 1920s (Fleming and Benedek, 1966, p. 10), "One learned, by identification with a highly libidinized object, ideas, and techniques which were emotionally invested not only with the wish for professional competence and recognition, but also with the excitement of continuing the discoveries which had begun with one's own analysis. Indeed, the known and formulated psychoanalytic knowledge constituted merely a foretaste of what was to come." Benedek was describing her own training experiences, which remained vivid in her memory, but she was also able to remain objective about teaching as being something similar to but different from "analyzing for therapeutic purposes." She was aware of the pitfalls which learning by identification with an idealized teacher can pose for an eager, excited student. Such a motivation has a tendency to strengthen affectivity at the cost of objectivity and cognitive thinking organized as secondary process. It supports learning by imitation without questioning (searching for reasons) and tends to reinforce group loyalty and fealty to a leader. Transferences and loyalty can approach in their intensity the dynamics of a cult, stressing the idealizing of authoritative bonds as more influential in the learning process than questioning, tolerance for uncertainty, and comprehension of a need for an expanding, spiraling evolution of theories of psychology and technique.

Every one of us has had to work through the regressive pulls of hero worship. Most of us are still engaged in that task. It was inherent in the beginnings of psychoanalysis, since the new science had its origins in one man who was the idol of his followers and who provided therapy, theory, and clinical learning for the second generation of analysts. The model of being all things to one's students began understandably with Freud and was continued by succeeding generations of isolated analysts scattered over Europe and by the early enclaves in the United States. The same situation continues in parts of the world today, since even a group of analysts only a few miles away from other groups can become inbred, provincial, tribally oriented, and ruled by a more or less closed system, which perpetuates barriors to growth of our science and our educational task.

In spite of these handicaps, there were great beginnings in the International Congresses, the International Training Commission, and the Four Countries Conferences. Those beginnings, devoted to reading papers about new formulations and new ideas to be shared with analysts attending the conferences, as well as with readers of journals and in libraries, were an excellent start at keeping communication open. The war interfered, as I have indicated. Other, more subtle unconscious factors interfered, too. Those who attended the Four Countries Conferences could (and I am sure they did) profit greatly by the ideas shared among themselves, but they did not publish or share more than locally with others in their own Institutes. Reading a published paper helps a beginner in the field; discussing ideas in a group conference opens up meanings and deepens what is learned. But no Four Countries Conferences (they met only twice), no national discussion groups by themselves, no national conference with all its printed reports, no COPE Study Group, no geographic or Three Institute Training Analyst Conferences can do the job. There must be continuing effort and leadership for an ongoing learning process. This is especially true for teachers.

It is imperative for the third phase of the tripartite system, the phase of clinical teaching and learning. One can learn a great deal by doing analysis, but, if it is done in isolation—not talking to anyone about what happens, what is interesting, what problems are being met, what questions cannot be answered, why one procedure seems to work and why another does not—then the analyst is left on a raft drifting with the current and threatened by unexpected rocks and rapids, or he possesses a most unusual and rare gift of being able to teach himself. I think it is easier to learn how to analyze with a supervisor, even if he is a poor teacher. Just reviewing for a supervisory hour helps, or writing a six-month report, or the like, even if it is not discussed with anyone. These are procedures built into the learning situation. They go side by side with clinical conference presentations, where discussion by teachers and peers is also built in with the hope of widening the range of clinical material observed.

From my experience as a student and as a supervisor, I am convinced a supervisor can be a very valuable assistant in a clinical learning experience. However, he is more valuable if he knows how to teach. That, of course, is a very complicated topic. How does one learn to teach? In the first place, a realistic attitude toward being a teacher is required.

I was fortunate to have a very relevant experience recently. Newly graduated residents were confronted suddenly with the job of becoming supervisors of new first-year residents, with only their own residency experience of being supervised as preparation for the new job. Anxiety was created, and they asked me for some help. I was intrigued, and we set up a seminar for six new faculty members.

I entered upon this project with an interest (even an ambition) to give them a systematic course in the aims, content, and pedagogic methods useful in teaching a beginning supervisor how to teach a beginning resident how to communicate and work with a patient. (After all, had I not written a book on the subject?) We met for an hour and a half every other week. My disillusionment with myself came quickly, and my goals and methods had to be revised. We were not on the same track. They were scared, and I wanted to talk about theories of teaching. When I turned on my empathic radar, listening to the anxiety, observing the regression in these young people, I made a diagnosis of transference distortions in their image of a supervisor. They saw a supervisor and a teacher as an exalted, omniscient, omnipotent authority. They were trying to see themselves as such and having realistic trouble. Their anxiety and sense of helpless inadequacy were interfering with their learning. Their need blocked effective use of what I knew they had already learned in residency experiences. They regressed to the level of mugs expecting to be filled from a jug when they said, "Please tell us what to do."

At that point I shifted my stance. As a teacher who also knew something about anxiety, regression, and overidealization, I decided to tackle the distortion in the exalted image of a teacher with which they were now identified and then go on to their feelings of inadequacy. So I replied to their appeal by saying, "I can't. I have no magic formulas. But it might help if we talk about what being a supervisor means to you." On exploring this question, it turned out the majority were afraid of not knowing enough about the technique of therapy. They were afraid they could not answer their supervisees' questions. They felt the administration that was expecting them to teach was expecting too much. They felt ignorant and helpless, and were afraid that their supervisees would also expect too much. Implicitly, I responded that it was all right not to know something. No one was as omnipotent as they were anticipating their supervisees would expect them to be. They began to objectify the situation more realistically.

One more topic was explored before they saw their assigned residents. I suggested we should try to recall what the experience was like when they were first-year residents and met their supervisors for the first time. This approach continued the effort to objectify certain fantasies and to make connections between what was blocked from current awareness and therefore not so useful. Each new supervisor began to feel better, because he remembered how anxious he had been, but how he recognized that his supervisor was anxious also. At this new level of functioning, they realized the anxieties were not intolerable—actually might be helpful in an empathic way—and that no supervisor was required to protect his supervisee totally from anxiety or ignorance. They also realized that, as residents themselves, they had learned to listen, to observe both explicit and implicit behavior, to evaluate and diagnose meanings, and to keep communication open. In July, as they left the security of the residency, they had regressed, but when they could focus on their own experience and explore their anxieties, they recovered and even enjoyed an exercise which involved "rehearsing" alternative tactics for becoming acquainted with their supervisees and introducing them to the tasks of the supervisory teaching–learning process.

As the seminar went on, my teaching strategies moved toward providing more "exercises" on which they could practice their capacities to describe and explain their own experiences in teaching. For about six months they were still somewhat anxious and therefore concerned with describing "a problem with a resident." In the seminar, we treated these accounts of "problems" as diagnostic challenges. The supervisor was expected to give us enough information on which to make an educational diagnosis. This step naturally came before a remedy for the student's problem. The group then discussed the diagnosis, tried to find a probable cause, and attempted to suggest a remedy. In the beginning, the "problem" was usually diagnosed as "an acting out of resistance to learning," especially to learning from the given supervisor. Discussion, however, enabled the group to be more precise about the learning difficulty. For example, was the "problem" with only one supervisor? If so, it was probably a character defense, a supervisory transference or countertransference reaction, and would require appropriate remedies. If not, was the difficulty a reflection of lack of sensitivity and aptitude, lack of knowledge, or inexperience? Each difficulty would offer a range of options for assisting the supervisee. In the experience of discussing the educational diagnosis and teaching remedies, this group of supervisors became aware of the fact that a positive attitude toward evaluation of the supervisee's competence as a therapist was intimately correlated with the teaching–learning process. It required the supervisor-teacher to know more explicitly what constituted therapeutic competence, and simultaneously increased his skill in assisting his student to achieve skills of his own (Weiss and Fleming, 1975 [see Chapter Six, this volume]).

It would be interesting to me to offer you for discussion in more detail an account of the events in this seminar, but we have probably extracted the essence. What I have written here is much more than was made explicit in the seminar or was available to me consciously. I learned much from review of the events. I could have talked to the group about the transference distortions. That they would have understood intellectually, but it would not have been integrated with experience, because the roots of each person's specific transference were in his own genetic history, and bringing that to consciousness belongs in another ball park. I could have described some of my teaching tactics in more conceptualized terms, but, as we moved along listening to the happenings in their teaching encounters, they were making observations on invaluable experiential data which could be generalized later (Waelder, 1962). They were exercising their analytic ego functions. They were like toddlers learning to walk. Later, they could conceptualize the process of teaching (walking). In fact, that is what we are planning to do this coming year. I hope we can spell out what we have already learned.

Learning how to supervise cannot be accomplished by reading a paper or a book or by listening to a lecture. It has to be learned by doing, as does any clinical work. But—and this is a big "but"—much of great value is lost to the specific supervisor and to the profession of psychoanalysis if there is no higher level of generalization of the teaching–learning process and no sharing with colleagues of what can become conscious. Freud's letters to Fliess (Freud, 1887–1902) served a comparable purpose for him, as did his notes and drafts of ideas originating in the consulting room. Later there were colleagues with whom Freud could discuss his ideas and teach them the new psychology.

The teaching–learning process has much in common with the therapeutic process, in that "making the unconscious conscious" is still primary in both, just as it was in the first period of psychoanalysis. However, for the early analysts, the experiential mode of learning (covering imitation and identification) was fundamental. Conceptualizing either the principles of the technique of psychoanalysis or the process of teaching and learning it waited for minds like Ferenczi and Fenichel in those days. Nevertheless, as more analysts became experienced in doing analysis, they were thrust into positions of teaching what they knew to others. Like my six new faculty members and myself, their teacher, the early teachers of analysis must have learned much from the necessity to put their observations and interpretations into words that an analytic student or a colleague could understand. From such attempts come new levels of understanding for oneself (often a very humbling experience).

Much progress has been made in the last 30 years, compared to what was accomplished from 1920 (Berlin and Vienna) to 1948 (London and the United States), although probably the rate of our learning about teaching has been slower from 1948 to 1978. The quantity of published knowledge has increased enormously; both the quantity of supervisory hours and the number of supervisors is constantly rising. But, like our plague of inflation, the quality of what is provided has not kept up with the cost. Nevertheless, interest in enhancing both knowledge and skill for educational work, particularly the strategy and tactics of teaching, has persisted from 1925 (the International Training Commission) and has been expanded by leadership on the national level and in the holding of such conferences as this one.

However, in spite of the evidence of persisting effort at the top, we must recognize a serious limitation in the inplementation of an overall program. There is very little diffusion to the local level, the individual supervisor. Some of this is inherent in the time demands of our professional practice and in the far-flung geographic distribution of our Institutes. These factors force us into an ad hoc approach to the continuing education of our educators. Conferences are stimulating and a beginning is made, but what about the follow-through? I have tried to stress that the beginning of a study of supervision is often anxiety-laden and that the group situation is burdened with transferences. A meeting limited to a one-time discussion stirs up questions and necessarily leaves them unanswered. For instance, there may never be another meeting of this group, and there may be little discussion locally. Questions raised at the Pittsburgh Three Institute Conference for new training analysts held in 1965 remain without much further exploration. The second such conference was in Topeka in 1969, four years later. This conference in Chicago on supervision comes 10 years after Topeka. Such a conference performs an important service for those who attend. But, ultimately, the doing (practicing) of supervision depends on the individual supervisor. He is the one who needs to learn how to teach his student how to conduct an analysis and how to know what he is doing while he analyzes. What is started at these conferences and study group meetings must be carried on locally by a sustained, ongoing, well-planned program which moves from general statements about purposes of supervision to the nitty-gritty of the events and phenomena that form the data base of a particular supervisory process. What really happens in the supervision of a particular student with a particular patient is what needs to be scrutinized and conceptualized as an interactive process of communication with teaching and learning as its goal. This process needs to be studied from several different angles, taken apart, discussed, criticized, and interpreted by the individuals in the group as they compare the supervision under examination with their own experiences.

. Let me emphasize two aspects of what I am advocating. The first is the planning of a local program for faculty development—for educating the educators in how to teach. The principle applies to both seminar teachers and supervisors. Since seminar teachers are often recently graduated candidates and have had relatively less experience in analyzing as well as teaching, compared to persons appointed to supervisory status, the program might begin with a study of seminar teaching and curriculum planning, then might progress to clinical conferences and supervision. Such a program for faculty development would offer a philosophy in sharp contrast to the prevailing philosophy of impressionistic selection of teachers, who are then left to sink or swim with little if any orientation to the curriculum plan, let alone any learning about how to teach in class or supervision.

Second, an essential part of the planning of such a program is its ongoing built-in continuity, which allows for follow-through on various questions, especially those which are controversial. There must be time for interim thinking, for coming back to the debate, and for working over the positions laden with personal bias. There must be time for examining different points of view, different styles of supervising—not for the purpose of defining *the one correct way* of proceeding, but to note differences, to have an opportunity to test out a given rationale. To describe, discuss, and formulate teaching goals and methods is an invaluable learning experience for a clinical teacher. It inevitably enriches one's grasp of psychoanalysis as a scientific theory.

One of the most important experiences is the opportunity to "practice" putting into communicable words how one understands the meaning of a patient's material and the student-analyst's handling of it. To explain technical concepts in relation to behavior of patient and analyst is a great challenge. A beginning seminar teacher or supervisor has had little experience in formulating basic concepts of technique as compared to basic concepts of development and psychopathology. For the most part, technical concepts have been stated as principles or rules (e.g., the rule of free association or abstinence). We all know the value of those technical procedures, but they need to be explained in relation to more general theories of therapy, and also connected with behavioral phenomena that indicate, for instance, that the rule of abstinence might be neglected. The analyst's response has many effects. It may be gratifying, may seem rejecting and critical, and so on. How does a student learn this important assessment of his own technical motivation and evaluate his competence? It is not enough for a supervisor to name the analyst's response to his patient as "countertransference." The supervisor needs to go at least one step further and demonstrate from the patient's responses that the analyst's departure from the rule of abstinence is producing a reaction that increases anxiety, reinforces the patient's transference resistance, or upsets his inner equilibrium to a point of rage that might threaten a breaking off of analysis.

Let me give you an example of how a student learned experientially in a supervisory session something he had not been able to integrate on a more cognitive and instrumental level until the supervisor helped him to reproduce with her the experience which his patient was responding to. The situation was as follows: The student-analyst had a habit of intervening with the question "Why do you say that?" When the patient responded with silence, changed the subject, and began to complain that her father never understood her but always expected more, the analyst felt misunderstood and irritated. He was unaware of reacting on the level of transferences just as the patient was. He interrupted the patient to ask, "Why did you change the subject? You are being defensive." In the supervisory hour, the supervisor said to him, "Why did you say that?" He looked startled and hedged. The supervisor went further, "You seem to be defensive." The next step in the teaching sequence was to objectify the immediate experience by asking, "Did you feel accused when I said, 'You seem defensive'?" "Yes, I did," he replied. "Is it possible your patient felt accused when you asked her, 'Why did you say that?' and 'Why did you change the subject?' " "I guess she did. I certainly did when you asked me that." The supervisor then discussed with the student the fact that his conscious aim was to "interpret the defense," but that the form of his intervention hit another target and stirred up feelings of fault finding and rejection which he was blind to, except that he, too, felt rejected when the patient changed the subject.

So far, the supervisor had catalyzed the student's associations and self-observation. There was a reliving of old responses to criticism in the supervisory relationship. There followed an exercising of his interpretive functioning with a practicing of alternatives and with play-acting responses by the supervisor in the role of patient. The student gained some insight into his countertransferences and the process of interpretation. He learned that to assess the resistance in a patient's response to an interpretation is an essential activity for an analyst and can be learned through experience and practice if the opportunity for "rehearsal" is provided.

Given the infinite variations in a patient's reactions with himself and his analyst, and the more focused but equally infinite responses from the analyst, there is no one "correct" or "perfect" interpretation (Calef and Weinshel, 1979, p. 419). Even an "inexact interpretation" (Glover, 1931) can be valuable if the reaction to it is noted and understood. Every intervention by the analyst aims at a target of which he is more or less aware, and which stimulates responses from the patient of which each is more or less aware. The task of the analyst is to be aware and to become more aware as he helps the patient to achieve a similar level of insight. In the process of working toward that goal, inevitable distortions of meaning occur, due to the anxieties, conflicts, and resistances which operate to produce a system of intrapsychic homeostasis whose economic value has been built up over the years by the patient. His responses to interventions are signals cueing his analyst to how that balance is maintained. An analyst who understands the principles of psychic structure and psychopathology, and who can tune in to developmental vicissitudes and their effects, can also enter the disarrayed world of his patient with responses and interpretations that in time shift the patient's intrapsychic organization toward a more personally and socially adaptive level.

The supervisory situation requires the supervisor to be sensitive to the many factors in the supervisory systems (Fleming and Benedek, 1966, Chapter IV), to think on multiple levels simultaneously, and to be able to go beyond expecting his student to do no more than be able to name transference phenomena or to demonstrate a "genetic reconstruction." Where can a beginning supervisor organize his knowledge and experience in a form useful to his student? Where does he learn to bring together in an integrated, insightful experience the processes of analysis and learning, and the creativity involved in both?

Up to this point I have talked about the supervisory teaching role in terms of information giving, in terms of correcting errors, or in terms of demonstrating procedures and interpretations that promote learning by imitation. I have recalled the early apprentice–master-craftsman relationship which represented the educational philosophy of psychoanalytic supervision in the early analytic Institutes. The International Training Commission and the Board on Professional Standards were mainly concerned with formulating professional standards and evaluating whether or not Institutes were accepting and maintaining them. Up to 1948 and the early 1950s, a person's local reputation as an analyst was enough to bestow upon him the "right to train" (Knight, 1953). Time passed and new difficulties arose. More analysts claimed to be analytic educators. In line with their diverse learning experiences, questions then arose about their competence as analysts, mostly on ideological grounds involving variations from classical techniques. Some were judged because of association with others of similar theoretical background. Few were questioned because they were considered poor teachers. It had been assumed that a good analyst was a good teacher and/or supervisor. No evaluations were made of a teacher's competence to teach.

Then, in the early 1950s, the tensions of ideological differences and arguments over the "right to train" resulted in the breaking apart of Institute faculties. Maintaining educational standards was at stake as Institutes multiplied by fission. The diminished faculty resources which resulted influenced the Board on Professional Standards to begin to evaluate local situations. The national survey and the program of periodic site visits by the Committee on Institutes required an Institute to examine itself and evaluate its curriculum and educational program. The question of quality of standards, as well as faithfulness to regulations by the Board, came under scrutiny. Doubts about the efficacy of these evaluative activities existed then and persist today. This has always been hard for me to understand, since evaluation seems such a logical part of education. The doubt was epitomized in a question with which a member of the first site visiting team confronted me in 1953 when we were discussing our agenda for the visit. With great skepticism in his voice, he asked me, "Do you really think you can learn anything about an Institute by visiting supervision?" Nevertheless, since then, site visits and auditing supervision by the site visitors have become standard procedures. Both sides have learned something, with, I hope, more to come.

However, a new dilemma was created. Should teachers and supervisors be prepared for the responsibility of teaching? Were there principles and techniques to be learned about teaching psychoanalysis? Or was it considered a narcissistic blow to intimate that there might be more to learn? Certainly, faculty selection by nepotism or elitism is not adequate to judge analytic competence or scholarship, nor is it healthy for a unified faculty working together. Nepotism, elitism, and failure to build provision for succession of leadership or for relaying the clinical baton in a program of faculty development create unrest and "splits." Today, leaders of Institutes have many resources at their command. The problem is how to use them. New knowledge and revised formulations are being presented from all sides. This fact alone makes continuing education imperative for our theoretical and clinical faculties. Otherwise, we teach what we learned as students and by a process of identification, as Benedek described for the 1920s.

Our problem is less ideological than it used to be, but there is some persistence of territoriality and narcissistic possessiveness toward ideas, plus a few cultist tendencies. These tendencies have been present from the early years of psychoanalysis, as represented in Alfred Adler's battle cry of "organ inferiority," Carl Jung's "collective unconscious," Otto Rank's "birth trauma," and so forth. All of these ideas, which were meaningful as parts of a whole, became limited in scientific value when they were presented as being the whole of the new science. The history of psychoanalysis is full of the overinvestment of ideas with personal possessiveness, which constructs isolating boundaries and sets up barriers for learning and scientific advance because we cannot communicate with each other across these prejudicial barriers. We cannot see and often do not try to find the relationship that ties the part to the whole.

Change is inevitable, and we want to go forward, not backward. We know that new knowledge is not created by spontaneous generation. Also, it conserves the best that has gone before if we give ourselves time and opportunity to test it out. What better way to do that than to set up opportunities for learning about teaching and to work together as a whole faculty? Under the present system, there are teachers who do not know what the others teach or what the student needs to be taught in seminars so that good supervision can be used most effectively.

Faculty development is an imperative in psychoanalytic education. We must keep up with the new knowledge that is available. It is also possible to communicate with each other more objectively than in the days around 1952 when, once upon a time, training analysts gathered in Atlantic City to discuss countertransference. The door was locked and a guard stood outside. Those of us little folk, not yet wearing the mantle of a training analyst, were aghast at the sounds of strife from inside the room. What were they doing in there? What were they saying that could generate that noise and such sounds of anger? Many of us never found out, since few from inside talked and the papers read on the program were held back from publication for several years.

Our problem today is primarily an adminstrative one. How shall we set up and maintain on a local level an atmosphere of open-mindedness, tolerance for uncertainty, and a searching curiosity in our faculty, which can be passed on to our students? How can we organize a situation in which faculty can pay attention to learning the skills of such creative teaching? What kind of learning experiences can be provided that will facilitate such fundamental attitudes and increase our teachers' ability to develop similar attitudes in students? Perhaps I am making an euphemistic reference to leadership, but I think the kind of leadership I am referring to involves more than skill at practical logistics. I am talking about a complex mixture of long-range vision, plus something that activates the latent creativity inherent in the science of psychoanalysis and the treatment techniques and their teaching. The general public supports the idea that creativity is necessary for an artist. Most of us would agree that it is necessary for a leader, a teacher, and an analyst, too. The problem is how to build an atmosphere and reinforce the potentials for "creativity." Paul Pruyser's recent essay on creativity . . . (1979) gives analysts, especially, much to think about.

I began this sketchy presentation on a philosophical note with the metaphor of a relay team traveling an interminable course, looking forward and backward, as each analytic supervisor passes on his clinical knowledge in his attempt to develop future generations of analysts. Let me close on a continuing philosophical and metaphorical note by outlining the elements of a bridge between learning and analyzing, with some specific suggestions for integrating them in a workshop for supervisors.

Learning to travel on such a bridge will test our ability to put the experience of analyzing in a cognitive framework. I think we would all agree that to use the basic tools of an analyst (introspection, empathy, and interpretation; Kohut, 1959) requires a kind of sensitivity and creativity which belong to the world of illusion (Pruyser, 1979) and metaphor (Arlow, 1979), the transitional world of play (Winnicott, 1951), and the symbolic fictional world of artists in all media. This world itself, according to Paul Pruyser, is a third world, a bridge between the inner world of the senses and emotions subjectively experienced and the outer world of real or consensually validatable experience. The as-if quality of transference phenomena puts transference in this third world and on this transitional bridge. The degree of as-if awareness indicates a position on the bridge, closer to the inner world of illusion or the external world of "reality." The analytic process in an actively progressing analysis requires both analyst and patient to work with transitional experiences for reorganization and integration on a new level of insight and maturation. Learning to communicate in these three worlds is the task of a student-analyst, and teaching this special form of communication is the task of an analytic supervisor (Fleming, 1961 [see Chapter Three, this volume]; Fleming and Benedek, 1966).

In the book which Therese Benedek and I wrote about supervision, we concentrated on the phenomena of the supervisory interactions rather than on a theory of learning or teaching reflected in the supervisory teaching–learning situation. Retrospectively, we could see that we progressed in "working through" to a new level of conceptualization of both analytic technique and teaching methods. We "created as we learned and learned as we created" (Fleming and Benedek, 1966, p. 239). What I am now advocating is setting up workshops locally for the training of supervisors, which will teach them how to facilitate the creative aspects of analyzing and of teaching others. Some Institutes have such workshops. We should hear more about their experiences.

The adventures in leadership and in communication among the participants would make signal contributions to the future community of analysts and to our science. As analysts we work with operations of association and introspection all the time, but we are not always cognizant of that ego functioning or that process of observation. It usually happens silently and outside of sharp awareness. Introspection usually needs to be developed. I refer you to the example offered earlier about the supervisor who was asked how she arrived at the meaning of the patient's associations. To become cognizant of the process of integrating a patient's associations with, for example, a diagnostic interpretation of their transference meaning is on a different level of thinking. This is a large topic. Consequently, for further elaboration of that statement, I refer you to Waelder's first four levels of observation and interpretation that give meaning to analytic data (Waelder, 1962, p. 620).

Waelder's discussion of levels of organization and generalization of analytic data touches on the process of coding, conceptualizing, and building clinical observation into theory and, perhaps, after repeated consensual validations, into a "scientific law." Most of us do not go that far into theory making. We do, however, use psychoanalytic theory to integrate clinical observations, to explain their meaning, and to form interpretations that will expand our patients' and our own insight into behavioral phenomena.

These interpretations can be considered as hypotheses, which are then tested for appropriateness and congruity with a patient's understanding of himself and his adaptive use of that understanding. Interpretations may be expressed in symbolic metaphorical language, which is often subjected to a second stage of interpretation, just as dreams or fantasies are. In this progressively creative stage, the as-if illusory quality of transference objectively observed by the analyst is translated and analyzed into previously repressed or disavowed drive derivatives and object needs. Facilitation by the analyst of a transference neurosis, with its regressed ego state, represents effective technical work in making transferences or illusions of current reproductions of past experiences observable to the analyst in the present and eventually to the patient. The picture of the past being acted out in the present must be observable and interpretable before it can be worked through and reintegrated for change in behavior. The unconscious must first be made conscious before a developing ego can take the place of the more primitively organized id, or before developing structure becomes a more stable and adaptively individuated self-system.

In a recent review of *The Evolution of Psychoanalytic Technique*, edited by Martin S. Bergmann and Frank R. Hartman (1976), Merton Gill (1979, p. 507) expresses his view that "analytic technique has not advanced beyond Freud and that the absence of systematic research in our field is a major reason for the lack of resolution" of the controversy over the basic model of an analyst's activity. Bergmann and Hartman frame the alternative models as either a "purveyor of interpretation" or an interactor. I tend to agree with Gill, and I believe one reason for this condition is our failure as teachers of the next generations of analysts to provide our faculty with an opportunity to study clinical material from supervisory situations. Study of such material will lead into the world of illusion, fantasy, and hypothesis making, and will make observable the process of interpreting and conceptualizing of technique. An ongoing workshop for supervisors will necessarily examine the data of interactions between analyst and patient and between a supervisor and his student. Alternative interpretations and supervisory teaching methods will necessarily come under discussion. If the goal of that discussion can be kept on an objective (perhaps even a research) level, there could be data available for various concepts and for theories of technique that recorded sessions and videotapes do not provide because they omit the account of the processing of data that goes on in the mind of the analyst or the supervisor. A workshop situation would take the participants into the transitional world of goal-directed vicarious contact with the creative imagination of another person. The possibilities for practicing empathy, introspection, alternative interpretations, and assessment of impactful responsiveness, as well as diagnosis of structural change, are enormous. Once the supervisor has experienced this exercise, he can carry it over to the more traditional supervisory situation, with benefit to all concerned.

Before I stop, I want to call your attention to two events which are happening in other disciplines. Both events could serve as models of the kind of learning experience I am talking about. Their goals and methods make use of the processes that create illusion and metaphor, that lean on the as-ifs of make-believe and dream work, that contribute to a sense of mastery and adaptive self-confidence—all of which as analysts we experience and as supervisors we teach to others. The first event is an educational TV program called *Meeting of Minds*, written and produced by Steve Allen. Different well-known historical figures meet together in the current time and carry on discussions of questions and problems solved in different ways in their different historical periods. The audience gains a perspective on past experiences and their influence on the respective participants in the dialogue being acted out. Occasionally, a participant reacts to immediate stimuli and expresses an opinion obviously limited by his own culturally determined attitudes. The listener can make his own prejudices conscious (if he knows how), can create new interpretations and new knowledge, and can even arrive at new solutions of old problems by comparison and contrast as he empathizes with the historical figures. Listening to this TV program is a most instructive and organizing experience as the perennial struggles of mankind come alive and evolve over time. Learning psychoanalysis—one might say especially, teaching it—follows a similar pattern.

The second event was also an educational TV program, on the air over the Labor Day [1979] weekend. It was the demonstration of data collection and interpretation as far as was possible during the entrance of Pioneer II through the rings of Saturn. The program was well organized for background information, simulated models that visualized problems, and the results of the spacecraft's progress. But the most exciting part of the experience of watching and listening was the demonstration of hypothesis generating in an effort to explain data collected by instruments millions of miles in space and never before available. More illusory ideas had been formulated by astronomers before on the basis of available data. Those explanatory interpretations were now subjected to confirmation or revision. This was the work of mature minds playfully operating in a transitional world of illusion. This kind of work and play is what I think belongs in the education of an analyst. At various levels of observation and interaction, it makes up the process of catalyzing the development of the work ego, which is the goal of an analytic supervisor.

·9·

ON THE TEACHING AND LEARNING OF TERMINATION IN PSYCHOANALYSIS

(with Stanley S. Weiss)

This paper deals with the criteria for evaluating a terminated analysis, and with the learning objectives and learning experiences for a seminar on termination. Correlating and connecting termination with the data of the analytic experience are stressed.

Dr. Fleming believed that to describe, discuss, and formulate teaching goals and methods is an invaluable learning experience for a clinical teacher and should be done for all courses and conferences. This paper describes how it should be approached and accomplished for a class on termination.

Dr. Fleming also felt that advanced candidates should be encouraged to engage in research or write a thesis. This would aid candidates in synthesizing all that they have experienced. The task of reviewing the literature critically and systematically, and of placing and evaluating the candidate's own contribution in the context of what is already known, is an important learning experience. Psychoanalytic educators, Dr. Fleming believed, need to encourage and help candidates achieve this advanced level of professional development.

INTRODUCTION

The teaching and learning of termination in psychoanalysis are most important and complex tasks. Yet only rather recently have most Institutes given the study of the terminal phase of psychoanalysis the proper emphasis that it deserves in their curriculum planning and teaching.

Reprinted by permission from *The Annual of Psychoanalysis*, 8:37–55. New York: International Universities Press, 1980.

Early in the history of psychoanalytic education it was taught that the analysis "just dies of exhaustion" (Ferenczi, 1927, p. 85). It was also assumed by many psychoanalytic educators that anybody who could conduct a proper analysis could surely terminate one. In fact, many Institutes did not require a terminated case for graduation, and termination was not taught in specific courses or even given special attention in supervision. The American Psychoanalytic Association, however, was aware of the educational advantages of supervision during the termination phase of analysis and believed that an applicant for membership should demonstrate an ability to conduct at least one analysis to a reasonably successful termination. However, if the membership application was sufficiently strong in other areas, the requirement for a terminated case was often waived.

The uncertainty about the significance of the termination phase in psychoanalysis may be traced to Freud's 1937 paper, *Analysis Terminable and Interminable*. Freud stated that "I am not intending to assert that analysis is altogether an endless business. Whatever one's theoretical attitude to the question [of termination] may be, the termination of an analysis is, I think, a practical matter. Every experienced analyst will be able to recall a number of cases in which he has bidden his patients a permanent farewell *rebus bene gestis* [things having gone well]. In cases of what is known as character analysis, there is a far smaller discrepancy between theory and practice. Here it is not easy to foresee a natural end, even if one avoids any exaggerated expectations and sets the analysis no excessive tasks" (pp. 249–250). It was in this same paper that Freud also suggested that "every analyst should periodically—at intervals of five years or so—submit himself to analysis once more, without feeling ashamed of taking this step. This would mean, then, that not only the therapeutic analysis of patients but his own analysis would change from a terminable into an interminable task" (p. 249). Today, of course, training analyses last significantly longer than in the early years of psychoanalytic training, but, in spite of that fact, even now, many analysts follow Freud's advice and return for further analysis. The lifetime practice of analysis requires the analyst to have a very deep grasp and mastery of his own unconscious as well as a significant ability to do self-analysis.

However, by 1950, Buxbaum reported that termination is an

important phase of analysis: "It is like the finale in a musical movement which repeats the leading motives of the piece" (p.190).

Glover, in his textbook, *The Technique of Psychoanalysis* (1955), was the first to stress that "unless a terminal phase has been passed through, it is very doubtful whether any case has been psycho-analyzed" (p. 140). He stated, "in all cases . . . our first concern must be to apply a *technical criterion* for termination, viz. the limits of psychoanalytic influence" (p. 154). Glover went on to say, "If we believe that this limit has been reached, it is our duty to terminate the analysis as soon as possible." Glover apparently did not appreciate at that time the full importance of setting a termination date or the significance of working through in the terminal phase as much as Buxbaum did with her musical analogy.

In Glover's questionnaire on technique of psychoanalysis, originally published in 1940 and included in his 1955 textbook, which he sent to those members of the British Psycho-Analytical Society who were engaged in active psychoanalytic practice, he asked about criteria for termination (1955, p. 327). It is significant that one-third of the contributors failed to answer this question and a majority admitted that their criteria were essentially intuitive. A few emphasized that they always tested these intuitions as intelligently and thoroughly as they were able. However, these few analysts did not spell out how they assessed a readiness for termination and what criteria they used.

In 1966, Fleming and Benedek, in their book on psychoanalytic supervision, presented a rather new view when they stated, "When the student has terminated a patient's analysis with a good resolution of the transference neurosis, he will have had the opportunity to learn how to differentiate progression from regression and psychological growth from resistance. This learning experience is a maturing one for him as well as the patient. For these reasons, we look upon the termination phase as crucial for the student-analyst" (p. 193).

Rangell, in an address on termination at the Pan-American Congress for Psychoanalysis in 1964, highlighted the posttermination period. He believed that it, too, was important enough to be considered a phase which also required further study (p. 158).

During this time there was a focus of attention on assessment of analyzability, ego structure, intrapsychic change, and prediction of outcome. This focus required follow-up studies, which were pioneered by Pfeffer (1959, 1961, 1963) and confirmed and continued by Schlessinger and Robbins (1974), Oremland, Blacker, and Norman (1975), and Norman, Blacker, Oremland, and Barrett (1976). These studies involved patient, analyst, and external observer.

In 1978, the first textbook devoted entirely to termination in psychoanalysis appeared. The author, Firestein, reported the analyses of eight adults, four men and four women, conducted by candidates under supervision at the New York Psychoanalytic Treatment Center. Firestein reviewed the clinical records and interviewed the analysts, the supervisors, and the patients. He was interested primarily in a study of termination and outcome of analyses, and did not attempt an evaluation of the ego organization or the analytic process of the cases, and did not discuss the educational issues which we believe to be crucial. In our view it is most important for candidates to be able to link the criteria for analyzability, the criteria for termination, and evidence for structural changes to the clinical and observational data. This was not done by many of the candidates whose cases were reviewed by Firestein, nor, it appears, was it encouraged by their supervisors.

However, we believe that Firestein's research offers a fertile field for the investigation of many complex and important issues involved in psychoanalytic education, and especailly for an extension of a student's learning experience in the area of evaluating the results of analytic work.

As peer review, third-party payment, and continuing education for recertification and relicensure gain wider acceptance, it will be most important for analysts to be able to clearly document why analysis is indicated in contrast to other forms of therapy and to be able to describe clearly all phases of the analytic process, to record the evidence of intrapsychic changes, and to fully assess and evaluate the analytic experience.

In three previous papers we have discussed the importance of evaluation and assessment as an ongoing process in psychoanalytic education. In 1975 [see Chapter Six, this volume], we (Weiss and Fleming) discussed the criteria for assessing progress in supervision and the problems involved in making an educational diagnosis of the candidate's learning difficulties which manifested themselves at the point of evaluation. In 1978 [see Chapter Five, this volume], we (Fleming and Weiss) discussed the evaluation of the training analysis to determine a candidate's readiness to analyze a patient under supervision. We have also reviewed selection criteria and the teaching and learning of the process of assessment of the potential to become an analyst (Weiss and Fleming, 1979 [see Chapter Seven, this volume]). In this paper we will review the criteria for evaluating a terminated analysis and discuss the teaching objectives for a seminar on termination.

In a terminated analysis, we hope patients will have acquired insight with conviction leading to lasting personality changes; this implies, of course, much more than symptom relief. We wish our students to assess accurately if this has been done and to what degree, or, if it has not been accomplished, why not. Freud in 1937 emphasized that the conditions for failure of analysis should be studied more thoroughly. We fully agree with this and would add that the conditions for success should also be able to be clearly documented. The development of this skill should take place in a termination seminar.

In Section I of this paper we will highlight what we feel a candidate should have been taught during the theroretical phase of the tripartite educational program before he attends a course on termination. Successful curriculum planning and teaching during the theoretical phase of psychoanalytic education should lead to genuine mastery of psychoanalytic psychology and effective integration with clinical concepts and techniques.

In Section II we will review what we feel the candidate should be taught in a course on termination and how his diagnostic and interpretive skills have to be developed.

In Section III we will discuss criteria for determining that a termination phase has been reached and that the important date setting and working through to the final good-bye can now be successfully accomplished.

In Section IV we will emphasize that candidates in a termination seminar must gain experience in correlating and connecting termination criteria with the data of the analytic process. We will (1) present an advanced candidate's case summary of a successfully terminated case, and (2) show the process of assessing the candidate's report as it is judged by the teachers of the course.

Dewald (1973), after several years of studying the case reports submitted to the Membership Committee of the American Psychoanalytic Association, has stated that these write-ups are poorly

executed: "Those case reports which indicate a good working concept of the process of psychoanalysis are indeed a rarity" (p. 266).
This observation would indicate that the learning objectives of
writing and summarizing analytic cases have not been given the
proper attention they deserve by psychoanalytic faculties. We believe that this learning experience of summarizing a terminated
case is an excellent way to learn about the analytic process. Such a
report can be a useful instrument in assessing and evaluating
clinical competence and analytic scholarship.

I. WHAT SHOULD A CANDIDATE KNOW PRIOR TO A TERMINATION SEMINAR?

By the time a candidate is ready to proceed in his psychoanalytic
education to a seminar on termination, it seems logical to expect
that he should (1) possess a strong foundation in the basic concepts
of psychoanalytic psychology and the basic theory of psychoanalytic therapy (COPER, 1974, pp. 32–33); (2) understand, recognize, and be able to assess the process nature of the analytic
experience; and (3) have achieved a growing appreciation of evidence and criteria for sturctural changes derived from a well-
conducted analysis and be able to describe the intrapsychic reorganization in dynamic, economic, genetic, and adaptive terms.

From the very beginning of their training, candidates should
appreciate the essential relation between clinical and theoretical
thinking. The teaching and learning of analytic process should
begin in the first year of training with a course on analytic technique and a clinical conference. We are aware that certain Institutes do not have a clinical conference or a course on technique in
the first year. However, we believe it is important throughout
training to link theoretical concepts to clinical data, and this can
be done most effectively in clinical-conference teaching. Teachers
and supervisors need to integrate the "how to" approach, which is
technical, with the "why" approach, which is conceptual.

The teacher of the termination seminar can logically expect
that the candidate should have learned about the establishment of
the analytic situation, the development of the working alliance,
the evolving of the transference neurosis, and the process of interpretation. Learning about the process nature of the analytic expe-

rience is not easily conceptualized. To treat this topic adequately requires further elaboration, which would take us beyond the scope of this paper. However, we will refer to a few learning experiences that touch on this learning objective.

A first step in teaching about the analytic process can be accomplished by presenting to beginning candidates the long-term perspective of a successfully completed case. Such a perspective begins to lay the groundwork for an understanding of the process nature of the analytic experience. This perspective on process helps a candidate at the beginning of training to build an "analytic cognitive map" (Tyler, 1974, p. 91) and serves as a useful prerequisite for his advanced learning in a termination seminar. This learning continues and deepens with the first case and the first supervisor. It continues throughout the theoretical and clinical phases of the educational process as basic and advanced courses are mastered and clinical experience is acquired.

The beginning courses should include the theory of development in early years and throughout the life cycle. The candidate begins to master the important task of making a structural diagnosis and acquires an ability to know where his patient is on a developmental line. This leads into the important area of criteria for analyzability and an appreciation of the importance of ego structure, which are important prerequisites for a course on termination.

As training proceeds, the candidate begins to learn more about interpreting, regression in the analytic situation, appreciation of the transference neurosis, and signs that the patient is changing. The candidate should appreciate the patient's growing ability to associate, to listen to his associations, and to begin to make some interpretations himself; i.e., as the analysis proceeds, the candidate should recognize the development of the patient's self-analytic skill. As the analytic process moves forward—with less acting out, improved synthetic functioning, increased insight, and uncovering of more childhood memories with accompanying ego strengthening—the candidate should be able to document crucial changes in the patient's self representation, object relations, and reality testing.

The candidate must also be able to recognize by the time he reaches a termination seminar when an analytic process is not moving or when it has gone awry. Of course, chaotic situations are easily identified; but many stalemates are not so easily recognized, and the candidate has to know how to identify them and how to intervene. In a Panel (1969) on "Problems of Termination in the Analysis of Adults," Wiedeman noted that some patients tend to assume an analytic "way of life" (p. 229), in which they engage in what is regarded as psychoanalysis but which, in fact, represents only a replacement of the early dependency on the parents.

In summary, by the time a candidate enters a course on termination, he should have a fairly sophisticated understanding that the aim of analysis is the lasting insight that comes from the ongoing exploration of the patient's unconscious, and that significant changes and growth are essentially the result of the science and art of interpreting defenses, resistances, content, and transference. The integrative function that is facilitated in a properly conducted analysis gives the ego better command of id, superego, and outer reality.

II. GIVEN THE PREREQUISITE LEARNING, WHAT ADDITIONAL OBJECTIVES BELONG IN A COURSE ON TERMINATION?

In a well-taught seminar on termination, the candidate has the opportunity to integrate all that he has learned about the theory and practice of analysis in previous courses, in clinical conferences, in supervision, and in his own training analysis. Analytic educators are aware that although synthesis must be individually accomplished by each candidate, it can be assisted by good teaching efforts.

The learning objectives of a termination seminar include not only a review of what the candidate has already learned, but the advanced objectives of mastering the theory and technique of the termination process. At the beginning of a termination seminar, it is important for the teacher to present to the candidates the signs that a termination phase has been reached and the indications for recognizing structural change which has occurred as the result of the process of analysis. Throughout the course, the significant literature about termination also needs to be read and discussed.

It is also important at the beginning of a termination seminar to discuss with candidates the educational value of the task of reviewing and writing a case report of a completed analysis which has been conducted without the introduction of parameters or manipulations and has been successfully terminated.

Another important objective of the termination seminar is the actual experience of writing and presenting a case report that is evaluated by colleagues and teachers for evidence of structural change, the ongoing process of the analysis, and the progress and learning of the candidate. In addition to a termination report, the candidate should also be given the opportunity to write up a completed case summary in about four or five pages. The candidate needs to learn how to condense significant analytic events and how to document the process of change during the beginning, middle, and end phases of the analysis. In the termination summary, the candidate must map the entire course of the analysis in language both cognitive and experiential, and be able to trace the beginning, development, and resolution of the transference neurosis. The summary should demonstrate the inner dynamics of the patient and the bringing to light of their origins. The report should also show the development of the candidate as he brings his growing knowledge, capacity for empathy, understanding, self-awareness, and self-analysis to the analytic situation.

The analytic termination of the patient should be the result of effective analysis and effective working through. The issue of termination should, of course, have been the subject of analytic work, and the decision to terminate should have been mutually agreeable to both patient and analyst. Countertransference problems and resolution, and details as to what the candidate learned from supervision and the analytic experience should be reported. The termination summary should include the candidate's assessment of the effectiveness of the analytic work, and follow-up data, if available, should, of course, be noted.

Initially, many candidates are somewhat anxious and awed by this assignment of having to condense an analysis that took place over many years and to describe its uniqueness, subtleties, and movement from initial interview through termination in a relatively few pages. However, the candidate should have achieved some experience in this important skill before reaching a termination seminar, through having written six-month and yearly summaries of his cases and having had them evaluated and discussed by his supervisors.

III. WHAT ARE THE CRITERIA THAT A TERMINATION HAS BEEN REACHED?

As we have noted, the learning about criteria that a termination phase has been reached and the manner in which it should be conducted are the special objectives of this advanced seminar. The movement of a properly conducted analysis leads to more conflict-free functioning, to autonomous functioning with more self-reliance and self-confidence, to secondary-process thinking with improved reality testing and improved sublimations, to an individuated sense of self and objects with improved object relations, and to a growing appreciation of the difference between analyst as analyst and analyst as transference imago.

If the analytic process has shown this progressive development over time and the working through of the middle phase has proceeded well, there comes a time in the analysis when the patient himself begins to recognize these changes and movements. The patient can now observe and comment on his improved ego functioning, especially his defenses and impulses. Insight has replaced acting out. The patient's unconscious has become more conscious, accessible, and controllable. During this time, the patient's associations deal more with present and future and less with past, and the patient usually begins to associate about wishes to complete the analysis, to separate from the analyst, and to go on to new experiences on his own. These associations about character changes, future plans, separations, etc., initiate the end phase of the analysis (Fleming and Benedek, 1966). The duration of the onset of termination varies, and the analyst is usually aware of the changes long before the patient is. The transforming of insight from an intellectual into a total experience takes time and is one of the essential parts of "working through" (Kris, 1956b, p. 337). The analyst, at this time, might begin to have a different feeling about the patient, i.e., a feeling of more equality (Weigert, 1952).

Evidence of this change or growth can be missed or not given proper attention by patient and/or analyst, since resistances regarding final separation may now come into play. However, if countertransference problems are not present in the analyst, and understanding and interpretation continue, both patient and analyst will soon be aware of important changes in the patient's total integrated psychic functioning.

When termination is approaching and when the termination phase is under way, "good analytic hours" become more frequent. They lead to new insights, new connections, new memories; the integrative function and the self-analytic function of the patient's ego are observable by both patient and analyst; and both are aware of the relation of these changes to the analytic material (Kris, 1956a).

The candidate, of course, has to know if associations about change and termination represent a true beginning of the end stage of analysis or a resistance against further significant analytic work and a wish for premature closure. In this vein, Kris (1956a) speaks of a need to differentiate the "good analytic hour" from the "deceptively good hour" which is due to resistance. Freud (1923), in discussing the theory and practice of dream interpretation, mentioned that associations "converge" when the analytic work is going well (p. 110). When the pressure of resistance is high, associations broaden instead of deepen, and, of course, at a time of high resistance the patient is not ready for termination.

If the analytic process reveals that structural changes in ego, superego, and drive organization do not parallel the patient's report of his improved external life, or if the analyst's observations indicate structural changes without corresponding improvement in the patient's real life, there is doubt that termination is really at hand. Greenson (1964, p. 265) has also noted that if talk of termination takes either the analyst or the patient by surprise, something is amiss.

By the time the termination phase is reached, the transference neurosis should be resolving and diminishing, the infantile amnesia should have been lifted, and the Oedipus uncovered, reworked, and resolved. Good analytic work should have prepared the patient for the final synthesis that will take place during termination (Nunberg, 1931).

In the end phase of the analysis, a specific time is set for termination, and the working through of the final separation takes place. Painful feelings of separation, estrangement, and mourning are usually part of the final work. Narcissistic rage, perfectionistic expectations, and infantile wishes might, once again, reappear and be reworked and mastered. In a panel on termination, Kanzer (Panel, 1974, p. 173) noted that besides anxiety, anger, and depression, there is also relief, joy, and hunger for new experiences for which time, money, and psychological preparedness are now available. In a good termination, separation from the analyst can be differentiated by the patient from a sense of being deprived or rejected. It is hoped that any analytic patient will have achieved enough insight and security to recognize a need for further analysis if it should arise and to be able to seek it.

IV. HOW CAN THE ACHIEVEMENT OF THE LEARNING OBJECTIVES ON TERMINATION BE EVALUATED?

The exercise of condensing significant analytic events and writing a summary of a completed case is a most important learning experience for candidates. It is from such a summary that an experienced analytic clinician and educator can assess a candidate's development as an analyst and his readiness to graduate. In our experience, the writing of such a summary as an assigned task in a termination seminar offers a view of the candidate's comprehension of the analytic process.

We will now present a case report written by an advanced candidate in a termination seminar, followed by the thinking of the teacher as he assesses the candidate's write-up and clinical data.

The learning–teaching material which we are presenting has been disguised and altered somewhat to protect and insure the confidentiality of the patient, candidate, and supervisor. The first-person pronoun in the following report refers to the candidate.

Termination Report—Mr. A. F.

Length of analysis—four years, nine months.

Frequency of analysis—five times a week.

Frequency of supervision—once a week for two years; once every two weeks for two years; once a month for six months; once a week for final three months.

The patient, a 29-year-old married high school teacher, had three evaluation sessions before starting on the couch.

The patient appeared friendly and pleasant-looking and was

dressed in a casual, sporty manner. He was neat and well-groomed and looked several years younger than his stated age. He related in an open, relaxed, and comfortable manner during the evaluation. This was in contrast to the start of the analytic work on the couch, when anxiety was evident in the rapid rush of associations.

In the first sitting-up session, the patient described regressive behavior at home and stated clearly and somewhat firmly that he wished and needed analysis because of "turmoil in the marriage" which he did not understand and could not control and many severe arguments with his wife over the question of having or not having children.

The patient's wife wanted to raise a family, and she believed the patient's wish to wait for "just the right time" was an emotional problem for her husband and that if he did not receive analytic help the right time would never appear. The patient stated that he knew his wife was right about his "fear of becoming a father," but only recently could he admit this to her and also actively seek analysis. However, in the first session he told me that not until his wife seriously threatened divorce did the patient call the analytic clinic for an appointment.

During the evaluation, I became impressed with this man's honesty, his ability to introspect, and his psychological-mindedness. This initial impression about his ego functions which pointed toward analyzability was confirmed during the beginning phase of the analysis. I thought it was an especially good sign for analyzability that he was so curious about his inner life and anxieties, and so unhappy and concerned about his regressive functioning in the marriage.

I did wonder about the meaning of his not applying for analysis until the wife threatened divorce, and I thought, is my impression about healthy motivation for analysis wrong? Might he be seeking analysis to placate his angry wife because of the threat of object loss? However, my overall impression was that this was not a passive, infantile man, and I thought that the marriage was basically solid and that both he and his wife understood that some "emotional block" (his term) was holding him back from continuing to grow. In fact, he seemed to be one of those sophisticated patients who even initially has some awareness that with insight he could change and improve his life and functioning. I was not surprised to learn that he had always been interested in psychology, had been a good student, and had even read some Freud in college.

The following history was obtained during the evaluation sessions and in the beginning phase of the analysis.

The patient was born and raised in a large Eastern city and moved West "to get away from the family and from all old friends." He wanted to make a new start in life in a part of the country where no one knew him.

The patient's father, an accountant, died suddenly of a coronary when the patient was 16 years of age. The patient had always been very close to his mother, "especially around tax time" when the father spent many extra hours at the office. On the way home from work during the busy time of the year, the father "suddenly fell over and died immediately."

After the father's death, a change took place in the closeness between mother and son. The patient began to withdraw more and more from his mother and from the home. He began to get very busy in school, indulged in sports and in many other extracurricular activities, but also continued to do well in classes. He was eager to go to college and insisted that the college be quite a distance from home. He began dating a girl in his high school class, and soon after graduation they married. His wife had a Catholic background but did not consider herself religious and did not attend church regularly. The patient came from a nonreligious Jewish family. Both families knew each other. In fact, the patient's father thought the patient's future wife was "extremely pretty and very bright." Two and one-half years after the father's death, the patient married.

Prior to the marriage, the patient experienced no sexual problems. However, once married, the turmoil began, and the patient also developed episodes of premature ejaculation and marked anxiety when he contemplated approaching his wife sexually. The arguments over raising a family also soon began.

My supervisor agreed with my diagnostic impression that the patient suffered from an anxiety neurosis tied to unresolved Oedipal issues. The healthy resolution of the Oedipus was interfered with by the sudden death of the father when the patient was 16 years of age. It seems that following the father's death the patient's Oedipal conflict intensified. He attempted to solve the problem by turning away from the mother to a non-Jewish girl friend who must have represented the yearned-for and feared incestuous object. I speculated that he also handled his traumatic object loss by identifying with the busy and hard-working father who had suddenly died. I also thought that he was feeling guilty for what he unconsciously perceived was an Oedipal victory which had been reinforced by the actual death of the father. His wish to leave home and start a new life elsewhere sounded like he felt himself to be a criminal who wanted to move where people would not know of his crime. The child he feared having could be the Oedipal baby who he felt would kill him and with whom he was also unconsciously identified.

The patient appeared to be analyzable, and my supervisor and I thought he surely deserved a trial of analysis.

Once he was on the couch, I gave him the basic rule about free association. He talked rapidly, seemed anxious, and stated that he "didn't expect to miss any sessions, never gets sick, never misses time at work, and plans to live for a long, long time." The initial associations about his excellent health sounded to me like a need to reassure himself, and I felt that he must need to defend against a fear of death. As the analysis progressed, this conjecture proved to be true. I had been taught in class about the importance of the initial associations, and that seemed to be clearly borne out in this case.

The patient focused early in the analysis on his father's death, and he was surprised that he had never really been overtly upset. The family had also commented on this. He was busy, working hard in school, soon dating and making plans for the future. He had thought that possibly he just had no time to indulge in mourning. It seemed to me that he had repressed all depressive affects at the time of the loss, and my supervisor suspected that at some time in the analysis this patient was going to experience much pain. He had obviously warded off the depression with activity.

Early in the analysis he joked often about "enjoying analysis" since he could "rest for an hour each day," and "I am in no rush to ever finish." He associated that my office "looked and felt" somewhat like his father's office and he had always enjoyed going regularly to visit his father. It became clear that in the transference I was becoming the replacement for the lost father and he did not wish to ever have to relinquish me.

Following the first summer vacation, he said that he missed

me and that he had experienced "some pain in the chest." He felt, at times, like he was going to faint but didn't want to worry his wife and didn't tell her about the frightening and painful symptoms. He also thought of trying to get in touch with me but rapidly rejected this thought. Instead, he went to his doctor for a checkup and to get some medication. The physical proved to be completely normal, and he wasn't given any medication, to his "disappointment and relief." I understood this important episode as an identification with his sick father, triggered by the anxiety, rage, and depression at our vacation interruption.

I interpreted to him his identification with his father. He confirmed this by bringing up new material: that his mother would get angry at his father since the father had the need to hide his symptoms and doctor's appointments from her, and she would become angry and hurt when she learned later about his symptoms. He could see that during the vacation break he had tried to hide his symptoms from me and could say, "I must have treated you like my father treated my mother." New material was brought forth. The father had angina for a "year or so" before his massive coronary, and he took "medication for the pain."

The patient "confessed" with embarrassment that he did worry "at times" that he would die at an early age like his father. I was able to connect for him, at this point, that his initial associations about never being sick and living for a long time were a defense against this fear of an early death. He was surprised and obviously pleased that I had remembered his first associations and stated that maybe he was not "fated and programmed" to die at the same time his father did. Actually, the physician had said that the patient was in very good health.

The summer vacation had brought out in bold relief his identification with his ill father and his fear of an early death. I wondered to myself how the termination work would eventually proceed, since his first long interruption had been so intense, yet so fruitful for the analysis.

After another vacation, he spoke of developing anxiety in the classroom as his students returned. He was upset when a fellow teacher commented that all these youngsters would be running the world before long. The teacher pessimistically stated that they probably would not do any better than their parents. He told his colleague that the new generation would surely be smarter,

kinder, and less angry and destructive than the present generation. He made an interesting slip. He meant to say children help
man to become "immortal." Instead, he said children help man
become "impotent."

The analytic work on this slip led to my being able to show
him that he became anxious at what the teacher said because it
triggered a fantasy that these students want to kill the parents. I
interpreted to him that he was frightened of parenthood because
he feared his child would kill him, and he magically attempted
to stay alive and avoid father's fate by not having children.

He responded to this interpretation in an interesting way. He
ignored the interpretation, which I understood as his wish to
destroy my interpretation. He also became anxious and associated
that I was planning to raise his fee since he had just bought a used
sports car and had not discussed it with me.

The "confession" about buying the sports car also brought up
some other associations that he had not brought into the analysis
because "they seemed too unimportant." These "unimportant
thoughts" were verbalized when I asked him if he had ignored any
other thoughts, such as the one about the sports car. He stated that
he had wondered about my house and my car, and had attempted
to figure out my income. He wondered how many hours a day I
work and how much each patient pays me. He said these associations "*usually* did not appear during the analytic sessions but at
other times." He also said that he spent one recent Sunday morning riding around my neighborhood attempting to view my house.

My supervisor was very helpful in discussing with me transference acting out, since I became anxious when I learned that the
patient was driving over to see my house. I had anxiously wondered how far the patient would act out instead of initially correctly evaluating this opportunity to impart insight with conviction through interpretation. I was able to identify my anxiety as
being tied to a fear of closeness that I had successfully worked out
in my own analysis. I enjoyed working with this patient, liked him,
and became anxious when the transference acting out began.

The patient, however, began to feel that I somehow did not
like him and wanted to get rid of him for a higher-paying patient.
He thought I must resent clinic patients.

Following analytic work on the "unimportant" associations
and the acting out, I was able to interpret to him that he thought I

should get rid of him since he wished to get rid of me and take over my home, wife, and children. I pointed out that he was the child who wanted to make the parent "impotent" instead of "immortal."

He laughed nervously and made an important genetic connection himself. "*Maybe* that's why I wanted to leave home after my father's death. I must have been very frightened and pushed by my guilt." I agreed with his interpretation and asked him about the *maybe*. He said that the impulse was so frightening that "I wanted to give myself an out but I know it's true. I knew my wife was right that I was frightened of becoming a father but I could not admit that to her for a long time. It was like admitting that I killed my father and that our child would kill me."

Well into the working through of the middle phase the patient reported that while having intercourse with his wife he thought, "I must be a better lover than my analyst." This thought caused much guilt and shame and led to recall of an adolescent fantasy in which an older woman appreciated him much more than her sick husband and both he and the woman forced the man to leave. This theme of being loved by the older woman and together sending the sickly husband away was the theme of his masturbation fantasies of adolescence. He associated his father to Van Gogh's picture of a depressed old man which had touched him deeply since he first saw it in a book when he was five years of age.

I was able to effectively connect the guilt over his masturbation fantasy with his premature ejaculation and marital problems. He also mentioned a family story from childhood that at age six he once told his father "in a very grown-up and cute way" that his father should not come home from the office since he was capable of taking care of his mother. As working through took place, I learned that his wife and mother had the same birth date. "Hadn't I told you that before? I thought I had." It turned out that both wife and mother were very similar women—bright, strong, maternal women—and I was able to show him that in the unconscious his wife and mother were felt to be the same. I interpreted to him that his fear of my retaliating had interfered with his telling me this important piece of data that linked wife and mother. He obviously viewed me not only as the depressed and weak father but as the angry and revengeful father.

Several years into the analysis he had a dream in which I appeared as a Nazi hunting out Jews to kill. The day residue was a newspaper story in which a fight broke out between two men following a traffic accident and one man killed the other.

This led to associations about the Holocaust and that my name sounded German. He felt horror and yet some "strange fascination" with that period of history. He had always been frightened of crowds and felt that aggression could suddenly erupt, inflicting death and suffering.

Following analytic work on this dream, I interpreted that he had felt he was responsible for the death of his father like the Nazis in the dream. In the dream, he had projected his own Nazi feelings onto me. He reported that at one time in the past he had a "peculiar thought" that the Nazis had killed his father, even though the family had had no direct contact with the Holocaust. He associated that he had been very interested in the story of SS Colonel Adolf Eichmann's capture by the Israelis, and he could never understand some feeling of compassion that he had for Eichmann. He now understood that he had made some "weird" kind of identification with Eichmann.

In an hour following an extra-analytic contact in the elevator, the patient associated to how surprised he was to notice that we were about the same size. His father was quite tall and he had always felt that I was taller than he was. I felt that this was a good example of the power of transference. He had always felt like a young boy in an adult's body and was not sure of the exact height or age of this young boy self-image. Much work was done on this interesting phenomenon, which seemed to have become more conscious since his father's death. At this particular point in the analysis, he bought a new watch and started wearing it regularly instead of the inexpensive watches that he "could afford to lose or break." His sense of time seemed to have taken on a more realistic view. I remembered from my reading on patients with "parent loss" that they have problems with time and seem to be "stuck" at the point of the loss. This was confirmed in this patient, and it was an important step for him when time was viewed more realistically.

The patient had improved in his sexual life. His self-object representations were more realistic. He had gained insight into his Oedipus. His life experiences had taken on new meaning and integration. He was for the first time very interested in his family history and also in his wife's history. Thoughts of termination began to cross my mind but had not yet been verbalized by the patient.

One day he came into the office elated. He thought his wife was pregnant and he was very pleased. He now knew that he had solved the riddle of why he had been so scared of having children, since a few years back he would have been "anxious and agitated" at the thought of becoming a father. His wife became pregnant four and one-half years after the analysis began. For the first time he spoke of terminating "before very long." Since I had also been thinking of termination, his associations had not surprised me, but I wondered if the talk of termination was tied in some way to the pregnancy and was possibly a resistance to further work.

Initially, I did not pursue the topic, and he dropped it for another three weeks. Then he brought it up again with humor, "Since I am becoming a real father in the real world, I should give up the luxury and pleasure of being a child five times a week."

He stated that he could now really accept the fact that his father was dead, and that the cause of death was heart disease, not a result of his son's wish to murder his father and take over his mother. The associations and the movement of the analytic process did not point to resistance, and several months after his wife had become pregnant we set a definite termination date.

Once the exact date was set, which was to be in four months, the patient became very tense and anxious, cried, and wondered if he could go on alone. The intensity of his affect surprised me, even though I knew from my reading that such phenomena could occur. My supervisor reminded me that we had discussed in the beginning that termination would be quite painful for this man. With the help of supervision, I was meaningfully able to tie this quite intense and vivid mourning reaction to the death of his father at age 16 when the patient could not experience any overt grief.

The patient could understand what was happening but also wanted me to know that at least some of the tears were meant for his sense of loss in the present. He went on to say that this analysis had been so helpful and that he would always remain very grateful.

Many of his associations dealt with future plans and with wishes to give his child the security of good parents and a loving home. I told him that I enjoyed our work together. I received a card following the birth of his daughter, thanking me again for my help. I sent a note congratulating him.

I believe he learned about himself and profited from the analysis. I, too, gained from the analytic work and the supervision.

Teachers' Assessment of This Report

The assignment of good analytic cases by psychoanalytic educators is an important task, and we feel this was successfully accomplished here. The candidate had a good case from which to learn the art and science of analysis.

The report is well written, and there is evidence throughout the report that the candidate was familiar with many important analytic concepts and that he has learned from previous cases and seminars. What is very positive in this report is that the candidate communicates his experience with patient and with supervisor. This was the candidate's third supervised case, and the candidate has shown that he can learn from supervision and use it well (pp. 182, 185). Obviously, a good supervisory alliance had been present. In our experience it is rare for the average candidate to bring into the write-up and presentation of a case report the experience of supervisory learning. There is a tendency in psychoanalytic education for candidates to isolate aspects of the tripartite educational experience. This was not the case with this candidate.

The candidate appears to have an appreciation and understanding of analyzability, as judged by his early assessment of the patient's ego functions and his motivation for change (p. 178). He showed throughout the report that he can interpret content, resistance, and transference, and that he understands the importance of connecting analytic data. The candidate also made conjectures about the psychoanalytic data, conjectures that would be confirmed or discarded at a later time (pp. 179, 181). In a poor report we usually do not see evidence of retrospective evaluation by the candidate.

We were impressed with the candidate's sensitivity to transference (p. 184) and his ability to identify the early manifestations of the transference (p. 180). The candidate has an appreciation of the developmental point of view in his understanding of the importance of the trauma of the father's death on concretizing unconscious fantasy and wishes and giving the transference a strong stamp of reality (p. 179). The report also demonstrates that the candidate appreciated the importance of the unresolved Oedipus complex in the formation of the patient's neurosis and a need to recover and rework this important constellation.

However, in this report practically nothing is reported from the infantile period, except for a significant memory about Van Gogh's "old man" from age five and a family story about the patient at age six (p. 183). The focus of the analysis, as reported, appeared to be mainly adolescence, the death of his father when the patient was 16 years of age, his marriage soon after, his reaction to death, and present difficulties. In the termination seminar this significant omission would be checked to see whether the infantile neurosis was not explored, recovered, or reconstructed adequately, or just does not appear in the write-up. In writing a report on the course of the analysis, analytic material from the infantile period is very relevant to evaluation of the analysis as well as to the analytic skill of the analyst. In this report, since there is no mention of siblings, it has to be assumed that the patient is an only child.

There is evidence in the report of the candidate's ability to use self-analysis successfully, which points toward a positive personal analytic experience for the candidate (p. 182). The candidate also briefly alludes to relevant literature (p. 184). Connecting the patient's material and analysis to appropriate literature is one sign of a good candidate. In our experience it is rather rare for a candidate to note the significant literature in a completed case write-up or presentation.

The patient through the analysis gained insight with conviction and made significant changes (p. 184). In this report, the candidate does not classify the changes brought about by the analysis specifically as structural changes, and we would discuss this omission in the termination seminar. However, the candidate did seem to recognize that a more realistic appreciation of time, a more realistic view of self and object representations, and the gaining of insight are evidences of important structural changes.

The candidate has learned that during termination old defenses may come back into play, such as regression and repetition of old patterns (p. 185). He also correctly wondered if the initial associations to termination were due to resistance (p. 185), and he did not set a definite date for stopping until he was sure that termination was an adaptive step toward growth and development and not a resistance against further analytic work (p. 185).

We believe that this candidate has shown a good appreciation of the analytic situation and the analytic process, and has a good grasp of the theory and technique of analysis for someone at his level of training, in spite of some partial negatives and omissions in the write-up. His sensitivity to the unconscious and his interpretive skill are developing well, and we would consider him from this report a candidate with high aptitude and potential.

CONCLUSION

We have discussed in the introduction how, in the early period of psychoanalytic theory and practice, the concept of termination as providing evidence of intrapsychic reorganization was much less in the foreground of analytic study than was the focus on the practical ending of the formal analytic work. Later, as structural and developmental theory became more sharply formulated and integrated with the theory of therapy, the significance of a terminal phase came into better focus (Hurn, 1971), and the importance of studying termination in supervision and in the classroom became more evident. We would like to emphasize that termination is much more than a study of the formal ending of the analytic situation, since the analytic process is an ongoing and even endless task, as Freud already noted in 1937. Today, termination encompasses a cross-section of the theory of development and takes in the full sweep of our present knowledge of psychoanalytic theory.

At the present time many psychoanalytic educators have begun to concentrate on a study of analyzability, analytic process, and outcome of analysis, involving assessment of structural development as well as evidence for structural change produced by the analytic experience. The concept of structural change as an outcome of psychoanalytic process has become an essential element in every phase of the tripartite educational program, including the training analysis. In this paper we have focused on the learning objectives and the learning experiences offered by a course on termination dealing with this essential concept.

EPILOGUE

Dr. Fleming's views on how best to teach and learn psychoanalysis are clearly expressed in her writings. However, in this closing chapter, I wish to present Dr. Fleming's position about certain important issues of psychoanalytic education that do not appear or are not sufficiently emphasized in the selected papers.

There is much that psychoanalytic educators agree upon, and much of this agreement we owe to the creative and pioneering work of Dr. Fleming. However, within the common framework of the 26 Institutes accredited by the Board on Professional Standards of the American Psychoanalytic Association, there also exists a broad spectrum of different educational philosophies, policies, and procedures. The dialogue about some of these differences produces an ongoing ferment and active debate, both locally and nationally. I believe it is of interest at this critical time in the history of psychoanalysis to review Dr. Fleming's thoughts on these matters.

Most educational organizations throughout the United States are actively involved in self-scrutiny with the aim of raising educational standards. The 1983 report of the National Commission on Excellence in Education, *A Nation at Risk*, called for action to reverse "a rising tide of mediocrity" (p. 5). However, psychoanalytic standards have remained high as a result of the deep commitment and energy the Board on Professional Standards has devoted over the years to setting and monitoring of standards. Despite high standards, Dr. Fleming and many other psychoanalytic educators have never ceased to worry about an increase in conformity in candidates and graduates and a decrease in originality, creativity, and scholarship. Also, many psychoanalytic educators are concerned about how successful Institutes will be in continuing to attract talented candidates at a time when enrollment in psychiatric residencies is decreasing and when psychoanalysis as a science and a profession is in a phase of diminished status.

189

Psychoanalytic education evolved from master–apprentice teaching and learning into the present tripartite system of psychoanalytic education comprising the training analysis, course work, and supervision. This framework for teaching and learning psychoanalysis has been evolving in American Institutes for over 50 years. Dr. Fleming believed, as do most psychoanalytic educators, that it still offers the very best setting for educating psychoanalysts. The goal of all Institutes is the same—to train and educate students to become excellent clinicians and scholarly analysts who can use the psychoanalytic situation and method for both therapy and investigation.

Over the years, psychoanalytic education has not remained static, and constructive changes in understanding and improving the educational process have gradually occurred. Today much less emphasis is placed on numerical requirements, and much greater focus is on the goals and quality of the educational experience. Psychoanalytic educators aim for more integration and synchrony of all aspects of the educational program. The principle of continuing assessment of all three phases of the educational experience is strongly endorsed. There is much more involvement of the candidate in the educational process, with greater emphasis on mutually determined decisions. Also, there is more attention to the individualization of the curriculum and the fostering of increasing independent activity as the candidate progresses through the educational process. Dr. Fleming played an important role in bringing about these changes, and she felt very positively about all of them. Dr. Fleming viewed psychoanalytic education as a developmental process that would continue to evolve.

At the present time, there are strong conflicting forces both inside and outside organized psychoanalysis, wishing to draw the Association and Institutes in what appears to be two different directions. On the one hand, there are strong and clear forces wishing psychoanalysis to move toward a greater involvement with psychiatry and medicine. Other forces wish to enlarge the applicant pool to include talented nonmedical candidates, and also to share our expertise and knowledge about psychoanalytic education with others. There are today many groups eager to participate in the science that Freud developed, and some of these new training centers would appreciate help from members of the American Psychoanalytic Association. Dr. Fleming was very interested in these phenomena; she hoped that the current state of flux would not lead to disruption, but would fuel creative solutions so that psychoanalysis would continue to advance.

Most psychoanalytic educators believe, as did Dr. Fleming, that medical–psychiatric training offers the best route for psychoanalytic education. However, Dr. Fleming thought that other paths should also be acceptable, and she hoped that the American Psychoanalytic Association would soon find a way to admit and educate highly qualified nonmedical applicants who possess the prerequisites and potential to become excellent psychoanalysts. The American Psychoanalytic Association has been studying this issue for many years, but at present still has not been able to resolve the question of training nonmedical candidates. This impasse persists, despite the fact that nonmedical research candidates continue to be successfully educated after having been carefully reviewed and granted a waiver to do clinical work by the Committee on Research and Special Training. Also, many Institutes have partial training programs for nonmedical colleagues who have achieved a high level of attainment in their own field and seek to enhance their work through psychoanalytic study but do not plan to practice psychoanalysis. Some Institutes have educational programs teaching analytically oriented psychotherapy for nonmedical candidates, and some of these programs deal with much that is taught in the psychoanalytic programs. At present the debate continues, and a definitive decision has still to be made. It appears, however, that the thinking has begun to turn in the general direction of Dr. Fleming's belief.[1]

Many psychoanalysts fear that their own medical identity, as well as the identity of the American Psychoanalytic Association, would be compromised or lost if the applicant pool were widened to include nonmedical applicants. Dr. Fleming had empathy for this point of view; however, she herself was not as concerned about the issue of medical identity, since her physician and psychiatric identities had been integrated into a firm and comfortable psychoanalytic identity. Dr. Fleming agreed with those psychoanalysts who consider psychoanalysis to be a separate scientific discipline and not a specialized branch of medicine and psychiatry.

1. At the 1985 midwinter meetings of the American Psychoanalytic Association, the Gaskill Proposal, which recommended full clinical training for carefully selected nonmedical candidates, was reaffirmed by both the Board on Professional Standards and the Executive Council, and it was decided to submit the proposal to the active membership for a vote. A

Another area of controversy within psychoanalytic education is the question of reporting or not reporting by the training analyst. This issue, too, has been going on for a long time; Dr. Fleming felt it had become, over the years, a spurious one. In Dr. Fleming's opinion, it is not reporting or the absence of reporting that is most significant. Instead, she believed that evaluation and assessment by the training analyst of the candidate's training experience within the analytic situation is most critical. Dr. Fleming was always pleased when she noted resistance to "reporting" being replaced by an interest in "evaluation," which she believed to be the principal educational issue.

Psychoanalytic educators believe that a successful training analysis is crucial for the candidate to conduct analyses at maximum capacity, but controversy exists as to how best to accomplish this, and also as to how best to assess progress and outcome. Periodic assessment of the analytic process is an important part of any analysis, but Dr. Fleming felt it takes on even more importance in those analysands who will be doing analytic work with patients. She stressed that the common goals and identifications of training analyst and candidate should become a meaningful part of the analytic work. Dr. Fleming believed that the candidate's motivation and the analysis of its transference roots can lead to a successful resolution of old conflicts and a new integration of development toward autonomy. In the later phase of training analysis, career choices and colleagueship must be differentiated from infantile transference resistances.

A majority of psychoanalytic educators take the position that the training analyst should have no role in decisions regarding the candidate and should not report an evaluation of analyzability or analytic progress, and possibly not even note whether the analysis is terminated or interrupted. Although these psychoanalytic educators may still value the principle of integrating the total educational experience into a goal-directed whole, they believe that the training analysis should be separated from the educational program. Reporting by the training analyst, they feel, mobilizes complex transference–countertransference problems that interfere with analytic progress and success.

---

significant majority voted in favor of the Gaskill Proposal and a newly established national waiver committee is being formed to implement the training of applicants from fields other than medicine.

The minority of educators believe that the training analyst should be involved in his candidate's progression and should have the option, *if desired*, to report about the progress of the analysis. Dr. Fleming belonged to this group and felt that absolute rules about reporting or not reporting should be avoided. She thought that the training analyst possesses unique knowledge about the candidate that can be helpful to his analytic education. Dr. Fleming also believed that the tranference–countertransference problems and resistances, especially those involving trust and confidentiality, can be successfully resolved, and that analytic work on these issues may even facilitate the analysis. In addition, Dr. Fleming believed that data from the successes and failures of training analyses would be most valuable for providing knowledge that could enhance general analytic theory. However, Dr. Fleming did feel that much work still needs to be done on how to communicate about analyses without violating basic principles of trust and confidentiality. Psychoanalytic educators are interested in the growth and development of ego functions necessary for understanding and applying the analytic method. In Dr. Fleming's opinion, this information is not in the real sense of the word "confidential," and that any student who does not wish his teacher to have this information is probably not ready to be a candidate-analyst. It was Dr. Fleming's belief that neither analysis nor education will be optimal if we cannot assume that the candidate is aiming for the same goal as his analytic educators; she also felt that we are in an untenable and deteriorating educational and analytic position if we cannot assume that the candidate trusts his analyst and that the training analyst is trustworthy.

Dr. Fleming hoped that analytic data would be gathered, that views would be exchanged, and that research would be done on the positions of the two camps. She was disappointed that thus far very little research has been done to resolve this controversy and also to study with candor both the process and the products of the training analysis. The debate continues.

In Dr. Fleming's judgment, training analysts analyzing candidates and candidates analyzing patients under supervision need to learn how to identify, interpret, and work through resistances and transferences complicated by the Institute structure and environment, so that a deep and positive analytic experience can take place. Dr. Fleming believed there is much evidence that this can be done, and that good analytic work continues to be accomplished in the training situation, despite all the hazards. The need for faculty development was always stressed by Dr. Fleming, and she hoped that all Institutes would offer a forum for training analysts to engage in continuous study and self-examination. It was her observation that the training analysis at times does not move past magical incorporative problems that appear as a manifestation of the transference neurosis, and that when this happens, a candidate's identity and sense of individuation may be compromised. The candidate may then hold his analyst to blame for failure to progress, or may attack psychoanalytic theory, or during his professional life may blindly imitate his analyst. The problem of excessive idealization and overidentification with the training analyst requires study and vigilance. Dr. Fleming thought that we may even increase this problem if we separate the candidate's training analysis from all other aspects of analytic education. Study groups can help training analysts, newly appointed as well as experienced, to become more skilled in analyzing candidates. Psychoanalytic educators who initially do not believe that there are any differences between analyzing a candidate and conducting a regular analysis usually agree after study that there are significant differences, or at least very special problems that require attention.

Although Dr. Fleming noted that our training structure and methods are working, she also felt that much can be done to make them work better. For example, Dr. Fleming felt that Institutes need to consider new ways and ideas to make the theoretical or curricular phase as important and meaningful to the candidate and faculty as the other two parts of analytic training. She believed that it is important to demonstrate to candidates that psychoanalysis is not a static affair, nor is it close to closure, but that it has grown, has changed, and is still changing in order to comprehend phenomena. She believed that data from other fields relevant to psychoanalysis need to be integrated into the core curriculum—for example, current child developmental research and new findings from the neurosciences. Also, Dr. Fleming believed that process material from child therapy and child analysis should be part of the basic curriculum.

Dr. Fleming emphasized that a healthy scientific skepticism and a mind open for discovery must be constantly encouraged by all psychoanalytic educators. Candidates need to appreciate that, following the revolutionary discoveries of Freud and the early pioneers, psychoanalysis entered a phase of normal science. This is the phase we are now in. In this stage, significant scientific advances have been made and continue to be made in both the theory and practice of psychoanalysis. These advances, even though not of a revolutionary character, should in no way be devalued. Dr. Fleming's recommendations are being implemented, and the curriculum has gained in importance.

Dr. Fleming introduced psychoanalysts to a new way of thinking about psychoanalytic education. Even though Dr. Fleming never de-emphasized psychoanalysis, her persistent emphasis on educational methods and goals and the teaching–learning process at times stirred controversy. Some analysts felt that there was a basic incompatibility between education and psychoanalysis and the body of technical principles used by each discipline. However, it was Dr. Fleming's opinion that there were important common denominators between therapy and education, between treating and teaching. She strongly believed that by helping analytic clinicians become analytic educators, psychoanalytic education would be improved and psychoanalysis advanced. Her vision prevailed, and psychoanalytic education and the science and profession of psychoanalysis have been enriched by her work. Dr. Fleming's strength, integrity, devotion to psychoanalysis, and scientific spirit became a model and source of inspiration for many generations of analysts.

At a symposium on psychotherapy at Tufts University in 1969, Dr. Fleming wondered aloud at what had given her the crucial impetus for the development of her very special interest in learning and teaching. She recalled from childhood a quote from Plato that had touched her deeply and that she had never forgotten: "Education is giving to the body and soul all the beauty and all the perfection of which they are capable." This quotation concisely represents Dr. Fleming's creed and her own philosophy of psychoanalytic education.

DR. FLEMING'S CURRICULUM VITAE

Date and Place of Birth:
  March 24, 1904
  Bloomington, Illinois

Education:

B.S., Wellesley College, 1924
M.A., Oberlin College, 1928 (Physiology)
M.D., University of Chicago, 1936

  Internship: University of Chicago, 1937–1938
  Residency: University of Chicago, 1938

  Psychoanalysis: Chicago Institute for Psychoanalysis, 1941–1945

Teaching:
  Biology: Illinois State Normal University,
                              1924–1925
                              Oberlin College, 1925–1926

  Physical Education: Rockford College, 1927–1930

  Anatomy & Physiology: Battle Creek College, 1931–1934

  Psychiatry: University of Chicago, Instructor,
                              1940–1943
                              University of Chicago, Social Service
                              Lecturer, 1942–1943 & 1947–1949
                              University of Illinois School of Medi-
                              cine, Assistant Clinical Professor,
                              1948–1952
                              Consultant, Family Service:
                                Evanston, 1943–1952
                                Milwaukee, 1943–1949
                                Racine, 1950–1951
                              Elgin State Hospital, Lecturer, 1950–
                              1951

Psychoanalysis: Chicago Institute for Psychoanalysis:
  Training & Supervising Analyst,
  1952–1969
  Staff member, 1952–1969
  Dean of Education, 1956–1969
University of Colorado Medical
Center:
  Professor of Psychiatry, 1969–1980
  Training & Supervising Analyst,
  Denver Institute for Psychoanalysis,
  1969–1980

Clinical Experience:
  Billings Hospital, University of Chicago, 1940–1943
  Private practice, 1943–1969
  Veterans Rehabilitation Center, Chicago, 1944–1946
  Presbyterian Hospital, Chicago, 1948–1952
  Chicago Memorial Hospital, 1949–1951
  Michael Reese Hospital, Chicago, 1951–1960

Certification in Psychiatry:
  American Board of Psychiatry and Neurology, 1943

Professional Societies:
  Illinois Psychiatric Society, 1940–1970
  American Medical Association, 1942–1980
  American Psychiatric Association, 1942–1980
  Sigma Xi, 1942–1980
  Chicago Psychoanalytic Society, 1946–1980
    Treasurer, 1954–1955
    President, 1957–1958
  The American Psychoanalytic Association, 1947–1980
    Secretary, Board on Professional Standards, 1953–1955
    Chairman, Board on Professional Standards, 1961–1964
    Many committees, 1948–1980
  Fellow American Psychiatric Association, 1954–1980
  Association of American Medical Colleges, 1959–1980
  Denver Psychoanalytic Society, 1969–1980
  American Association for the Advancement of Science, 1948–
  1980
  Phi Beta Kappa (A), 1974

· Appendix B ·

WORKS BY DR. FLEMING

PAPERS

(1940). Observations on the use of finger painting in the treatment of adult patients with personality disorders. *Character and Personality*, *8*:301–310.

(1943). Observations on the use of chess in the therapy of an adolescent boy (with S. M. Strong). *Psychoanalytic Review*, *30*:399–416.

(1946). Confusional states seen in consultation in a general hospital. *Journal of the American Medical Women's Association*, *1*:173–181.

(1946). Observations on the defenses against a transference neurosis. *Psychiatry*, *9*:365–374.

(1949). Mental hygiene implications of the effect of unemployment on the family and child. *Mental Health Bulletin* (Illinois Society for Mental Hygiene), *27*(5):1–4.

(1953). The role of supervision in psychiatric training. *Bulletin of the Menninger Clinic*, *17*:157–169.

(1953). What is a supervisory analysis? (with N. L. Blitzsten). *Bulletin of the Menninger Clinic*, *17*:117–129.

(1958). An analysis of methods for teaching of psychotherapy with description of a new approach (with D. A. Hamburg). *Archives of Neurology and Psychiatry*, *79*:179–200.

(1959). Review of *The Teaching and Learning of Psycho Therapy*, by R. Ekstein and R. S. Wallerstein. *Bulletin of the Menninger Clinic*, *23*:78.

(1961). What analytic work requires of an analyst: A job analysis. *Journal of the American Psychoanalytic Association*, *9*:719–729.

(1963). Activation of mourning and growth by psycho-analysis (with S. Altschul). *International Journal of Psycho-Analysis*, *44*:419–431.

(1964). Supervision: A method of teaching psychoanalysis (with T. F. Benedek). *Psychoanalytic Quarterly*, *33*:71–96.

(1967). Teaching the basic skills of psychotherapy (Frieda Fromm-Reichmann Lecture, Palo Alto, California, March 24, 1966). *Archives of General Psychiatry*, *16*:416–426.

(1972). The birth of COPE as viewed in 1971 (Plenary session of the American Psychoanalytic Association, May, 1971). *Journal of the American Psychoanalytic Association*, *20*:546–555.

(1972). Early object deprivation and transference phenomena: The work-

198

ing alliance (Sandor Rado Lecture, Columbia University, April 6, 1971). *Psychoanalytic Quarterly, 41*:23–49.

(1973). The training analyst as an educator. *The Annual of Psychoanalysis, 1*:280–295. New York: Quadrangle.

(1974). The problem of diagnosis in parent loss cases. *Contemporary Psychoanalysis, 10*:439–451.

(1975). Review of *Psychoanalytic Investigations: Selected Papers*, by Therese Benedek. *Contemporary Psychoanalysis, 20*:161–162.

(1975). Some observations on object constancy in the psychoanalysis of adults. *Journal of the American Psychoanalytic Association, 23*:743–759.

(1975). Evaluation of progress in supervision (with S. S. Weiss). *Psychoanalytic Quarterly, 44*:191–205.

(1976). Chicago selection research: The group interview. *The Annual of Psychoanalysis, 4*:347–373. New York: International Universities Press.

(1976). Chicago selection research: The post-group interview. *The Annual of Psychoanalysis, 4*:375–382. New York: International Universities Press.

(1978). Assessment of progress in a training analysis (with S. S. Weiss). *International Review of Psycho-Analysis, 5*:33–43.

(1979). The teaching and learning of the selection process: One aspect of faculty development (with S. S. Weiss). *The Annual of Psychoanalysis, 7*:87–109. New York: International Universities Press.

(1980). On the teaching and learning of termination in psychoanalysis (with S. S. Weiss). *The Annual of Psychoanalysis, 8*:37–55. New York: International Universities Press.

BOOKS AND BOOK CHAPTERS

(1956). Discussion of teaching psychoanalytic concepts in psychiatry. In *Psychoanalysis and Psychotherapy*, F. Alexander, Ed. New York: Norton, pp. 217–222.

(1963). The evolution of a research project in psychoanalysis. In *Counterpoint: Libidinal Object and Subject*, H. S. Gaskill, Ed. New York: International Universities Press, pp. 75–105.

(1966). *Psychoanalytic Supervision: A Method of Clinical Teaching* (with T. F. Benedek). Reissued New York: International Universities Press, 1983.

(1966). Discussion of "The phobic reaction" by L. Ovesey and "Resistance to transference in hysterical character neurosis" by Drs. R. Easser and S. Lesser. In *Developments in Psychoanalysis at Columbia University*, G. S. Goldman and D. Shapiro, Eds. New York: Hafner Publishing Co., pp. 81–86.

(1971). Freud's concept of self-analysis: Its relevance for psychoanalytic training. In *Currents in Psychoanalysis*, I. M. Marcus, Ed. New York: International Universities Press, pp. 14–47.

(1972). Discussion of "Group rivalry between analysts and its influence on candidates in training," by A. Garma. In *The Psychoanalytic Forum*, Vol. 4, J. Lindon, Ed. New York: International Universities Press, pp. 192–194.

UNPUBLISHED PAPERS AND PRESENTATIONS

(1958). The influence of parent loss in childhood on personality development and ego structure (with V. S. Altschul, V. Zielinski, M. Forman). Paper read at the American Psychoanalytic Association meeting.

(1969). Seminar on Supervision. Presented at the Washington Psychoanalytic Institute, Washington, D.C., February 7–8.

(1969). Planned teaching in supervision. Paper read at Fourth Symposium on Psychotherapy, Boston, April.

(1969). Sequelae of Parent-Loss in Childhood. Panel discussion presented at the American Psychoanalytic Association meeting, Miami, May.

(1974). Some observations on object constancy in the psychoanalysis of adults. Paper read at Mahler Symposium, Philadelphia, May 18.

(1974). Planned teaching of clinical skills. Paper read at meeting of supervisors, Michael Reese Hospital, Chicago, October 21.

(1975). Panel on Parent Loss. Presented at Colorado Society for Clinical Social Workers, Denver, October 4.

(1975). The mutual influence of developmental and structural concepts on the diagnosis and treatment of parent-loss patients. Paper read at Pittsburgh Symposium on Parent and Sibling Loss, Pittsburgh, October 24.

(1975). Psychoanalysis: Some general contributions to psychiatry and some recent advances. Paper read at Colorado Psychiatric Society meeting, Denver, November 13.

(1977). Discussion of "Transference and object replication" by Gertrude and Rubin Blanck and "The therapist as object for facilitating change" by Paul A. Dewald. Presented at Tufts University Symposium, Boston, April 1.

(1977). Discussion of *The Psychological Birth of the Human Infant* by Margaret S. Mahler, Fred Pine, and Anni Bergman. Presented at the Meet the Author Panel, the American Psychoanalytic Association meeting, Quebec, Canada, April 29.

(1978). Early object deprivation and Transference Phenomena: Pre-Oedipal object need. Paper read at annual meeting of New Orleans Psychoanalytic Society, New Orleans, May 12.

(1978). Different forms of transference interpretation. Paper read at Aspen Conference, August.

(1978). Changes in psychoanalytic perspectives in the first years of life: The Oedipus revisited. Paper read at Bertram D. Lewin Symposium, Philadelphia Psychoanalytic Society, Philadelphia, November 11.

(1979). Early object deprivation: Object need and developmental diagnosis. Paper read at the Denver Psychoanalytic Society meeting, June 4.

(1979). The education of a supervisor. Paper read at Chicago Symposium on Supervision, Chicago, November 9–11.

REFERENCES

Arlow, J. (1963). The supervisory situation. *Journal of the American Psychoanalytic Association, 11*:576–594.

Arlow, J., Ed. (1973). *Selected Writings of Bertram D. Lewin.* New York: Psychoanalytic Quarterly.

Arlow, J. (1979). Metaphor and the psychoanalytic situation. *Psychoanalytic Quarterly, 48*:363–385.

Babcock, C. G., Ed. (1965). *Training Analysis: A Report of the First Three Institutes Conference, Chicago, Pittsburgh, Topeka.* Pittsburgh: Pittsburgh Psychoanalytic Institute.

Balint, M. (1948). On the psychoanalytic training system. *International Journal of Psycho-Analysis, 29*:163–173.

Balint, M. (1954). Analytic training and training analysis. *International Journal of Psycho-Analysis, 35*:157–162.

Bandler, B. (1960). The American Psychoanalytic Association, 1960. *Journal of the American Psychoanalytic Association, 8*:389–406.

Bateson, G. (1942). Social planning and the concept of "deutero learning." Second Symposium, Conference on Science, Philosophy, and Religion, New York.

Benedek, T. (1954). Countertransference in the training analyst. *Bulletin of the Menninger Clinic, 18*:12–16.

Benedek, T. (1960). Personal communication.

Benedek, T. (1969). Training analysis—past, present and future. *International Journal of Psycho-Analysis, 50*:437–445.

Benedek, T. (1976). Chicago selection research: The individual interview as an instrument for the selection of candidates for psychoanalytic training. *The Annual of Psychoanalysis, 4*:333–346. New York: International Universities Press.

Beres, D. (1957). Communication in psychoanalysis and in the creative process. *Journal of the American Psychoanalytic Association, 5*:408–423.

Bergmann, M. S., and Hartman, F. R., Ed. (1976). *The Evolution of Psychoanalytic Technique.* New York: Basic Books.

Bernfeld, S. (1946). An unknown biographical fragment by Freud. *American Imago, 4*(1):3–19.

Bernfeld, S. C. (1952). Discussion of Buxbaum: "Freud's dream interpretation in the light of his letters to Fliess." *Bulletin of the Menninger Clinic, 16*:66–73.

Bibring, G. L. (1954). The training analysis and its place in psychoanalytic training. *International Journal of Psycho-Analysis, 35*:169–173.

Blitzsten, N. L., and Fleming, J. (1953). What is a supervisory analysis? *Bulletin of the Menninger Clinic, 17*:117–129.

Breuer, J., and Freud, S. (1895). Studies on hysteria. *Standard Edition, 2*:1–307. London: Hogarth Press, 1962.

Bruner, J. S. (1957). Going beyond the information given. In *Contemporary Approaches to Cognition*. Cambridge, Mass.: Harvard University Press, pp. 151–156.

Buxbaum, E. (1950). Technique of terminating analysis. *International Journal of Psycho-Analysis, 31*:184–190.

Buxbaum, E. (1951). Freud's dream interpretation in the light of his letters to Fliess. *Bulletin of the Menninger Clinic, 15*:197–212.

Calef, V., and Weinshel, E. M. (1973). Reporting, nonreporting, and assessment in the training analysis. *Journal of the American Psychoanalytic Association, 21*:714–726.

Calef, V., and Weinshel, E. M. (1979). The new psychoanalysis and psychoanalytic revisionism. (Book review essay on *Borderline Conditions and Pathological Narcissism* by Otto Kernberg.) *Psychoanalytic Quarterly, 48*:470–491.

Console, W. A. (1963). A study of one hundred consecutive applications. Unpublished paper.

COPER (Conference on Psychoanalytic Education and Research). (1974). *Commission I: Tripartite System of Psychoanalytic Education*. The American Psychoanalytic Association, unpublished.

DeBell, D. E. (1963). A critical digest of the literature on psychoanalytic supervision. *Journal of the American Psychoanalytic Association, 11*:546–575.

Dewald, P. A. (1973). The clinical conference in teaching and learning the psychoanalytic process. *The Annual of Psychoanalysis, 1*:265–279. New York: Quadrangle.

Eisendorfer, A. (1959). The selection of candidates applying for psychoanalytic training. *Psychoanalytic Quarterly, 28*:374–378.

Eissler, K. R. (1951). An unknown autobiographical letter by Freud and a short comment. *International Journal of Psycho-Analysis, 32*:319–324.

Eitingon, M. (1926). An address to the International Training Commission. *International Journal of Psycho-Analysis, 7*:130–134.

Ekstein, R. (1953). On current trends in psychoanalytic training. In *Explorations in Psychoanalysis*, R. Linder, Ed. New York: Julian Press, pp. 230–265.

Ekstein, R., and Wallerstein, R. W. (1958). *The Teaching and Learning of Psychotherapy*, revised edition. New York: International Universities Press, 1972.

Farrow, E. P. (1942). *A Practical Method of Self-Analysis*. London: Allen & Unwin.

Ferber, L. (1974). Remarks about the role of the training analysis and the psychoanalyst in the candidate's progression in the institute. (Appendix to COPER, *Commission I*, pp. 81–87). The American Psychoanalytic Association, unpublished.

Ferenczi, S. (1911). On the organization of the psychoanalytic movement. In *Final Contributions to the Problems and Methods of Psychoanalysis*, Vol. 3, M. Balint, Ed. New York: Basic Books, 1955, pp. 299–307.

Ferenczi, S. (1919). On the technique of psychoanalysis. In *Further Contributions to the Theory and Technique of Psychoanalysis*. New York: Basic Books, 1953, pp. 177–188.

Ferenczi, S. (1927). The problem of termination of an analysis. In *Final Contributions to the Problems and Methods of Psychoanalysis*, Vol. 3, M. Balint, Ed. New York: Basic Books, 1955, pp. 77–86.

Ferenczi, S. (1928). The elasticity of psychoanalytic technique. In *Final Contributions to the Problems and Methods of Psychoanalysis*, Vol. 3, M. Balint, Ed. New York: Basic Books, 1955, pp. 87–101.

Ferenczi, S. (1930). The principles of relaxation and neocatharsis. In *Final Contributions to the Problems and Methods of Psychoanalysis*, Vol. 3, M. Balint, Ed. New York: Basic Books, 1955, pp. 108–125.

Ferenczi, S., and Rank, O. (1924). *The Development of Psychoanalysis*. New York: Nervous and Mental Disease Publishing Company, 1925.

Ferenczi, S., and Rank, O. (1927). *The Development of Psychoanalysis* (NMD Monograph Series #40). New York: Nervous and Mental Disease Publishing Company.

Firestein, S. K. (1978). *Termination in Psychoanalysis*. New York: International Universities Press.

Fleming, J. (1967). Teaching basic skills in psychotherapy. *Archives of General Psychiatry, 16*:416–426.

Fleming, J. (1969). Seminar on Supervision. Presented at the Washington Psychoanalytic Institute.

Fleming, J. (1972). The birth of COPE as viewed in 1971. *Journal of the American Psychoanalytic Association, 20*:546–555.

Fleming, J. (1976a). Chicago selection research: The group interview. *The Annual of Psychoanalysis, 4*:347–373. New York: International Universities Press.

Fleming, J. (1976b). Chicago selection research: The post-group interview. *The Annual of Psychoanalysis, 4*:375–382. New York: International Universities Press.

Fleming, J., and Benedek, T. (1966). *Psychoanalytic Supervision: A Method of Clinical Teaching*. Reissued New York: International Universities Press, 1983.

Fliess, R. (1942). The metapsychology of an analyst. *Psychoanalytic Quarterly, 11*:211–227.

Freud, A. (1951). The problem of training analysis. In *The Writings of Anna Freud*, Vol. 4. New York: International Universities Press, 1968, pp. 407–442. (Original work published 1938)

Freud, A. (1971). The ideal psychoanalytic institute: A utopia. In *The Writings of Anna Freud*, Vol. 7. New York: International Universities Press, pp. 73–93.

Freud, S. (1887–1902). *The Origins of Psychoanalysis: Letters to W. Fliess, Drafts, and Notes*, M. Bonaparte, A. Freud, and E. Kris, Eds. New York: Basic Books, 1954, pp. 168–345.

Freud, S. (1899). Screen memories. *Standard Edition, 3*:303–322. London: Hogarth Press, 1963.

Freud, S. (1900). The interpretation of dreams: Preface to the second edition. *Standard Edition, 4*:xxv–xxvi. London: Hogarth Press, 1953.

Freud, S. (1905). Prefatory remarks to "Fragment of an analysis of a case of hysteria." *Standard Edition, 7*:7–14. London: Hogarth Press, 1956.

Freud, S. (1910). The future prospects of psycho-analytic therapy. *Standard Edition, 11*:141–151. London: Hogarth Press, 1957.

Freud, S. (1912). Recommendations to physicians practicing psycho-analysis. *Standard Edition, 12*:111–120. London: Hogarth Press, 1958.

Freud, S. (1914a). On the history of the psycho-analytic movement. *Standard Edition, 14*:7–66. London: Hogarth Press, 1957.

Freud, S. (1914b). Remembering, repeating and working through. *Standard Edition, 12*:145–156. London: Hogarth Press, 1958.

Freud, S. (1916). Fixation to trauma—the unconscious (Introductory lectures on psycho-analysis, Lecture 18). *Standard Edition, 16*:273–285. London: Hogarth Press, 1963.

Freud, S. (1916–1917). Introductory lectures on psycho-analysis. *Standard Edition*, 15–16. London: Hogarth Press, 1963.

Freud, S. (1923). Remarks on the theory and practice of dream interpretation. *Standard Edition, 19*:109–121. London: Hogarth Press, 1961.

Freud, S. (1926). Foreword to E. Pickworth Farrow's *A Practical Method of Self-Analysis*. *Standard Edition, 20*:200–250. London: Hogarth Press, 1959.

Freud, S. (1932). New introductory lectures on psycho-analysis. *Standard Edition, 22*:5–182. London: Hogarth Press, 1964.

Freud, S. (1935). The subtleties of a faulty action. *Standard Edition, 22*:233–235. London: Hogarth Press, 1964.

Freud, S. (1936). A disturbance of memory on the Acropolis. *Standard Edition, 22*:239–248. London: Hogarth Press, 1964.

Freud, S. (1937). Analysis terminable and interminable. *Standard Edition, 23*:210–253. London: Hogarth Press, 1964.

Freud, S. (1940). An outline of psycho-analysis. *Standard Edition, 23*:141–208. London: Hogarth Press, 1964.

Gill, M. (1979). Review of *The Evolution of Psychoanalytic Technique*, Martin S. Bergmann and Frank R. Hartman, Eds. *Psychoanalytic Quarterly*, 48:506–507.

Gitelson, M. (1948). Problems of psychoanalytic training. *Psychoanalytic Quarterly, 17*:198–211.

Gitelson, M. (1954). Therapeutic problems in the analysis of the "normal" candidate. *International Journal of Psycho-Analysis, 35*:174–183.

Gitelson, M. (1964). On the identity crisis in American psychoanalysis. *Journal of the American Psychoanalytic Association, 12*:451–476.

Glover, E. (1931). The therapeutic effect of inexact interpretations. *International Journal of Psycho-Analysis, 12*:397–411.

Glover, E. (1952). Research methods in psychoanalysis. *International Journal of Psycho-Analysis, 33*:403–409.

Glover, E. (1955). *The Technique of Psychoanalysis.* New York: International Universities Press.

Goodman, S., Ed. (1977). *Psychoanalytic Education and Research: The Current Situation and Future Possibilities.* New York: International Universities Press.

Greenacre, P. (1954). The role of transference. *Journal of the American Psychoanalytic Association, 2*:671–684.

Greenacre, P. (1961). A critical digest of the literature on selection of candidates for psychoanalytic training. In *Emotional Growth,* Vol. 2. New York: International Universities Press, 1971, pp. 670–694.

Greenacre, P. (1966). Problems of training analysis. *Psychoanalytic Quarterly, 35*:540–567.

Greenson, R. R. (1960). Empathy and its vicissitudes. *International Journal of Psycho-Analysis, 4*:418–424.

Greenson, R. R. (1964). Discussion. In *Psychoanalysis in the Americas,* R. E. Litman, Ed. New York: International Universities Press, 1966, pp. 263–266.

Greenson, R. R. (1965). The working alliance and the transference neurosis. *Psychoanalytic Quarterly, 34*:155–181.

Greenson, R. R. (1967). *The Technique and Practice of Psychoanalysis.* New York: International Universities Press.

Grotjahn, M. (1949). The role of identification in psychiatric and psychoanalytic training. *Psychiatry, 12*:141–151.

Henrick, I. (1955). Professional standards of the American Psychoanalytic Association. *Journal of the American Psychoanalytic Association, 3*:561–599.

Hilgard, E. R. (1948). *Theories of Learning.* New York: Appleton-Century-Crofts.

Holt, R., and Luborsky, L. (1958). *Personality Patterns of Psychiatrists,* 2 vols. New York: Basic Books.

Horst P. (1941). *The Prediction of Personal Adjustment* (Bulletin 48). New York: Social Science Research Council.

Hurn, H. T. (1971). Toward a paradigm of the terminal phase: The current status of the terminal phase. *Journal of the American Psychoanalytic Association, 19*:332–348.

Isakower, O. (1963a). Minutes of the Faculty Meeting of the New York Psychoanalytic Institute, October 14, unpublished.

Isakower, O. (1963b). Minutes of the Faculty Meeting of the New York Psychoanalytic Institute, November 20, unpublished.

Jones, E. (1953). *The Life and Work of Sigmund Freud.* New York: Basic Books.

Jones, E. (1962). The role of self-knowledge in the educative process. *Harvard Educational Review, 32*:200–209.

Kairys, D. (1964). The training analysis: A critical review of the literature and a controversial proposal. *Psychoanalytic Quarterly, 33*:485–512.

Keiser, S. (1969). Psychoanalysis—taught, learned, and experienced. *Journal of the American Psychoanalytic Association, 17*:238-267.

Klein, H. R. (1965). *Psychoanalysts in Training: Selection and Evaluation.* New York: Psychoanalytic Clinic for Training and Research, Department of Psychiatry, Columbia University, College of Physicians and Surgeons.

Knight, R. (1953). The present status of organized psychoanalysis in the United States. *Journal of the American Psychoanalytic Association, 1*:197-221.

Kohut, H. (1959). Introspection, empathy and psychoanalysis. An examination of the relationship between mode of observation and theory. *Journal of the American Psychoanalytic Association, 7*:459-483.

Kramer, M. (1959). On the continuation of the analytic process after psychoanalysis (a self-observation). *International Journal of Psycho-Analysis, 40*:17-25.

Kris, E. (1952). *Psychoanalytic Explorations in Art.* New York: Basic Books.

Kris, E. (1954). *Introduction to the Origins of Psychoanalysis.* New York: Basic Books.

Kris, E. (1956a). On some vicissitudes of insight in psychoanalysis. *International Journal of Psycho-Analysis, 37*:445-455.

Kris, E. (1956b). The recovery of childhood memories in psychoanalysis. In *The Selected Papers of Ernst Kris.* New Haven: New York: Yale University Press, 1975, pp. 301-340.

Kubie, L. (1958). *Neurotic Distortion of the Creative Process.* Lawrence: University of Kansas Press.

Langer, M., Puget, J., and Teper, E. (1964). A methodological approach to the teaching of psychoanalysis. *International Journal of Psycho-Analysis, 45*:567-574.

Lewin, B. D. (1962). American psychoanalytic education: Historical comments. *Journal of the American Psychoanalytic Association, 10*:119-126.

Lewin, B. D., and Ross, H. (1960). *Psychoanalytic Education in the United States.* New York: Norton.

Lewis, H. (1964). Personal communication.

Loewenstein, R. M. (1957). Some thoughts on interpretation in the theory and practice of psychoanalysis. *The Psychoanalytic Study of the Child, 12*:127-150. New York: International Universities Press.

McLaughlin, F. (1967). Addendum to a controversial proposal. Some observations on the training analysis. *Psychoanalytic Quarterly, 36*:230-247.

McLaughlin, J. (1973). The nonreporting training analyst, the analysis, and the institute. *Journal of the American Psychoanalytic Association, 21*:677-712.

National Commission on Excellence in Education. (1983). *A Nation at Risk.* Washington, DC: Department of Education.

Norman, H. F., Blacker, K. H., Oremland, J. D., and Barrett, W. G.

(1976). The fate of the transference neurosis after termination of a satisfactory analysis. *Journal of the American Psychoanalytic Association, 24*:471–498.

Nunberg, H. (1931). The synthetic function of the ego. *International Journal of Psycho-Analysis, 12*:123–140.

Oberndorf, C. P. (1953). *A History of Psychoanalysis in America.* New York: Grune & Stratton.

Oremland, J. D., Blacker, K. H., and Norman, H. F. (1975). Incompleteness in "successful" psychoanalysis. *Journal of the American Psychoanalytic Association, 23*:819–844.

Panel (1961). The selection of candidates for psychoanalytic training (R. R. Greenson, reporter). *Journal of the American Psychoanalytic Association, 9*:135–145.

Panel (1969). Problems of termination in the analysis of adults (S. K. Firestein, reporter). *Journal of the American Psychoanalytic Association, 17*:222–237.

Panel (1974). Termination: Problems and technique (W. S. Robbins, reporter). *Journal of the American Psychoanalytic Association, 23*:166–176.

Pfeffer, A. (1959). A procedure for evaluating the results of psychoanalysis: A preliminary report. *Journal of the American Psychoanalytic Association, 7*:418–444.

Pfeffer, A. (1961). Follow-up study of a satisfactory analysis. *Journal of the American Psychoanalytic Association, 9*:698–718.

Pfeffer, A. (1963). The meaning of the analyst after analysis. *Journal of the American Psychoanalytic Association, 11*:229–244.

Pollock, G. H. (1961). Historical perspectives in the selection of candidates for psychoanalytic training. *Psychoanalytic Quarterly, 35*:481–496.

Pruyser, P. W. (1979). An essay on creativity. *Bulletin of the Menninger Clinic, 43*:294–353.

Quen, J., and Carlson, E. T. (1978). *American Psychoanalysis: Origins and Development.* New York: Brunner/Mazel.

Racker, H. (1968). *Transference and Countertransference.* New York: International Universities Press.

Ramzy, I., Ed. (1973). *Training Analysis: A Report on Psychoanalytic Education—the Second Conference of the Chicago, Pittsburgh, and Topeka Institutes.* Topeka: Topeka Institute for Psychoanalysis.

Rangell, L. (1964). An overview of the ending of an analysis. In *Psychoanalysis in the Americas,* R. E. Litman, Ed. New York: International Universities Press, 1966, pp. 141–165.

Reik, T. (1937). *Surprise and the Psychoanalyst.* New York: E. P. Dutton.

Ross, H. (1956). Comments on Supervision. Presented at Chicago Training Analysts' Seminar. March 20, unpublished.

Sachs, H. (1942). *The Creative Unconscious.* Cambridge, Mass.: Sci-Art Publishers.

Sachs, H. (1947). Observations of a training analyst. *Psychoanalytic Quarterly, 16*:157–168.

Schafer, R. (1959). Generative empathy in the treatment situation. *Psychoanalytic Quarterly, 28*:342–373.

Schlessinger, N., and Robbins, F. (1974). Assessment and follow-up in psychoanalysis. *Journal of the American Psychoanalytic Association, 22*:542–567.

Shapiro, D. (1974a). Summary of pilot study—the analyst's own analysis (Appendix to COPER, *Commission I*, pp. 61–69). The American Psychoanalytic Association, unpublished.

Shapiro, D. (1974b). The training setting in training analysis: A retrospective view of the evaluative and reporting role and other "hampering" factors. *International Journal of Psycho-Analysis, 55*:297–306.

Sharpe, E. (1930). The technique of psycho-analysis: Seven lectures. In *Collected Papers on Psycho-Analysis.* London: Hogarth Press, 1950, pp. 9–106.

Shouksmith, G. (1960). A validatory criterion for a group selection procedure. *Australian Journal of Psychology, 12*:34.

Simmel, E. (1949). The "doctor game," illness and the profession of medicine. In *The Psychoanalytic Reader*, R. Fliess, Ed. New York: International Universities Press, pp. 291–305.

Steckel, W. (1923). *Pychoanalysis and Suggestion Therapy.* Trans. by J. S. Van Teslaar. London: Kegan Paul, Trench, Trubnert.

Stone, L. (1974). The assessment of students' progress. *The Annual of Psychoanalysis, 2*:308–322. New York: Quadrangle.

Strachey, J., Ed. (1934). The nature of therapeutic action of psycho-analysis. *International Journal of Psycho-Analysis, 15*:127–159.

Strachey, J., Ed. (1957). Footnote to "On the history of the psycho-analytic movement. *Standard Edition, 14*:20. London: Hogarth Press.

Survey Steering Committee. (1955). *Report of the Survey Steering Committee to the Board on Professional Standards of the American Psychoanalytic Association* (the "Rainbow Report"). Unpublished.

Szasz, T. S. (1958). Psychoanalytic training: A sociopsychological analysis of its history and present status. *International Journal of Psycho-Analysis, 39*:1–16.

Thompson, C. (1955). Introduction to Ferenczi's *Final Contributions to the Problems and Methods of Psychoanalysis*, Vol. 3, M. Balint, Ed. New York: Basic Books, pp. 3–4.

Tyler, R. W. (1974). Teaching and learning (Appendix to COPER, *Commission I*, pp. 88–101). The American Psychoanalytic Association, unpublished.

Waelder, R. (1962). A review and discussion of *Psychoanalysis, Scientific Method and Philosophy: A Symposium*, Sidney Hook, Ed. *Journal of the American Psychoanalytic Association, 10*:617–637.

Wallerstein, R. S., Ed. (1981). *Becoming Psychoanalyst: A Study of Psychoanalytic Supervision.* New York: International Universities Press.

Weigert, E. (1952). Contribution to the problem of terminating psycho-analysis. *Psychoanalytic Quarterly,* *21*:465–480.

Winnicott, D. W. (1951). Transitional objects and transitional phenomena. In *Collected Papers: Through Pediatrics to Psychoanalysis.* London: Tavistock, 1958, pp. 229–242.

INDEX